CHARIOTS OF GOD

Alan Cairns

God's Law in relation to the Cross & the Christian

Chariots of God:
God's Law in Relation to the Cross and the Christian

Published by

Ambassador-Emerald International

427 Wade Hampton Blvd.
Greenville, SC 29609 USA
www.emeraldhouse.com

and

Ambassador Productions
Ardenlee Street
Belfast, Northern Ireland BT6 8QJ
www.ambassador-productions.com

Cover and internal design by Animotion Studios
www.astudios.com

To my faithful congregation in Faith Free Presbyterian Church,
who delight in nothing more than to hear of the imputation to them of
Christ's perfect obedience to God's law for their justification,
and who use that truth as their motivation to live in
obedience to God by the faith of the gospel.
No preacher has better hearers who are not hearers only,
but doers of God's word.

CONTENTS

ACKNOWLEDGMENTS

I am deeply indebted to many people for helping to bring this book to publication. I have to thank Debbi Spears and my wife, Joan, for typing the initial drafts of each chapter. I must also thank my editor, Sara Elliott, for the incredible amount of work she put into this project. Her professionalism, patience, help, and encouragement at every stage of the work were a constant source of strength to me. Sara analyzed every sentence and every idea, questioning and suggesting, and doing all she could to make the finished work better. I am grateful to Dr. Michael Barrett for kindly checking the transliteration of Hebrew and Greek terms. Sara Elliott and Carolyn McNeely undertook the early proof readings, a tedious but essential task, and to both of them I express my sincere gratitude. The final stages of proof reading fell to Judy Brown, and I thank her for her diligent oversight in the preparation of the work for the printer. The cover design and page layout are the work of Steven Lee of Animotion Studios, Greenville. Steven never ceases to amaze with the speed and skill of his work. I deeply appreciate his unfailing courtesy and patience as he found time in a busy schedule to produce such an attractive book. I must also thank Samuel Lowry of Ambassador Productions for waiting without complaint while the book was being prepared and for his understanding that the demands of a busy pastoral ministry often upset the best laid publication schedules of writers and publishers.

Most of all I give thanks to God for His blessing on the preaching of these studies in Faith Free Presbyterian Church, Greenville, South Carolina, and on the wide distribution they enjoyed by means of tape recording. I trust that He will greatly use them in this printed form and through them lead many to a biblical understanding of the important subject of His law and commandments.

The chariots of God are twenty thousand, even thousands of angels: the Lord is among them, as in Sinai, in the holy place.

— Psalm 68:17

PREFACE
THE CHARIOTS OF GOD

It was a day like no other. Thunder rumbled and lightning flashed. Some three million people stood in awe, and even Moses, the man with whom God spoke face to face, quaked with fear. To mark the giving of His law to His covenant people, God came down on Mount Sinai with awesome majesty and did something He had never done before and has never done again. He spoke audibly so that the gathered company could actually hear Him as he solemnly stated His Ten Commandments.

Most of us know that the Lord brought Moses up into the mount and gave him the two stone tables on which He had written His law with His own hand. But few stop to think of the stupendous miracle of God's actually addressing the Israelites and reciting the Ten Commandments in their ears. The Bible tells us that is exactly what He did. "God spake all these words" (Exodus 20:1); "Did ever people hear the voice of God speaking out of the midst of the fire, as thou hast heard, and live? . . . Out of heaven he made thee to hear his voice, that he might instruct thee: and upon earth he shewed thee his great fire; and thou heardest his words out of the midst of the fire. . . . The Lord talked with you face to face in the mount out of the midst of the fire. . . . These words the Lord spake unto all your assembly in the mount out of the midst of the fire, of the cloud, and of the thick darkness, with a great voice: and he added no more. And he wrote them in two tables of stone, and delivered them unto me" (Deuteronomy 4:33, 36; 5:4, 22).

The Psalmist David described the scene: "The earth shook, the heavens also dropped at the presence of God: even Sinai itself was moved at the presence of God, the God of Israel. . . . The chariots of God are twenty thousand, even thousands of angels: the Lord is among them, as in Sinai, in the holy place" (Psalm 68:8, 17). The "chariots of God" is a metaphorical description of the glorious majesty of the Lord. Scripture clearly associates the idea of the divine chariot with the Lord's presence in supernatural majesty (2 Kings 2:11, 12). Psalm 68 describes the angels as chariots because they are manifestations of that awesome majesty that set Mount Sinai on fire (Hebrews 12:18).

We pass from one unique day to another, from Mount Sinai to Mount Calvary. Once again the earth was convulsed with a powerful shaking and the mount was shrouded in supernatural darkness. Once again God came down on the mount in awful majesty. This time, however, there were no angels present. That was by the choice of the Son of God who hung upon the cross. Our Saviour could have called more than twelve legions of angels to His aid (Matthew 26:53), but He suffered and died alone. He had to if He were to pay the penalty of the broken law and redeem our souls from its curse. Once again, as at Sinai, God's law stood paramount. And here, just as on Mount Sinai, God spoke.

The voice of God heard at Sinai would forever have been the voice of condemnation had not God something more to say. He had, and He said it at Calvary. From the midst of the darkness the Lord Jesus Christ cried with a loud voice, "It is finished" (John 19:30). At Sinai God had spoken thunderously, spelling out the demands of His law and establishing a standard of perfect righteousness that we could never attain. At Calvary He spoke triumphantly, announcing the satisfaction of His law and the perfect righteousness He had attained for us.

At Sinai, the angels were symbols of God's glory; the law was the essential revelation of it. The Ten Commandments, even more than the angels, were God's chariots. At Calvary, though the angels were absent, the chariots of God were still there. God's law and commandments were never more in force and never more fulfilled than at the cross.

Thus, though the world in the blindness of its unbelief could not see it, God's majesty was even more striking at Calvary than at Sinai. The majesty of the law satisfied at the cross is even greater than the majesty of the law stated at the mount that burned with fire. Think of it like this:

God rode down from glory to Mount Sinai in chariots of fire to state His law, closing heaven against us as law-breakers. Christ our Saviour rode up to glory from Mount Calvary in those same chariots of God, opening heaven for us by His perfect satisfaction of the law.

May we find ourselves praying with Moses, "I beseech thee, shew me thy glory" (Exodus 33:18) and experience the Lord's gracious answer as we consider *The Chariots of God,* a study of the law in relation to the cross and to the Christian.

Part I
The Law

CHAPTER ONE

THE PURPOSE OF THE LAW

"Wherefore then serveth the law?"
Galatians 3:19

God promised Israel that if they would give due attention to His law He would bring the nation back from the abyss of moral and spiritual declension (Deuteronomy 30:1ff). He fulfilled His promise repeatedly to them and has continued to fulfil it for His church, "the Israel of God." The Puritan revival in England and America provides an outstanding example. In times of deep spiritual darkness and moral laxity the Puritans, perhaps more than any other generation of theologians, paid particular attention to the place of the law in relation to the gospel. While it is common for their detractors to mock their piety, Puritan preachers won the hearts and minds of their countrymen and laid the foundations of their nations' progress and prosperity. Whenever the threat of declension arose again they and the heirs of their legacy called the people back to God's law. They expounded it at length and, fully aware that the law had no saving power, used it as the backdrop against which they displayed the glories of the gospel. It is not too much to say that the past success of the gospel was in direct proportion to the extent of the recognition of the proper place and purpose of the law.

That is a lesson we need to learn today. A generation ago most people in Europe and America made moral judgments on the basis of a general acceptance of the Ten Commandments, but not any more. Today the usual framework for making such decisions is thoroughly secular and humanistic. Rebelling against the moral absolutes of God's law, Western civilization is adrift on a sea of relativism and is reliving the disastrous experience of Israel in the days of the judges: "In those days there was no king in Israel: every man did that which was right in his own eyes" (Judges 21:25). With no moral or spiritual rule to govern the behaviour of individuals or of society in general, everyone is pressured to conform to a politically correct public policy that is dictated by the theories of secular humanism.

On the religious front, many churches see their role as reflecting current cultural mores and even of justifying them by a misapplication of Scripture. "The Bible says" used to be the final authority in deciding right and wrong for professing Christians, but today even some evangelicals set aside the plainest statements of Scripture as "culturally conditioned"—in plain English, the products of the social prejudices of the time of their writing, not the timeless statements of God's truth. For example, it is common for churchmen to pervert such biblical terms as "compassion" and "justice" to justify utterly unbiblical positions. *Compassion*, they tell us, will not allow us to deny practising homosexuals a place in the fellowship of the church. And *justice* demands that we must not marginalize or condemn, but rather welcome them. These allegedly biblical principles take precedence over any Scripture texts that denounce homosexuality as an abominable sin upon which God has pronounced His abiding wrath. Consequently, in many churches, practising homosexuals no longer are viewed as sinners needing to be transformed by the gospel, but are received as Christians, even though they do not acknowledge or abandon their sin.

Here is the difference between the method of confronting moral decadence that God directed Moses to use (and which the Puritans employed) and the method adopted by modern churchmen. The old way may be derided as harsh and judgmental, but it actually is the way of love, for it alone offers the hope of radical change. The modern method of reflecting the culture, instead of calling for its conformity to the word of God, abandons sinners to their sin and dooms society to further decay. If we are ever to become a force for real spiritual good in society we must start where God starts, and that is by calling men to repentance for breaking His law. Some may object that "we should simply preach the gospel." However, we cannot preach the gospel without reference to God's law.

Such terms as *sin, atonement, righteousness,* and *justification* are incomprehensible apart from the law. Without knowing what the Bible teaches about the law we cannot know what it teaches about God, grace, the gospel, or salvation. This makes the study of the law particularly urgent and important.

Before we consider the Ten Commandments we must seek to understand the more general questions of the place and function of the law. We must commence with the reasons God has given for revealing His law and for placing the emphasis that He does upon it.

The Law Shows Men They Are Accountable to God

First, God gave His law to make men know that they are responsible and accountable to Him for all they are and do. The law did not commence with Moses but with God who gave it first, not to Moses, but to Adam. This means that the law is not limited to the Jews. The fact that God gave it to them in written form on Mount Sinai does not mean that no one else ever had the law. Paul tells us in Romans 2:15 that the Gentiles "shew the work of the law written in their hearts, their conscience also bearing witness, and their thoughts the mean while accusing or else excusing one another." A fundamental truth lies on the surface of this text: no man—Jew or Gentile, Greek or barbarian, religious or infidel—can escape the authority of his Creator. The law clearly expresses the Lord's right to command. When He gives His law He is saying in effect, "I am God. I am your supreme Creator and your constant sustainer. I am, and because I am and because of my will and my work, you are. I am the Creator, you are the creature. I am the sovereign, you are the subject." When God writes His law on the table of every man's heart He is saying, "It is my right to command my creature."

This law, written on the heart of man and later on the tables of stone, manifests a holy and majestic God. It proves that this holy God actually requires obedience to His revealed will from His creatures. It shows each of us the unpalatable truth that man has spent the whole of his history vainly trying to escape, namely that God will hold men accountable to His standards, not theirs. Why does God give the law? First, to make men know that they are responsible and accountable to Him. The very existence of conscience in every man tells us that God holds us responsible. We are not mere victims of circumstances, but responsible, moral agents whom God will call to account by the standard of His inviolable law.

The Law Reveals God's Standard of Right and Wrong

Second, God gives His law to make clear His standard of right and wrong. This also is apparent from Romans 2:15. God's moral law is the unchangeable standard of right and wrong. This standard is not defined by contemporary society. Today people commit some of the most heinous crimes and moral perversions with little if any shame, and often with no social or legal penalty. But however societies, governments, judges, and court systems change, God's law never changes; it declares the ultimate standard of right and wrong.

One of the most vexing questions society faces is how to square the constitutional right of free speech with the public good. The airwaves are polluted every day by the foulest trash imaginable. The results are there for all to see. We have now an increasing number of ten-, eleven-, and twelve-year-old rapists and murderers who can receive expert instruction in the commission of their crimes in their own homes from godless, money-grubbing companies and film producers who hide behind their right of freedom of expression. Even pornographers, we are told, have a right to express their perversion. If we speak of laws to shut down their vicious operations we hear the howl of protest that if people wish to read or watch moral filth they have the right to do so without censorship. "You cannot legislate morality" is the mantra of the permissive society. Apparently, we may legislate immorality but not morality. This raises the greatest question any nation can face and that is the question of ultimate moral authority. When we deny God and His word and ban both from the education of our children, as has happened in the public schools of America, we remove the very foundation of moral authority. Only God can authoritatively establish the standard of right and wrong. That is why He gave His law. Paul tells us in Romans 3:20, "By the law is the knowledge of sin." James likens the law of God to a mirror (James 1:23–25). It lets a man see himself as he truly is. Why did God give the law? To establish for man what is right and what is wrong.

We should all consider a very personal application. Ultimately we will not stand before any human judiciary but before God. It does not matter how acceptable our lives are to our corrupt and vile society. It does not matter how morally superior we may appear to other people. In the end they will not be our judges. We will stand before God to be judged according to His law, the standard of right and wrong that never changes.

The Law Establishes the Only Standard of Acceptance with God

Third, God gave His law to establish the only standard of acceptance with Him. Micah tells us, "He hath shewed thee, O man, what is good; and what doth the Lord require of thee, but to do justly, and to love mercy, and to walk humbly with thy God?" (Micah 6:8). The law sets forth God's standard of holiness. It shows what God expects and demands—the only standard He will accept. Paul says, "It is written, Cursed is every one that continueth not in all things which are written in the book of the law to do them" (Galatians 3:10). That is the standard of acceptance with God: total, perfect, absolute, and impeccable obedience. That means obedience not merely in what the Puritans used to call the substance or the matter of the commandment, but also in the motive.

In the light of this we must all confess that there is not a single thing we have ever done that we can present to God and say, "Lord, here is an act of full obedience." Obedience does not consist in a mere form but also in the inward desire of the heart to do what God commands, solely for His honour and glory. What a standard for acceptance with God! The Bible knows nothing of the myth that has long been popular among the Jews and now has become a point of orthodoxy among professed Christians, that God will weigh good deeds against bad deeds and if our good deeds outweigh our bad He will accept us. This notion is neither Christian nor orthodox; it is the lie of the devil. When God weighs our deeds they will *all* be on the same side of the balance, the wrong side. His standard of acceptance is absolute, perfect, unblemished obedience, short of which there is no hope of our being acceptable to God.

The Law Establishes Man's Guilt

Fourth, God gives His law to establish the guilt of fallen man. Paul made this abundantly clear: "We know that what things soever the law saith, it saith to them who are under the law: that every mouth may be stopped, and all the world may become guilty before God" (Romans 3:19). Why does God reveal His law? He reveals His law so that His witness against every man who fell in Adam may be clear: Guilty! Guilty! Guilty before God! In John 5:45 the Lord Jesus says, "There is one that accuseth you, even Moses," that is, the law. The law accuses the lawbreaker.

Many people deceive themselves with the thought, "No one has seen the wrong I have done. No one knows the evil thoughts I have entertained. My life is hidden from view." Such people go through life wearing the bland smile of the hypocrite, forgetful of the truth of Hagar's words, "Thou God seest me" (Genesis 16:13). God's law, which is written in their hearts, will rise up as a powerful advocate of their doom. It will accuse them and then, as we have seen in Galatians 3:10, condemn them. So, by His law God establishes the guilt of every man by nature.

The Law Slays All Self-Righteousness

Fifth, God gives His law to slay all self-righteousness. By His law God established the standard of acceptance with Him as absolute, sinless, undeviating perfection in obedience to the substance and spirit of the law. In so doing He established the guilt of every man by nature. The conclusion is inescapable that He also slays the self-righteousness behind which we all naturally love to hide. Judged by the standard of someone else's conduct we may convince ourselves that we are upright and good. However, God does not allow us to judge ourselves by others but by the standard of His immutable law. By that standard He declares, "All your righteousnesses are as filthy rags." There is sin in the holiest desires we have ever felt. There is corruption in the most upright things we have ever done. There is selfishness in the most selfless actions we have ever taken. There is rebellion in our fullest submission to God. That is why Paul states, "By the deeds of the law there shall no flesh be justified in his sight, for by the law is the knowledge of sin" (Romans 3:20).

Jesus said to the Jews of His day, "Except your righteousness shall exceed the righteousness of the scribes and Pharisees, ye shall in no case enter into the kingdom of heaven" (Matthew 5:20). While it is easy for us to condemn the scribes and Pharisees, honesty requires us to confess that by the standards of churchmen today they would be acclaimed as paragons of virtue. Yet Jesus said that if our righteousness does not exceed theirs, we cannot be saved. That must have sounded like a death knell to the Jews of Christ's day. Our Lord was teaching them the truth that Paul later spelled out in Titus 3:5–7, "Not by works of righteousness which we have done, but according to his mercy he saved us, by the washing of regeneration, and renewing of the Holy Ghost; which he shed on us abundantly through Jesus Christ our Saviour; that being justified by his grace, we should be made heirs according to the hope of eternal life."

This brings us to the heart of the message.

The Law Leads Sinners to Christ

Sixth, God gave His law to lead sinners to Christ. The law of God exposes sin and the sinner. It tears away the veil from the heart. It convicts. If you have not begun to feel just how great a sinner you are, you have good cause to fear. If you can listen to what the Bible says about the law of God and glibly dismiss it, you stand in grave danger. Anyone who honestly, carefully, and humbly studies God's law finds that it weighs heavily on his soul, destroying all hope he may have placed in himself. But by God's grace it also points him to Christ. Paul says, "The law was our schoolmaster to bring us unto Christ" (Galatians 3:24). A schoolmaster was not only an instructor but a strict disciplinarian who made liberal use of the whip to subdue his student. He was something of a slave driver until the student graduated from his school. Just as a schoolmaster drove his student to learn, so the law whips and wounds in order to lead us to Christ. In the law, God demands a perfect righteousness. In the gospel, He reveals Christ as the One in whom He has provided that righteousness for us. God says in effect, "My standard of acceptance is impeccable obedience." Christ rendered impeccable obedience, as His Father testified from heaven, "This is my beloved Son, in whom I am well pleased" (Matthew 3:17). The gospel message is essentially the truth that Christ is made righteousness unto His believing people (1 Corinthians 1:30). Augustus Toplady's great hymn, "Rock of Ages, Cleft for Me," expresses the same message:

Nothing in my hand I bring,
Simply to Thy cross I cling.

That is the gospel way of acceptance with God. The law tells us what we need and drives us to the foot of the cross where we learn that Christ has met our need. The law is satisfied and all believers are justified in Him who fully kept God's law.

Why did God give the law? So that we would not be foolish, sinful wretches, self-righteously boasting of our imagined good works. Our best works fit us only for hell. God has given us His law so that, deprived of every hope in ourselves, we may rush to the cross and cry, "Wash me, O Lamb of God, from all my sin and cover me with the robe of Thy righteousness to make me acceptable to God."

The Law Directs Believers in Holy Living

Finally, God gave us His law not only to lead us to Christ for salvation but also to direct us in holy living. The preface to the Ten Commandments shows that God addressed them to a people already redeemed. "I am the Lord thy God, which have brought thee out of the land of Egypt, out of the house of bondage" (Exodus 20:2). Since these commandments then were given to a people already redeemed, they were obviously not intended as a means of obtaining redemption. This yields a far-reaching truth: Christians are not under the law as a covenant to obtain eternal life. They are not under the law as a way of salvation. The law can have no *condemning* power over them because they are justified in God's sight through Christ Jesus. But the law has a *commanding* power because it is a revelation of the holy will and nature of our God. Paul said, "I delight in the law of God after the inward man" (Romans 7:22). Only a Christian could say that. Not another soul on earth delights in the law of God after the inward man, only one who has been justified freely by God's grace and has been delivered from any dependence on his own works-righteousness.

Once we are saved we can rejoice with Paul who said, "Ye are not under the law, but under grace" (Romans 6:14).

Some people interpret these words in a way that the apostle never intended. They jump to the conclusion that a Christian is under no obligation to keep the law as a standard of holiness—he is "free" from any submission to the law. This notion raises very serious questions. Why would a Christian desire to be free from the commands of God? Why would a Christian seek to be free from the constraints of perfect holiness of life? In a word, why would a Christian want to resemble the people of this world instead of reflecting the character and beauty of his Redeemer who perfectly kept God's law? Paul testified, "I delight in God's law." The Psalmist said, "Thou hast commanded us to keep thy precepts diligently. O that my ways were directed to keep thy statutes!" (Psalm 119:4–5). God has given His law to delight the hearts of His people and to direct their steps in holy obedience to Him.

Here then are some reasons God gave us His law. President Harry Truman put a notice on his desk, "The buck stops here." As Christians we would do well to realize that the responsibility of re-establishing a biblical perspective of God's purpose in the giving of His law lies with us. It is useless for us to lament the moral declension of the nation without actively seeking to lead people to recognize the authority of God's law. And it is hypocritical to call others to do this while we ignore it in our private lives. We need to come to a deeply humbling understanding of the holy law of God as the Bible fully expounds it. We should profit and learn from it so that with the Psalmist we will fervently pray, "O that my ways were directed to keep thy statutes." The law will then have served its purpose well.

CHAPTER TWO

THE PERMANENCE OF THE LAW

"Think not that I am come to destroy the law, or the prophets: I am not come to destroy, but to fulfil. For verily I say unto you, Till heaven and earth pass, one jot or one tittle shall in no wise pass from the law, till all be fulfilled."
Matthew 5:17–18

The term *law* sounds deceptively simple. In fact, with its wide variety of meanings it is one of the most complex terms in Scripture. For example, in Ephesians 2:15 the apostle Paul says that the Lord Jesus Christ by His death abolished "the law of commandments." But in Romans 3:31 he vehemently denies that faith—and by faith he means the gospel—makes void the law. The term translated "makes void" is precisely the one he uses in Ephesians 2:15, "abolished." At first sight it appears that Paul taught in one place that Christ by His gospel abolished the law and in another place that He did not abolish it, but rather established it. Actually, the apostle was not contradicting himself; he was simply using the term *law* in two different ways.

At times the word *law* denotes the entire word of God, while at other times it refers to the Old Testament revelation. Sometimes it means the Ten Commandments and sometimes it speaks of the Levitical ceremonial law. In some passages it signifies a general governing principle within a person (Romans 7:23). Thus it has a wide variety of meanings.

Our study concerns the law in the sense of divine commandment. Perhaps the easiest way to summarize what the Bible teaches about the law is to think of it in its three categories—the moral law, the ceremonial law, and the civil law. The moral law embodies divine directives by which God commands men and governs their beliefs, worship, and practices both in private and in public life. The ceremonial law consists of the sacrificial system that God gave to Israel to foreshadow the coming realities of the gospel. The ceremonial or ritual laws of Israel were passing pictures of permanent principles for faith and practice. In other words, the ceremonial law is the shadow of which the New Testament revelation is the substance. The civil law contains the system God gave through Moses to govern the nation of Israel under the theocracy He had instituted among them.

The Bible teaches that Christ fulfilled and therefore abolished the ceremonial law. Having offered one sacrifice for sins for ever (Hebrews 10:12), He triumphantly proclaimed from the cross, "It is finished" (John 19:30) and so pronounced the passing of Jewish types. That is what Paul meant in Ephesians 2:15 when he said that Christ abolished the law of commandments. The shadow has given place to the substance.

The civil law was addressed to no other nation but Israel. Its specific dictums were limited to that one national body chosen by God to live under a theocracy. It is significant that the apostles never attempted to impose the civil code of Israel on those who received the gospel. Nevertheless, many of those civil enactments provide illustrative applications of the abiding moral principles of the Ten Commandments and as such are of continuing authority in the church. For example, it is not binding on all nations to adopt stoning as a method of capital punishment, or to criminalize ploughing with an ox and an ass together, or to demand that every house should have a battlement for its roof (Deuteronomy 22:8). It is easy to see the spiritual principles in such commandments, but the actual laws were limited to the nation of Israel. Some today deny that Israel's civil law has ever been abrogated and advocate a return to the precise details of the Mosaic civil code. Some of these theonomists go so far as to accuse Calvin of "heretical nonsense" on this point (R. J. Rushdoony, *The Institutes of Biblical Law,* p. 9). Most theonomists are Presbyterian and therefore on this subject they must reject their own *Westminster Confession of Faith* (chap. 19, sec. 4) which teaches exactly what Calvin taught—that

Israel's ceremonial and civil laws are not binding on the consciences of men today.

Certainly our nation should conform its laws to the moral and spiritual truths of God's law. If there is to be any hope for this country it will be because God raises up such a spiritual consciousness in the nation that her political leaders will be brought to the place of conforming our legal code to the spiritual truths God revealed to the only nation He ever personally ruled on earth, the nation of Israel. Those spiritual standards still hold good. This means—in direct opposition to humanistic propaganda—that we should legislate morality. It is true that legislating morality does not make men moral. Sometimes the best we can do is to make the price of being immoral too high for them to pay. If that is the case in this nation, then let us pray God for leaders with vision and courage enough to do it.

Having said all that, it is dangerous to bind the consciences of God's people to the civil code of ancient Israel. The danger is made more acute by the theonomist's assertion that while justification is by grace, sanctification is by law. That notion is entirely foreign to the word of God which teaches that salvation, including sanctification, is all of grace through faith in Jesus Christ (Ephesians 2:8; Romans 8:28–30; Galatians 2:20). Grace will produce a conformity to God's moral law, whereas the law has no power to produce such conformity.

So civil and ceremonial laws were temporary, adapted to particular people with particular needs at a particular time. The moral law is something entirely different. It is permanent; it is immutable. "Till heaven and earth pass, one jot or one tittle shall in no wise pass from the law, till all be fulfilled." That seems a simple and straightforward statement but the truth of it has long been controverted. Therefore, we must seek to establish from Scripture the vital doctrine of the permanence of God's law.

Evidence for the Permanence of the Law

The evidence for the permanence of God's law is clear. First, *the Lord gave the moral law in Eden*. His command to Adam and Eve, "Of the tree of the knowledge of good and evil, thou shalt not eat of it" (Genesis 2:17), could have made no sense unless it rested on the basis of moral law. That commandment included a clear understanding that Adam should love God with all his heart—more than he loved himself or his wife, more than he desired immediate sensual pleasure. It was clear also in that commandment that Adam was to have no other gods before the Lord. In addition, we can see that at his creation Adam received the sabbath law. Since he was created at the end of the sixth day of the creation week his first day on earth was marked by the observance of the Lord's sabbath, a part of God's law. Paul's assertion that the new man is created in righteousness and true holiness (Ephesians 4:24) clearly suggests that righteousness and true holiness defined the moral constitution of Adam at his creation. Since righteousness is conformity to God's law and holiness is conformity to God's nature, it is evident that the Lord gave the moral law at the dawn of human history in Eden.

Second, *the Lord maintained the moral law throughout patriarchal times.* The days between Adam and Moses were long. The peoples of the earth were widely dispersed and quickly fell into great apostasy. Sin began to do its leavening work. Increasingly, darkness and ignorance pervaded humanity. Nevertheless, through all that time the Lord maintained His moral law. Long before the time of Moses the statutes of the Lord were already known. In addition to the sabbath law men were aware of the law against idolatry (Genesis 35:2), the law of parental authority (Genesis 9:24–27; 18:19), the law against murder (Genesis 9:5, 6), and the law against adultery (Genesis 12:18f; 20:3, 9). Add to these a host of what are generally called positive commands (arbitrary expressions of God's sovereign will on a variety of subjects) found later in Moses' civil and ceremonial code: the difference between clean and unclean animals (known to Noah), the law of circumcision (revealed to Abraham), and the rituals of the Old Testament sacrificial system (fully revealed to Moses but known in many of its parts since the days of Adam). So in addition to all the great moral enactments that would appear in the Ten Commandments, many of the positive commandments that God gave later to Israel were known in patriarchal times. In this way, throughout that period when there was no written word, the Lord was maintaining the integrity of the moral law.

Third, *the Lord reissued the moral law at Mt. Sinai.* A fact often overlooked is that God actually spoke the Ten Commandments out of the thick darkness and the burning fire of Sinai. The gathered thousands of Israel actually heard the very voice of their God. That was the only time in the history of the world that such a thing ever happened. In this way God indelibly impressed His law on the consciences of His people. Unlike the ceremonial and civil enactments of the Mosaic code which would change with the passage of time, this law was forever. And not only did God speak the Ten Commandments, He also wrote them on tables of stone, once again bearing witness to their permanence.

Fourth, *the Lord repeated the moral law through the prophets.* The ministries and messages of the prophets called Israel back to the law. The prophetic books of the Old Testament begin and end with this call. Isaiah stands at the head of the prophets. He says, "Give ear to the law of our God" (1:10). Malachi closes the book of the prophets. He says, "Remember the law of Moses my servant" (4:4). The prophetic ministry begins and ends with the exposition of God's law and His call to the people to return to it.

Fifth, *the Lord established the moral law in Christ.* Jesus said, "I am come not to destroy the law, . . . but to fulfil [it]." God established His law in Christ, who obeyed it perfectly in thought, word, and deed.

Sixth, *the Lord Jesus Christ summarized the moral law in two great, enduring commandments.* Deuteronomy 6:5 says, "Thou shalt love the Lord thy God with all thy heart." The Lord Jesus quoted this to summarize the first four commandments of the decalogue. He stated our duty to our fellow man according to the second table of the law by quoting Leviticus 19:18, "Thou shalt love thy neighbour as thyself." These two commandments will never pass away while we live on this earth. No one in his right senses could ever argue that there has been the slightest abrogation of them. On them hang all the law and the prophets. And, as we shall see, the gospel revelation of the New Testament emphasizes their abiding authority over all men. Since these two commandments comprehend the entire moral law, the Saviour's reference to them demonstrates the permanent and enduring value of the law.

Seventh, *the Lord confirmed the moral law through the apostles.* Every one of the Ten Commandments is repeated in the New Testament (including the fourth commandment, as we shall see in due course). That confirmation establishes the permanence of the law.

Eighth, *the Lord writes the moral law in the hearts of men.* The Gentiles, who have not the written Mosaic law, show the works of the law written in their hearts (Romans 2:14–15). That is as true today as ever before.

Ninth, *the Lord puts the moral law into the hearts and minds of His people at regeneration.* "This is the covenant that I will make with the house of Israel after those days, saith the Lord; I will put my laws into their mind, and write them in their hearts" (Hebrews 8:10). When God saves a man He writes His law in his heart. The unsaved man has the law of God in his heart as a witness against him. The saved man has the law of God written in his heart as a delight to his soul. God intends His law to be permanent.

The final piece of evidence in support of the permanence of God's moral law is this: *The Lord will use that law as His standard for judgment.* "Let us hear the conclusion of the whole matter: fear God, and keep his commandments: for this is the whole duty of man. For God shall bring every work into judgment, with every secret thing, whether it be good, or whether it be evil" (Ecclesiastes 12:13–14). Today we entertain very loose views of the judgment of God. There is a striking absence of the fear of God. Most people can take the Bible in their hands, read of the reality and terror of God's law, and never tremble. When we stand before God and the books are opened (Revelation 20:12), the first book opened will be the book of God's law. God does not open the door to heaven for any man by abrogating one tittle of His moral law. He will open this book of the law and then He will open the book of each person's life. Millions of people, ignorant of the stringent strictness of divine judgment, slide carelessly toward their appearance at the great white throne, confident that God will judge them as indulgently as they judge themselves. They could not be more wrong. Unless He finds in those who appear before Him an absolute righteousness and perfection with which He can find no fault, His law will call for their destruction. God will place every sinner on the scales of strict justice. The standard against which He will weigh them will not be the deeds or opinions of others; it will not be the standards of the society in which they lived. It will be His own immutable and holy law. Weighed against that standard, every sinner who consoled himself with the thought that he had nothing much to fear at the judgment bar of God will hear the same dread sentence that sealed Belshazzar's doom: "Thou art weighed in the balances, and art found wanting" (Daniel 5:27).

God gave the law at the very commencement of time. He will maintain the law until the day of final judgment. Nothing could be plainer: God's law is permanent.

The Consequence of the Permanence of the Law

Now let us come to the consequence of that truth. What does this mean to us? Simply this: God's law is still in effect. No man on earth, saved or unsaved, can avoid the authority of the law of God. But believers in the Lord Jesus Christ stand in a completely different relationship to God's law from unbelievers. To unbelievers the law of God is still a covenant of works. As we have seen, on the judgment day the law will demand absolutely perfect conformity in both nature and practice, with all the words, the inner meanings, and the spirituality of its enactments. No fallen man can personally meet such a standard, but that is God's standard of judgment for sinners according to the covenant of the law. To the people of God, however, the law is no longer a covenant of works. Christ has fulfilled that covenant. He has satisfied the law. He is the end of the law unto righteousness to His believing people (Romans 10:4). To believers the law of God stands not as a witness against them but as a rule of righteous living. Thus believers and unbelievers stand in different relationships to the law. But the fact remains that for both, God's law is still in full effect, and nothing in heaven, earth, or hell can annul it.

The Fall did not abrogate the moral law. Some people imagine that because man by his fall became incapable of obeying the law he is no longer under any obligation to obey it. It has been put like this: God would not come to a man who cannot see and command him, "See, or I will condemn you." So God will not come to fallen man and say to him, "Keep the law or I will condemn you." But this illustration misses the point entirely. How foolish it is for men to think that Adam's sin in breaking God's law actually freed his depraved posterity from any obligation to keep it! God holds all men truly responsible to His law, to the necessity of an absolute and perfect obedience, as He did Adam in the garden of Eden. The Fall did not abrogate the law.

Time does not erode the moral law. The law reflects the eternal perfection of the nature of God. Since divine perfection is unchangeable, the inescapable conclusion must be that the law which expresses it is unchanging. Some things are right merely because God commands them. Such commands are what theologians call positive laws. Positive laws express God's *will* for given situations, rather than His *nature.* They are therefore temporary and changeable. For example, God commanded, "Thou shalt not let thy cattle gender with a diverse kind: thou shalt not sow thy field with mingled seed: neither shall a garment mingled of linen and woollen come upon thee" (Leviticus 19:19). Again, He commanded His people to give one-tenth of their income to His work. These are positive laws. Why did the Lord forbid the mingling of linen and wool? Why did He ordain a tithe and not an eighth? Not because of His perfection of nature but because of the exercise of His sovereign will. That makes them law. In contrast, the moral law is not merely positive. In other words, in the moral law God does not say, "This is right only because I command it." He commands it because it is eternally right and expresses the eternal perfection of His nature. So the moral law is rooted in the nature of God. Has God changed with time? He says, "I am the Lord, I change not" (Malachi 3:6). Paul said, "Jesus Christ [is] the same yesterday, and today, and for ever" (Hebrews 13:8). God is eternally immutable because He is eternally perfect. Only if He changed could His law change. The great issues of the Ten Commandments are not matters that change with the climate of public opinion, or with religion, or with culture. They are the absolutes to which God holds every man and nation. Time does not erode God's law.

Furthermore, *grace does not annul the moral law.* The Lord Jesus did not come to destroy the law. For believers the law is not a covenant of works whereby we work our way to heaven. God does not say to us as He said to Adam before the Fall, "Here is a standard of personal obedience whereby you will enter into the blessing of eternal life." We are not justified by obeying the law. Anyone who tries to get to heaven by personal obedience to the law will perish, for who can keep God's law? No man can honestly say, "Lord, look into my heart, I am sinless. Look into my thoughts, I am sinless. Examine my actions, I am sinless. I have left nothing undone that I should have done. I have not done anything that I ought not to have done. I have not deviated a hair's breadth from the absolute standard of divine perfection." No, we must admit that we stand condemned as guilty lawbreakers, rebels against the throne of heaven. But the Lord Jesus Christ can make that claim with perfect honesty. In His person, His life, His thoughts, His feelings, His motives, His actions, His sorrows, and His sufferings He maintained absolute moral perfection. What a Saviour! Having fully honoured and satisfied the precept of God's law in His life, He presented Himself to God as the perfect sacrifice and paid the penalty of the broken law for His people in the shedding of His blood at Calvary. Thus He saves His people from the condemnation of the law. God made Him to be sin for us; that is, He imputed our sin to Him. Conversely, He imputes Christ's righteousness to every believer, and so makes us the righteousness of God in Him. He imputes His perfect righteousness to us because since believers are one with Christ, the law reckons all He did as ours. In Him we have fully met the perfect standard of God's law.

It was pure grace that put us in Christ and so justified us. That same grace places the law in the hearts of all true believers as we have already noted from Hebrews 8:10. In other words, an inevitable mark of people who are genuinely trusting Christ is their regard for God's law. They love it and by God's grace strive to keep it. The Bible knows nothing of the glib, cheap, easy, meaningless professions of salvation by a faith falsely so called that leaves men without any concern to obey their God. Churches have received as Christians too many people who have made decisions of some sort but who have imbibed the theology that denies God's law any authority over their lives. Is it any wonder that in many churches adulterers and other gross sinners stand in the pulpit and sit in the pew? A church pew is a good place to bring an adulterer or a thief or any other kind of sinner to let him hear the gospel of saving grace. Christ gladly received sinners and ate with them (Luke 15:2) and He still does. So churches should ever be open and welcoming to sinners. But to receive into fellowship people who live in open defiance of the law of God as professing Christians is a very different matter. Such professions are lies. No man is trusting Christ if his heart has no concern to glorify Him in a life of obedience. We are not saved by our works, but when we are saved through the work of Christ He writes His law in our hearts and in our minds and gives us a desire to fulfil it in a life of godliness and holiness. No true Christian can ever desire to be free from the directives and moral imperatives of God's law. Anarchy has no part in the makeup of a genuine believer. A man who has been washed in the blood of Christ and has obtained a gracious standing with God by the imputation of Christ's righteousness will say with Paul, "The law is holy, and the commandment holy, and just, and good" and therefore, "I delight in the law of God after the inward man" (Romans 7:12, 22). In 1 Corinthians 9:21, Paul said that he was "not without law to God, but under the law to Christ." What a statement! We are not under the law as a covenant of works to work our own way to heaven, because the Lord Jesus Christ worked our way to heaven for us. But as those who have been freed from the curse and condemnation of that covenant of works and have been freely justified by the grace of God, we find our hearts bound to obey God in Christ. So even grace does not annul God's moral law.

One final thought: *Rebellion does not remove God's law.* In Hosea 8:12 we read one of the most terrible statements God ever made regarding Israel: "I have written to him the great things of my law, but they were counted as a strange thing." Men may ignore, blaspheme, mock, or utterly despise God's law, but one thing they cannot do is destroy it. Its permanence is guaranteed by the eternal God who gave it.

CHAPTER THREE

THE SPIRITUALITY OF THE LAW

"We know that the law is spiritual."
Romans 7:14

Human self-righteousness is truly amazing. It is as unblushing as it is universal. A little child needs no training to act the part of the innocent or to blame his wrong on someone else. As we grow older, this is a proclivity we never lose. It is natural for us to evade responsibility for our sins, to measure ourselves by other people, to shift our blame on to others, and even to compliment ourselves on a moral goodness that is entirely imaginary—and to expect God to reward us on that illusionary basis.

We have lived through an ethical and cultural revolution that has made immorality acceptable. Shame is an almost forgotten thing in Western society—certainly in its public life. And yet in this age of almost untrammelled wickedness people have the audacity to act shocked and hurt at the thought that perhaps God may be angry with them. Anyone who suggests that AIDS among homosexuals is God's judgment on their perversion will discover that the censure withheld from the sodomite is swiftly visited on him (this despite the fact that the acronym stands for "*Acquired* Immune Deficiency Syndrome").

The truth is that man is very much a self-righteous sinner. He does not face the reality and nature of his sin. He has believed the lie that even God has little reason to be displeased with him. And it is a lie. People who have never faced up to the enormity of their sin in the sight of God need to hear God's law. They need to stand at Mount Sinai and hear the thunder of its proclamation. They need to stand at Mount Calvary to see the evidence of its penalty.

This is what the Lord Jesus makes us do in the Sermon on the Mount (Matthew 5:2–48). He makes us face up to the true meaning of the law of God. This passage is so important that each one of us should be careful to read and understand it for himself. We may summarize the Saviour's teaching as follows: "Do not let the law's well-known phrases dull your conscience. Do not hide behind a superficial regard for the letter of the law. I have come to make you face the full force and scope of its meaning. If you refuse to do so you are deceiving yourself and will pay for your self-deception with your soul—for any man who is unwilling to face the full force of God's law is equally unwilling to receive the grace of God revealed in the gospel."

That was the essential message of the Saviour. His apostles preached the same truth. In Romans 7:14 Paul really encapsulates all that Christ taught in Matthew 5—the law is spiritual in that it governs and holds us accountable not only for our external actions but also for our internal desires and motives. The doctrine of this statement may be expressed in one simple sentence: The law of God searches to the depths of our souls and destroys every vestige of self-satisfaction and self-righteousness. This is what theologians call the spirituality of the law.

The Law Is Spiritual in Its Search of the Soul

First, the law of God is spiritual in its search of the soul. "For the commandment is a lamp; and the law is light; and reproofs of instruction are the way of life" (Proverbs 6:23). The commandment of God is a lamp. Paul made this point in writing to the Ephesians: "It is a shame even to speak of those things which are done of them in secret. But all things that are reproved are made manifest by the light: for whatsoever doth make manifest is light" (Ephesians 5:12–13). God beams His law like a searchlight from heaven into every corner of the soul, shining the rays of absolute truth into every part of the life. The law of God exposes what is in our souls.

The law regulates our behaviour. That is its clear object. God says, "Thou shalt" and "Thou shalt not." This is the true regulator of our actions. The question for us is not what is fashionable, acceptable, or even legal in the eyes of men. Neither is it what is easy or profitable in the short term. The question is, what does the law of God command? This is the permanent regulator of our behaviour. We would all do well to remember this. It is foolish to compare our behaviour with someone else's, or to make it comply with the mindset of this ungodly age. Rather we must set our behaviour alongside the unchanging commandments of God's law and judge it in that light.

The law regulates much more than our actions. *It regulates our thoughts, desires, and motives, the hidden springs of the mind and heart.* This is the clear meaning of Christ in Matthew chapter 5. Many people jump to the conclusion that Christ added to the law making it more severe. That is a false conclusion based on a superficial reading of this passage. Our Lord was showing what the true meaning of the law of Moses was and always has been and always will be.

The Pharisees had externalized the law and their obedience to it. They had reduced obedience to the law to mere fleshly deeds, neglecting its "weightier matters," as Jesus put it. Outwardly they appeared clean but inwardly they were corrupt. The Lord Jesus repudiated all external compliance that left the heart still unclean. He was not deceived by outward appearances. As God said to Samuel, "Man looketh on the outward appearance, but the Lord looketh on the heart" (1 Samuel 16:7).

How this devastates glib self-righteousness! Men today are much like the Jews of Ezekiel's day. The Jews had come under judgment because of apostasy and sin yet they would not acknowledge that they were under judgment. They paraded their vaunted righteousness. Even after God allowed the Babylonians to take many of them captive and reduce Judah to the level of a vassal state, they had no sense of their sin. They continued to parade their imagined virtue. When Jeremiah preached against their sin they cursed him, imprisoned him, and threatened him with death. Faced with the exiled Ezekiel's similar message from Babylon they called attention to their self-righteous show. But the Lord soon tore away the mask as Ezekiel chapter 8 records. From that chapter of devastating rebuke one verse demonstrates God's exposure of the sin the Jews hid under a cloak of self-righteousness: "Then said he unto me, Son of man, hast thou seen what the ancients of the house of Israel do in the dark, every man in the chambers of his imagery? for they say, The Lord seeth us not" (Ezekiel 8:12).

The law searches out the depths of the soul. Paul wrote to the Hebrews, "The word of God is quick, and powerful, and sharper than any two-edged sword, piercing even to the dividing asunder of soul and spirit, and of the joints and marrow, and is a discerner [critic, or judge] of the thoughts and intents of the heart. Neither is there any creature that is not manifest in his sight: but all things are naked and opened unto the eyes of him with whom we have to do" (Hebrews 4:12–13). The Lord Jesus made the same point to the scribes and Pharisees in Luke 16:15 as He prepared to tell the story of the rich man and Lazarus: "Ye are they which justify yourselves before men; but God knoweth your hearts." So God's law regulates behaviour and even judges the deepest motives of the soul. Even then it has not finished.

It goes beyond what we do and think. *The law examines and judges what we are.* Most of the enactments of the law are prohibitions. Why? The reason is simple: God's law recognizes the natural bias of fallen man towards sin. In other words, what is wrong with man goes deeper than his thoughts, words, and deeds. He does wrong because he is wrong. The law lays man's soul low, condemning it as depraved and spiritually dead.

There is an important practical implication in all this. Clearly the law of God holds a man responsible not only for what he does, thinks, and feels, but for what he is. "All the ways of a man are clean in his own eyes; but the Lord weigheth the spirits" (Proverbs 16:2). The Lord goes to the very depths of our nature to lay bare the moral and spiritual state of the soul in His sight. His law is spiritual in its search of the soul.

The Law Is Spiritual in the Scope of Its Statutes

Second, the law is spiritual in the scope of its statutes. God's law has an obvious meaning. When it says, "Thou shalt have no other gods before me; thou shalt not make unto thee any graven image; thou shalt not take the name of the Lord thy God in vain; remember the sabbath day, to keep it holy; honour thy father and thy mother; thou shalt not kill; thou shalt not commit adultery; thou shalt not steal; thou shalt not bear false witness; and thou shalt not covet," its meaning is perfectly plain. There is no difficulty in understanding it. No one can honestly say that God's commandments are ambiguous.

But the law includes a lot more than the obvious meaning. *Every prohibition implies the contrary precept.*

When the first commandment decrees, "Thou shalt have no other gods before me," it not only prohibits the worship of false gods but it requires that we worship and love the true God above all.

When the second commandment says, "Thou shalt not make unto thee any graven image," it not only prohibits all use of idols and representations of deity, but it also establishes the principle that we must worship God scripturally and spiritually.

When the third commandment prohibits all vain use of the Lord's name, it also calls for the positive honouring of that name.

When the fourth commandment calls on us to "remember the sabbath day, to keep it holy," it clearly requires us to recognize the sovereignty of the Lord over all the affairs of men, to use our time to serve and obey Him, and to ensure that we enter into His rest.

When the fifth commandment says, "Honour thy father and thy mother," it not only lays down the duty of children to parents but also calls for all family relationships to be scripturally based.

When the sixth commandment decrees, "Thou shalt do no murder," it clearly prohibits the unlawful taking of human life. But it goes further and requires us to protect and guard human life as the gift of God.

When the seventh commandment says, "Thou shalt not commit adultery," it goes further than prohibiting the physical act of committing adultery. It teaches that we should live in moral purity and contain sexual gratification within the limits of marriage to a lawful spouse.

When the eighth commandment says, "Thou shalt not steal," it clearly prohibits the unlawful seizure of another's property. But it also teaches that we should have regard for the rights of ownership of legally held property and that we should exercise a just and godly stewardship of all properties within our control.

When the ninth commandment requires, "Thou shalt not bear false witness," it prohibits lying and establishes the principle set forth by Paul in Ephesians 4:25: "Putting away lying, speak every man truth with his neighbour."

When the tenth commandment dictates, "Thou shalt not covet," it not only prohibits all envious desire but teaches us to be content with such things as we have.

Each commandment represents a whole class of duties. For example, the law commands, "Thou shalt not kill." The Lord Jesus Christ teaches that this commandment includes many other actions as well as actual murder. "Ye have heard that it was said by them of old time, Thou shalt not kill; and whosoever shall kill shall be in danger of the judgment: but I say unto you, That whosoever is angry with his brother without a cause shall be in danger of the judgment: and whosoever shall say to his brother, Raca [a term of reproach meaning an empty-headed person], shall be in danger of the council: but whosoever shall say, Thou fool [impious rebel, one destitute of divine light and knowledge], shall be in danger of hell fire" (Matthew 5:21–22). Here the Saviour makes it clear that if we allow our passions to get out of control so that we curse a brother whom God has blessed, we have broken the sixth commandment. The apostle John makes the same point: "Whosoever hateth his brother is a murderer: and ye know that no murderer hath eternal life abiding in him" (1 John 3:15).

In the light of this, who can stand before the holy law of God and plead his innocence? Where is the man who has never been unjustly angry? Where is the man who has never hated a brother? Except for the God-man, Jesus Christ, no such man has ever lived. Clearly, the law is spiritual and none of us can silence its thunders by such futile means as the Pharisees employed. They sought to stultify the condemning witness of the law by meagre observance of the letter of the law. All of us tend to behave as they did, but such shifts are powerless to evade the spirituality of God's law.

Each commandment of the law requires us to attend to the means God has made available for obedience to its prohibitions and precepts. In other words, the law includes everything that incites us to do what it commands or forbids. When God says, "Thou shalt not do such and such," He means that we must maintain a thoroughgoing separation from everything that tends toward the breach of His command. We must not only obey His prohibition but eschew everything that would tempt us to disobey it. Equally, we must cultivate those things that lead us in the path of obedience to God's commands.

This has a wide application. It brings every area of our lives under the divine statute. What we watch, what we read, and what we listen to is regulated by the law of God. The same is true of the places we go, the clothes we wear, and the companions we keep. "My son, if sinners entice thee, consent thou not. . . . My son, walk not thou in the way with them; refrain thy foot from their path" (Proverbs 1:10, 15). Many people defend carnal actions and attitudes with the claim that the Bible does not state a direct prohibition of their particular sin. But does it not? When God's law says, "Thou shalt have no other gods before me," and "Thou shalt love the Lord thy God with all thy heart," it includes everything that incites us either to obey or to disobey. While it is true that the Bible may not make specific mention of the television programmes people watch, or the music they listen to, or the literature they read, it does require us to evaluate these things in the light of the fundamental question, "Does this lead me God-ward or sin-ward?"

The application of this principle lifts much of the decision-making that we face out of the realm of what is popular or fashionable and into the realm of spiritual obedience to God's unchangeable standards of holiness. God's law commands us not to commit adultery, and the Lord Jesus Christ warns us that to look upon a woman with lust is to break that commandment. That being the case—and remembering that each commandment includes all that incites us to obey or disobey it—all immodesty and all wilful exposure to immodesty breaks the eighth commandment. Thus the man who gazes at immodest or pornographic pictures is guilty of adultery. The lustful thought is the same in essence, though perhaps not in implementation, as the act. The same principle should guide women in their choice of clothes. If the law of God requires men to avoid all that would incite to sinful lust, it also requires women not to provoke that lust by immodest dress. What incites to sin is itself sin.

Of course the converse is true. What incites to God and to an obedient observance of His law is itself good. We should spend our time and energy pursuing such things. "Whatsoever things are true, whatsoever things are honest, whatsoever things are just, whatsoever things are pure, whatsoever things are lovely, whatsoever things are of good report; if there be any virtue, and if there be any praise, think on these things" (Philippians 4:8).

The Law Is Spiritual in the Stringency of Its Standards

Third, the law is spiritual in the stringency of its standards. In every area it demands perfection. It knows no compromise. It reflects the absolute holiness of God. It cannot accommodate itself to any lower standard. It has no place for an easygoing attitude that may accept what sinners are pleased to term "their best." Doing our best is not good enough to satisfy God's law if our best is a breach of that law. In fact, such a "best," far from winning the approval of the law, calls forth its condemnation. "It is written, Cursed is every one that continueth not in all things which are written in the book of the law to do them" (Galatians 3:10).

The Lord Jesus Christ summarized the standard of the law in Matthew 22:37–39: "Thou shalt love the Lord thy God with all thy heart, and with all thy soul, and with all thy mind. This is the first and great commandment. And the second is like unto it, Thou shalt love thy neighbour as thyself."

Here then is the spirituality of God's law: It demands a perfect, selfless love for God and our fellow men. That is the inflexible standard by which it judges men.

The Law Is Spiritual in the Satisfaction of Its Sentence

Finally, the law is spiritual in the satisfaction of its sentence. Here we need to attend very carefully to the teaching of Scripture for at this point we lay bare the depths of hell and see the open door to heaven.

God's law carries heavy sanctions. Its penalty is terrible beyond description. It falls on men both in this world and in the world to come. The temporal judgment of God on sin is well documented in Scripture. God slew the sons of Judah for their sin (Genesis 38:7, 10). He smote Gehazi with leprosy for his sin (2 Kings 5:27). He inflicted sickness and even death on members of the Corinthian church because of their constant wickedness (1 Corinthians 11:30). While disease and sickness may not be the direct result of a particular sin, as the case of the man born blind proves (John 9:3), in the final analysis all the sickness and suffering in the world are the results of the entrance of sin. Therefore, every child of Adam feels the temporal sanctions of God's broken law.

However, whether or not men suffer much of these temporal sanctions, the law of God will inevitably and inexorably execute its full sentence against their sin. Its penalty is not merely temporal but eternal. Hell is real. It is the necessary place of punishment for the breakers of God's law. We cannot escape it by "being good," or by "doing our best." The Pharisees could have claimed as much, but the Lord Jesus Christ said, "Except your righteousness shall exceed the righteousness of the scribes and Pharisees, ye shall in no case enter into the kingdom of heaven. . . . If thy right eye offend thee, pluck it out, and cast it from thee: for it is profitable for thee that one of thy members should perish, and not that thy whole body should be cast into hell. And if thy right hand offend thee, cut it off, and cast it from thee: for it is profitable for thee that one of thy members should perish, and not that thy whole body should be cast into hell" (Matthew 5:20, 29–30).

If the message of the law of God ended there, it would be a bleak word indeed. But God's word emphasizes an additional theme with regard to the spirituality of the law: *the law declares its spirituality by receiving the vicarious obedience of Christ for all His believing people.* This is the unambiguous testimony of Scripture: "As by the offence of one judgment came upon all men to condemnation; even so by the righteousness of one the free gift came upon all men unto justification of life. For as by one man's disobedience many were made sinners, so by the obedience of one shall many be made righteous" (Romans 5:18–19); "Christ hath redeemed us from the curse of the law, being made a curse for us: for it is written, Cursed is every one that hangeth on a tree" (Galatians 3:13). In other words, Calvary is the final quenching of the fire and fury of Sinai. In the words of the old hymn, "In one almighty draft Christ drank damnation dry."

Thus once again we find that the law leads us directly to Christ. *He bore the scrutiny of the law.* The searchlight of the law examined every word, thought, action, and motive of Christ and declared Him perfectly sinless. *Christ also obeyed the statutes of the law.* He fulfilled its strictest standards in all their moral and spiritual implications. Then *He suffered its severest sentence.* As Peter put it, "Christ . . . hath once suffered for sins, the just for the unjust, that he might bring us to God" (1 Peter 3:18).

Here then is the way of salvation: "To him that worketh not, but believeth on him that justifieth the ungodly, his faith is counted for righteousness" (Romans 4:5). The holy God of absolute justice justifies the ungodly, not on the basis of any personal obedience but solely on the merit of Christ's obedience. The faith of believers is "counted for righteousness" or, as Paul is careful to interpret the phrase, God imputes the righteousness of Christ to them by faith alone. That is the gospel. God justifies sinners, not by lowering the law's standards, but by fulfilling them in Christ; not by abrogating its penalty, but by having it fully executed upon our Substitute.

So we need to stand at two places, Mount Sinai and Mount Calvary. At Sinai we hear the law's loud thunder as it proclaims its spiritual standards and sanctions. At Calvary we see how inflexibly earnest God is about inflicting the penalty of His law, for "He . . . spared not his own Son" (Romans 8:32) when the Son stood as our sin-bearer. But there also we see God's glorious plan of salvation whereby He can be just and yet justify sinners who deserve His wrath (Romans 3:26). Because Christ satisfied the law both as to its precept and its penalty, God can justify sinners who have no personal merit to commend them. Albert Midlane beautifully expressed this theme:

The perfect righteousness of God
Is witnessed in the Saviour's blood;
'Tis in the cross of Christ we trace
His righteousness, yet wondrous grace.

God could not pass the sinner by,
His sin demands that he must die;
But in the cross of Christ we see
How God can save us righteously.

The sin is on the Saviour laid,
'Tis in His blood sin's debt is paid;
Stern Justice can demand no more,
And Mercy can dispense her store.

The sinner who believes is free,
Can say: "The Saviour died for me;"
Can point to the atoning blood,
And say: "This made my peace with God."

CHAPTER FOUR

THE CURSE OF THE LAW

"As many as are of the works of the law are under the curse: for it is written, Cursed is every one that continueth not in all things which are written in the book of the law to do them."
Galatians 3:10

There is an awful majesty about God's law. It is a transcript of the nature of the one who gave it. It not only states what God commands, it reveals what He is. It is the voice of heaven's authority on earth. It is not a statement of options or preferences but the imperial declaration of right and wrong from the King of kings to all men. The law is the rule and standard by which God judges men, and that standard is infinitely more spiritual and exacting than a cursory glance at the Ten Commandments may lead us to think. Understood in its spiritual fulness, God's law is a terrifying thing to sinners. But depraved men refuse to consider the spiritual fulness of the law. In the mistaken belief that God's holiness will not be too hard on human sinfulness, sinners lose all true sense of their sin and their need. Thus they proudly try to obtain eternal life by the works of the law.

This is the deadly error Paul combats in Galatians 3:10: "As many as are of the works of the law are under the curse: for it is written, Cursed is every one that continueth not in all things which are written in the book of the law to do them." This is a quotation from Deuteronomy 27:26, the last of the twelve curses of God on disobedience that are listed in that chapter: "Cursed be he that confirmeth not all the words of this law to do them. And all the people shall say, Amen."

Clearly the law imposes a solemn curse on all who break its commandments.

God's Law Exposes Sin

The law of God exposes sin for what it really is. It unmasks sinners and sets their sin in its true colours. No smugness or self-righteousness can withstand its penetrating conviction. Paul spoke from experience. Looking back on his own life he remembered a time when he had felt complacent in his own imagined righteousness: "Sin, taking occasion by the commandment, wrought in me all manner of concupiscence. For without the law sin was dead. For I was alive without the law once: but when the commandment came, sin revived, and I died. And the commandment, which was ordained to life, I found to be unto death" (Romans 7:8–10). In other words, before the law brought a true conviction of sin to Paul's heart he felt at ease with himself and was proud of his righteous attainments. "Sin was dead," that is, it lay unrecognized. It did not perturb or accuse him. He was unafraid of God's judgment, being perfectly convinced of his personal worthiness before his Maker. He felt good about himself, or in the jargon of today, he had high self-esteem.

Then the Lord taught him the true meaning of His law, and it shattered his pride. That new understanding of the law made the formerly self-satisfied Pharisee tremble under the fear of God and of death. He felt himself condemned by the law that he had previously imagined smiled its blessing on his righteous life. For the first time in his life, Paul, who as a Pharisee had learned every technical detail of the Ten Commandments, knew "the curse of the law." He saw sin as God saw it. It was a life-changing experience.

Paul never forgot the lesson he learned. Writing to the Corinthians he said, "The sting of death is sin; and the strength of sin is the law" (1 Corinthians 15:56). In Romans 8:2 he even describes the law as "the law of sin and death." How can he call God's holy law "the law of sin"? He makes it clear that he does not mean that the law is sinful. "Is the law sin? God forbid. . . . The law is holy, and the commandment holy, and just, and good" (Romans 7:7, 12). Paul means that the law stands related to sin in something like a cause-and-effect relationship. "Sin is the transgression of the law" (1 John 3:4). "Where no law is, there is no transgression. . . . Sin is not imputed when there is no law" (Romans 4:15; 5:13). It is the existence of God's law that gives our actions their moral quality. The law makes sin sinful. It reveals sin's true viciousness and exposes its rejection of God's holiness. The law destroys any view of sin but its own. It rips the self-righteous mask off sinners and exposes their wickedness as it truly is. It allows for no excuses.

This "law work" is what it means for a sinner to come under conviction of sin. Regrettably, most modern evangelistic efforts leave little room for true conviction of sin. Preachers are so eager to register "decisions for Christ" that they seem afraid to allow sinners to groan under the terrible weight of realized guilt. Henry Moorehouse was undoubtedly right in insisting that he would "not put even a tear between a sinner and the Saviour." We may not tell a sinner that he must have a certain feeling or expression of sorrow before he may come to Christ for salvation. It is always wise to point sinners directly to the Lord Jesus, with no man-made hindrances placed in their way. But it is also wise to allow the law of God to do its proper work of exposing sin and making the sinner realize that he is guilty and without excuse before God. As long as a man makes some excuse for his sin, he has not experienced the convicting power of the law. The very first thing the law does is to make us see our sin for what it really is.

God's Law Condemns Sinners

Second, the law condemns sinners for their sin. "Cursed is every one that continueth not in all things which are written in the book of the law to do them." This means exactly what it says. All who fail to render complete and perfect obedience to God's law come under its curse. By this standard all men fall under the curse of God's law, for what the Lord Jesus Christ said of the Jews of His day is equally true of all men: "None of you keepeth the law" (John 7:19).

The word *curse* is one that should inspire awe. Among men it denotes something spoken with ill will or malevolence, a malediction, a pronouncement of evil upon its object. But that is not the meaning when we speak of God's curse on sinners who break His law. When God curses He does not express a mere wish but pronounces a righteous judgment on people who are worthy of His wrath. That is what Paul means in Galatians 3:10, "Cursed is every one that continueth not in all things which are written in the book of the law to do them." This curse is the righteous judgment of a holy God pronounced in strict accordance with His law.

That makes the text we are considering a very serious statement for all sinners. By nature, sinners are inveterate rebels. They are determined sinners. Sin is not only what they do; it is what they heartily serve. Sin rules in their hearts, governing the principles of action in their souls.

Paul describes the powerful principle of sin in the natural man, a principle so powerful and persistent that it continued to oppose all holiness in him even when he had become a new creature in Christ: "But I see another law in my members [flesh], warring against the law of my mind [i.e., his renewed mind, what he calls "the inward man" in the preceding verse] and bringing me into captivity to the law of sin which is in my members" (Romans 7:23). This "law of sin" is the evil principle of inbred wickedness that rules as a monarch in every unconverted soul and impels it to rebel against God.

So deep is this evil principle in fallen man that it makes even God's holy law an occasion for sin. "Sin, taking occasion by the commandment, wrought in me all manner of concupiscence. . . . And the commandment, which was ordained to life, I found to be unto death. For sin, taking occasion by the commandment, deceived me, and by it slew me" (Romans 7:8, 10–11). Sin makes the law an occasion for expressing itself in a variety of ways. It makes the very mention of what God has prohibited the occasion for lusting after it. It makes the forbidden desirable. It decries all divine authority, emboldening the sinner to declare his independence from God, saying in effect, "I will be free to be my own master. I recognize no authority higher than myself. I will decide and act according to my own beliefs and purposes. I do not admit the right of any code of law, any Bible, to dictate to me what is right and wrong." In this way the sinner views God's "perfect law of liberty" (James 1:25) as a curtailment of his own liberty and a threat to his imagined autonomy.

Thus, governing the soul of fallen man is the law of *rebellion* against which God has written the law of *retribution*. He calls His law "the law of sin and *death.*" Here is a solemn truth. God's law is a law of death for every sinner. It utterly condemns him and sentences him to death for his sin. In 2 Corinthians 3:6 Paul says, "The letter killeth." By *letter* he means the written law of God, that same law which he terms "the ministration of death" (v. 7) and "the ministration of condemnation" (v. 9). Some superficial expositors of this passage interpret the letter of the law to mean strict compliance with the law's requirements. On that basis they conclude that such close observance of God's law is a deadly thing, that we should not be concerned with strictness as long as we honour "the spirit of the law." Such nonsense has no place in Paul's thinking. We cannot observe the spirit of God's law if we ignore what His Spirit has actually written! In the context of 2 Corinthians 3 we are left in no doubt about what the apostle means by the expression "the letter killeth." The letter means the law of God itself, not merely a punctilious observance of it.

The law kills. It condemns sinners to death. Paul draws the connection between God's law, our sin, and the sentence of death in Romans 7:5: "When we were in the flesh, the motions of sins, which were by the law, did work in our members to bring forth fruit unto death." Simply put, "The wages of sin is death" (Romans 6:23). That is the sentence of God's law. For sinners it is a law of death.

This death is real, personal, and total—that is, spiritual, physical, and eternal. The apostle John described how he saw the fate of sinners condemned by God's law: "I saw the dead, small and great, stand before God; and the books were opened: and another book was opened, which is the book of life: and the dead were judged out of those things which were written in the books, according to their works. And the sea gave up the dead which were in it; and death and hell delivered up the dead which were in them: and they were judged every man according to their works. And death and hell were cast into the lake of fire. This is the second death. And whosoever was not found written in the book of life was cast into the lake of fire" (Revelation 20:12–15). This is the law of death in operation. This is the curse of the law in its final expression.

God's Law Condemns Partial Obedience

We must carefully note a third important truth as we consider the curse of the law: God's law condemns sinners who seek salvation by partial obedience to it. "Cursed is every one that *continueth not in all things which are written in the book of the law to do them.*"

It comes very naturally to fallen man to try to do something to place God under obligation to him and thus to earn his way to heaven. Men often speak glibly about keeping the Ten Commandments or about living by the Sermon on the Mount or by the example of Jesus. They parade such efforts as sure ways of gaining heaven. By this they propose that God should accept and justify them on the basis of their flawed and sinful attempts at legal obedience. A flawed and sinful attempt at keeping God's law is the best sinners can do, but it is not enough. The law demands perfect obedience and it condemns partial obedience as actual disobedience. That is why the Bible adamantly declares that "no man is justified by the law in the sight of God" (Galatians 3:11). In Romans 8:3 Paul makes the same point: "What the law could not do, in that it was weak through the flesh, God sending his own Son in the likeness of sinful flesh, and for sin, condemned sin in the flesh." In the Greek text, the phrase *what the law could not do* is literally "the impossibility, or inability, of the law." What is it that the law has no power to do? The answer of Scripture is clear: The law is incapable of freeing sinners from its condemnation. It cannot justify them. It offers no hope of salvation on the basis of their partial obedience. Rather, it makes their vaunted, flawed obedience an added ground of condemnation. That is the sole power of the law toward the eternal destiny of sinners.

If that were all that the Bible had to say about the curse of the law we would all be lost in hopelessness and despair. But it is not. There is yet one more truth we must consider about the curse of the law, a truth that sheds the light of grace to dispel the darkness of our guilt.

God's Law Commends and Accepts Perfect Obedience

The implication of Galatians 3:10 is that God's law commends and accepts perfect obedience. If "it is written, Cursed is every one that continueth not in all things which are written in the book of the law to do them," then we must logically conclude, "Blessed is he who does continue in all things that are written in the book of the law to do them." We know that this conclusion is valid because we read, "The commandment . . . was ordained to life" (Romans 7:10; compare Leviticus 18:5; Galatians 3:12).

Wherever the law finds perfect obedience it commends and accepts it. But where can it find such obedience? Is there one who is free from the guilt of Adam's first transgression? Is there one who is sinless in nature, principle, and practice? Is there any such person?

There is. There is only one, the Lord Jesus Christ. He kept the law of God absolutely perfectly. From heaven God the Father testified to His perfect obedience, "In him I am well pleased" (see Matthew 3:17; 17:5). When God's law searched the humanity of Christ and sifted His thoughts, feelings, motives, words, and actions it found nothing but absolute sinlessness. Here is the perfect man. "Mark the perfect man" says the Psalmist (Psalm 37:37). The law of God marks the Lord Jesus Christ as perfect in every way. Thus it blesses Him. He is the blessed one who continues in all things that are written in the book of the law to do them.

If there were some way that we, who stand condemned by the law, could be united to Christ, who has merited its blessing, we could escape the condemnation of the law. If there were some way that we could be invested with His righteous merit we could be justified.

Is there such a way? There is! Indeed, this is the whole point of the gospel. "Christ hath redeemed us from the curse of the law, being made a curse for us: for it is written, Cursed is every one that hangeth on a tree: that the blessing of Abraham might come on the Gentiles through Jesus Christ; that we might receive the promise of the Spirit through faith" (Galatians 3:13–14). By His life, Christ fulfilled the precept of the law. By His death, He paid the penalty of the law that He had kept and that we had broken. He did all this for us. All His work in satisfying the highest demands of the law of God were vicarious. Christ stood as one with us, His believing people. God imputed our sin to Him so that He might impute His righteousness to us. "He hath made him to be sin for us, who knew no sin; that we might be made the righteousness of God in him" (2 Corinthians 5:21).

Christ bore the curse of the law and merited its blessing for all those who believe on Him. What we could never obtain by our feeble, sinful attempts at law-keeping, Christ has obtained for us by His perfect obedience to both the law's precept and penalty. We receive that free righteousness by faith, not by works. Working in order to obtain acceptance with God brings us back under the law and under the curse. Believing in Him who has merited the blessing of the law frees us from the curse and places us on redemption ground.

CHAPTER FIVE

THE UNLAWFUL USE OF THE LAW

"We know that the law is good, if a man use it lawfully."
1 Timothy 1:8

The law of God is good. The New Testament goes to great lengths to make that clear. "The law is holy, and the commandment holy, and just, and good [Greek *agathos*]. . . . I consent unto the law that it is good [Greek *kalos*]" (Romans 7:12, 16). "We know that the law is good [*kalos*]" (1 Timothy 1:8). By using these two Greek words to describe the goodness of the law the Scripture shows us that the law is good and excellent in itself, well fitted for the purpose for which God gave it and beneficial to those who use it for that purpose. It could not be other than good for it is the expression of the character and will of Him who is supremely good.

However, even a good thing may be put to an evil use. There is a good use of God's law. There is also an evil use of it. And such is the perversion of man's depraved nature that he inevitably tends to misuse and abuse it.

Paul had all of this in mind in writing 1 Timothy chapter 1. As the minister of the church in Ephesus Timothy was having a difficult time combating the spurious doctrine of certain people who posed as "teachers of the law" (verse 7) but who were ignorant of the true meaning and purpose of the law. They were *perverters* of the law, given to wild and fanciful interpretations of the Pentateuch. Worse still, they sought to bring the Ephesian believers from the liberty of grace to the bondage of law.

The predictable results of their activities were confusion and division in the church.

1 Timothy 1:1–11 was Paul's response to the challenge presented by these false teachers. It has much to teach us today for it emphasizes a sobering truth: The misuse of God's law poses a real danger to any church that tolerates it. *When men go wrong on the law they also go wrong on the gospel because they distort the true relationship between the two.* That makes Paul's statement in 1 Timothy 1:8 a matter of urgent importance. In this passage, the apostle does not give a full, theological exposition of the functions of the law, but as he replies to some Jewish perversions of the law he makes four telling points.

First, *the law burdens sinners.* The statement in 1 Timothy 1:9 that "the law is not made for a righteous man, but for the lawless and disobedient" means that God directs His law against sinners. It does not mean that God does not address His law to justified men as a rule of life; it is not a support for antinomianism. Later in these studies we will address the biblical proof against the antinomian attitude toward the law. For the moment we simply note that the Greek verb *keimai,* translated "made" in the Authorised Version, literally means "to lie upon." Thus we may render Paul's statement, "The law does not lie [as a burden] upon a righteous man, but upon the lawless and disobedient." God's law is not a heavy burden bearing down on the justified, because their burden has been removed through the obedience of Christ. But His law does weigh heavily on unjustified lawbreakers, who labour under the load of their own guilt. So the law burdens sinners, not saints.

Second, *the law exposes sin.* Paul's listing of specific sins in verses 9 and 10 plainly infers this. Even though society may accept such things as normal or tolerable, the law of God exposes them for what they are. John Calvin comments, "The Law is like the mirror in which we first contemplate our own weakness, then the iniquity that proceeds from the same, and finally the malediction which comes of both, even as in a mirror we perceive the blemishes upon our face" (*Institutes,* 2.7.7). To a Christian the exposing power of the law is a welcome light, not a frightening threat. David wrote, "By them [Thy judgments] is thy servant warned: and in keeping of them there is great reward" (Psalm 19:11). To an unbeliever, on the other hand, the exposing power of the law is a divine indictment that foreshadows a certain judgment. Even sinners who have no access to the written word of God know the law's power to expose their sin: "[The Gentiles] shew the work of the law written in their hearts, their conscience also bearing witness, and their thoughts the mean while accusing or else excusing one another" (Romans 2:15).

Third, *the law condemns sinners.* The language of our passage is unmistakably the language of condemnation. The bearing down of the law on sinners carries the idea of a heavy punishment. Paul makes the same point in other places: "We know that what things soever the law saith, it saith to them who are under the law: that every mouth may be stopped, and all the world may become guilty before God" (Romans 3:19); "Cursed is every one that continueth not in all things which are written in the book of the law to do them" (Galatians 3:10). In the light of all this, the law cannot save sinners. It has no power to deliver sinners from the condemnation it imposes on them. As Paul says in Romans 8:3, it is "weak through the flesh."

One particular aspect of the law's condemning function is its role in restraining sinners. There can be no doubt that the law's restraining power is a benefit to mankind. So how can it be a condemning work? We know that the purpose of hindering the commission of sin was obviously in God's mind when He thundered forth the stern prohibitions of the law, especially when He pronounced His curse on every breach of it. As earthly rulers and judges are—or ought to be—a terror to wicked works (Romans 13:3) and use their laws to promote civil righteousness, so the Lord uses the terror of His law to restrain sinners. But—and this is what further condemns unregenerate men—though they curb the expression of their lust they do so only by *compulsion.* Their need of compulsion witnesses against them so that their restraint, far from making them more righteous before God, actually makes them doubly condemned. As Calvin well says of those who are hindered from doing evil by the terror of the law, "Their heart is not touched." Indeed, it is inflamed to deeper sinfulness: "Not only does their heart still remain evil; they also have a mortal hatred of the law of God, and for as much as God is its author they hold him in execration. . . . This feeling shows itself more openly in some, in others it is more hidden, nevertheless it is in all those who are not regenerate. . . . This constrained and forced obedience is necessary to the community of men, for the tranquillity which our Saviour provides by preventing all things from being overturned in confusion—which is what would happen if everything were permitted to everyone" (*Institutes,* 2.7.10). As God's gift to human society, the restraining function of the law is good. Nevertheless, it is an added factor in the condemnation of sinners.

Fourth, *the law directs sinners to the gospel.* It shuts them up to the gospel as their only hope for salvation. In 1 Timothy 1:10–11 Paul speaks of "sound doctrine according to the glorious gospel of the blessed God." This glorious gospel stands in sharp contrast to the "vain jangling" (verse 6) of those who make the law the means of justification. As in all his epistles, Paul's message continues to be salvation by grace alone through faith alone in Christ alone. He made this clear in his ministry to the Ephesians from the very beginning (Ephesians 2:8–9) and in meeting the challenge of these Judaising teachers of the law, he does not shift his ground one hairbreadth.

Having said that we are saved by grace through faith and not by works, Paul continues, "For we are his workmanship, created in Christ Jesus unto good works, which God hath before ordained that we should walk in them" (Ephesians 2:10). He not only declares that the gospel alone can save, but he also insists that it, not the law, can sanctify. The law may show us what sin is. It may point out what displeases God. But it cannot create in us the power to be holy. It may set the standard, but only the gospel can empower us to strive after holiness. The ability to do good works is the direct result of the new creation. The law cannot save us in any sense of the word. It cannot justify, sanctify, or glorify. Only Christ can do these things, and the law itself witnesses to this truth (Romans 3:21).

These four points represent a lawful use of the law. Any deviation from these basic truths in our handling of the law of God is an unlawful use of the law. There are four ways in which men frequently use the law unlawfully.

Using God's Law as an Occasion for Sin

It is unlawful to make God's law an occasion for sin. Yet this is invariably the way in which self-righteous sinners use it. "What shall we say then? Is the law sin? God forbid. Nay, I had not known sin, but by the law: for I had not known lust, except the law had said, Thou shalt not covet. But sin, taking occasion by the commandment, wrought in me all manner of concupiscence. For without the law sin was dead" (Romans 7:7–8). Many commentators take this to mean that when we understand the spirituality of the law we will acutely feel the greatness of our lust and wickedness. It is true that a person who perceives the spirituality of the law will feel how great a sinner he is, but this does not exhaust Paul's meaning.

He says that sin took occasion by the law to work in him all manner of evil desire. *Take occasion* is an interesting expression. It means that sin took the law as its point of departure, as its fulcrum, or, to use a military term, as its base of operation. Such is the innate wickedness of our hearts that we abuse the commandment of God's law to lust after the very thing it prohibits! We give our attention, not to God's law, but to what it forbids. We begin to think on the prohibited thing as something desirable and then we fall to lusting after it. This is surely an unlawful use of the law.

Using God's Law as the Way of Salvation

Second, it is unlawful to use God's law as a way of salvation. That was the practice of the Jews, Judaisers, and the Ephesian would-be teachers of the law. As Romans 10:3 explains, "They being ignorant of God's righteousness, and going about to establish their own righteousness, have not submitted themselves unto the righteousness of God." This is the error that the New Testament constantly opposes. It is unlawful to use the law as a ground of acceptance with God. "By the works of the law shall no flesh be justified" (Galatians 2:16). We tend to think of justification by works-righteousness as a dogma peculiar to Judaism or Roman Catholicism. But the notion of establishing merit with God by the works of the law may also be found in churches that pay lip service to the truth of a free, gracious justification received by faith alone in the merits of

Christ. Whoever adopts salvation by law-keeping comes under the condemnation of the New Testament, which rejects every scheme of human meritorious law-keeping as unlawful. To give place to such a scheme would have devastating consequences.

To use the law as a way of salvation would steal the glory of God. According to Romans 8:33, "It is God that justifieth." But if salvation is by law-keeping, we justify ourselves. To use the law against God is plainly unlawful.

To use the law as a way of salvation would deny the grace of God. Nowhere does the New Testament more clearly distinguish between the false gospel of salvation by works and the true gospel of salvation by grace than in Romans 4:4–5: "Now to him that worketh is the reward not reckoned of grace, but of debt. But to him that worketh not, but believeth on him that justifieth the ungodly, his faith is counted for righteousness." If salvation were by law-keeping, God would justify the *godly.* But thankfully the Bible does not teach the justification of the godly, for that would leave all of us without hope. No, God "justifieth the ungodly." That is grace. There would be no grace in justifying the godly or in giving salvation to those who had earned it. To use God's law to deny His grace is plainly an unlawful use of the law.

To use the law as a way of salvation would destroy the gospel of God. What is the gospel? It is the good news of what God did for sinners in the person and work of the Lord Jesus Christ. "I delivered unto you first of all that which I also received, how that Christ died for our sins according to the scriptures; and that he was buried, and that he rose again the third day according to the scriptures" (1 Corinthians 15:3–4). That is the good news. Anyone who embraces the law as a way of salvation is seeking to work his own way to heaven. Effectively he declares, "I do not need the gospel." Thus salvation by law-keeping is an attack on Christ's atonement. It is a rejection of His shed blood. It is a blasphemy that robs the incarnation, obedience, death, resurrection, and intercession of Christ of all saving merit. To use the law of God to attack the gospel of God is plainly an unlawful use of the law.

Using God's Law to Condemn Believers

Third, it is unlawful to use God's law to condemn believers. Paul must have had this in mind when he opposed the Judaisers who were troubling the church and trying to bring believers under guilt. This was happening even in the church at Ephesus, a church well taught in the doctrines of grace. The Ephesians had heard from Paul himself the glorious truths of union with Christ, acceptance with God on the sole merits of Christ, redemption through the blood of Christ, and salvation by grace through faith without works (see Ephesians 1:4–2:10). Yet even among these people, perverters of the gospel were trying to rob believers of the freedom and assurance they enjoyed by grace. They were seeking to use the law to bring believers back under condemnation. That is a vicious and unlawful thing to do. The law does not bear down on God's people. The use of the law to beat Christians into the ground and to rob them of the assurance they have in Christ is a wicked misuse of the law.

One would think that this would be self-evident. However, there are preachers who delight in manufacturing legal missiles to launch against Christian confidence. Some Arminian "holiness" preachers do this. So do some Calvinists who seem to consider it great success to send believers away from their meetings consumed by doubt. To hear them, one would think that doubt, not assurance, was a Christian virtue. What a perversion of God's law to use it to bring Christians under guilt!

That abuse of the law was the essence of the Galatian error. The Galatian Christians had placed their faith in the Lord Jesus Christ to the saving of their souls. Now perverters of the gospel undermined their assurance of His all-sufficient merit by making them feel condemned by the law and in need of establishing their own merit with God by personal legal obedience. These false teachers professed to believe on the Lord Jesus Christ, but they taught that faith alone in Him alone was not enough to place a soul in a right relationship with God. According to these perverters of the gospel, believers had to have Christ *plus,* the blood *plus,* faith *plus* something. That *plus* was always some work of legal obedience that was necessary to make them acceptable with God.

Against all such misuse of the law of God Paul stated the gospel in radical terms. "There is therefore now no condemnation to them which are in Christ Jesus" (Romans 8:1). *No* condemnation! It is significant that Paul makes this statement immediately after his treatment of the believer's ongoing battle with indwelling sin. The apostle confesses that a believer is not sinless. He does things that he should not do and fails to do things that he should do. He consents to the law that it is good but finds "another law"—indwelling sin—warring in his body. Paul identifies himself with the rest of God's people in this battle and goes so far as to say, "In me (that is, in my flesh,) dwelleth no good thing" (Romans 7:18). He cries out, "O wretched man that I am! who shall deliver me from the body of this death?" (Romans 7:24), and laments, "With the mind I myself serve the law of God; but with the flesh the law of sin" (verse 25).

The verdict of all human religions upon this confession is that such a man could not possibly be free from condemnation. While he still serves the law of sin in his flesh he must stand condemned. Thus, human religion declares that man must work to atone for his sin and thereby escape condemnation. That is the response of human religion, but it is not the response of the inspired apostle. To the believer still battling with inborn sin he says in effect, "Christ is our righteousness, Christ is our merit, Christ is our perfection. God has imputed Christ's righteousness to us and placed all His merit to our account. This is the ground of our legal acceptance with God, not anything that we have personally done. Therefore, there is no condemnation to them that are in Christ Jesus."

Later in Romans 8 Paul issues the challenge, "Who is he that condemneth?" (verse 34). His answer is devastating to everyone who would bring believers in Christ back under the condemnation of the law. What is the Christian answer to the challenge the apostle lays down? Fleshly religion would tell us that we must do something to silence the accuser of our soul. But that only brings us under more condemnation and guilt, for we can never do enough. Thus Paul's answer to the challenge he issues is the all-sufficient merit of Christ: "Who is he that condemneth? It is Christ that died, yea rather, that is risen again, who is even at the right hand of God, who also maketh intercession for us" (Romans 8:34).

Here are the four pillars of the gospel: Christ died, Christ rose again from the dead, Christ ascended to the right hand of God, and Christ makes intercession for His people. The entire edifice of Christian theology stands secure on these four pillars of grace. On the basis of this all-sufficient work of Christ there is no condemnation to those who are in Him, to those who believe on His name. To use God's law to rob them of what Christ has given them and thereby bring them back under the burden of guilt is unlawful. It is to commit the sin that Isaiah condemns: "[Woe to them] which justify the wicked for reward, and take away the righteousness of the righteous from him!" (Isaiah 5:23). Woe to the preacher who blinds God's people to the righteousness they have in Christ and to the assured acceptance they have on the basis of that righteousness! Woe to the man who takes away the righteousness of Christ from a justified man and substitutes some legal observance for it! That is an unlawful use of the law.

Using God's Law as a Burden on Believers

Finally, we must realize that it is unlawful to use God's law as a burden on the backs of believers. This is Paul's clear meaning in 1 Timothy 1:9–10: "The law is not made for a righteous man, but for the lawless and disobedient, for the ungodly and for sinners, for unholy and profane, for murderers of fathers and murderers of mothers, for manslayers, for whoremongers, for them that defile themselves with mankind, for menstealers, for liars, for perjured persons, and if there be any other thing that is contrary to sound doctrine." We have noted that the force of the verb is that the law does not lie as a burden on believers. While this text does not support the antinomian notion that Christians have no obligation to keep God's law, we must state emphatically that according to the plain meaning of the apostle any attempt to lay legal burdens on believers apart from grace and the gospel is both evil and unlawful. We may put that another way: *Any attempt to persuade Christians to live by rule and not by faith is unlawful.* A Christian observes God's law because God has placed it in his heart as something he loves, not on his back as a burden he bears. David testified, "I delight to do thy will, O my God: yea, thy law is within my heart" (Psalm 40:8). In Psalm 37:31 he says of the righteous man, "The law of his God is in his heart; none of his steps shall slide."

One of the most alarming defects of the modern church is the widespread misunderstanding of the gospel. We may even say, the *misrepresentation* of the gospel. In many "good" churches, with saved and sincere preachers, God's people constantly hear sermons that burden them with rules and regulations—*principles,* they are usually called. As a result, many imagine that the gospel is something that tells sinners how to be saved, while Christian principles are what direct Christians how to live once they have been saved. Anything further from the New Testament approach would be difficult to imagine. The New Testament invariably sets before Christians the gospel of grace and faith in Christ as He is revealed in that gospel. On that basis it calls believers to obey God. We live by faith. That simply means that what we believe concerning Christ and our position in Him governs what we do. We respond to God's word and God's law in the light of the cross. Calvary controls our response to Sinai.

Any attempt to set up a system of rules or principles in the place of a life lived by faith in Christ will bring bondage and bitterness. C. H. Spurgeon's comment (on Psalm 37:31) about God's law is memorable: "In the head it puzzles, on the back it burdens, in the heart it upholds." Believers keep God's law because they love it and the One who gave it, the One who in love for them gave His Son to be their Saviour. The gospel motivates believers to observe God's law as a delight to their soul, an expression of the very will of God they find written on their hearts. The law may tell us what to do, but it cannot give us the desire or power to do it. Only gospel grace can do that. To divorce obedience from the gospel and from Christ is blatant legalism. It is an unlawful use of God's law.

A common sin unites all these abuses. Ultimately, each of them substitutes the law for Christ. *Christ, not the law, should be for us the way of salvation, the base of all our operations, the ground of our freedom from condemnation, and the source of our motivation and power to live holy lives.* We must never allow anyone to set the law in Christ's place.

Let the weight of the law fall on sinners. God intends that it should. He did not give it to bear down on His redeemed people, because it has already fallen in all its force on their Saviour and Substitute. Did not

Christ perfectly fulfil the law for His people? Did He not then go to the cross and pay the full penalty for all their breaches of the law? If the law lay hard on Christ—if it bore down on Him—and He satisfied it, then it is unlawful for any man to make it bear down on a believer in Christ.

We must ever be watchful lest anyone move us from the lawful to the unlawful use of God's law.

CHAPTER SIX

THE LAW IN THE LIFE OF THE BELIEVER

"Whoso looketh into the perfect law of liberty, and continueth therein, he being not a forgetful hearer, but a doer of the work, this man shall be blessed in his deed."
James 1:25

The relationship of believers to God's law has always been a matter of heated controversy in the Christian church. At one extreme, legalists teach that it is by law-keeping that we gain acceptance with God. While denying that it teaches salvation by works, the Roman Catholic Church adopts this legalistic position. The *Catechism of the Catholic Church,* Rome's most recent authoritative and exhaustive statement of her beliefs, says, "*No one can merit the initial grace* of forgiveness and justification, at the beginning of conversion. Moved by the Holy Spirit and by charity, *we can then merit* for ourselves and for others the graces needed for our sanctification, for the increase of grace and charity, and for the attainment of eternal life" (¶2010, emphasis in the original).

At the opposite extreme, antinomians hold that the law has been entirely abrogated for Christians. They do not mean merely that justification is not by our law-keeping. They mean that the law is no longer even a rule of life for those who have been justified by faith, that it has nothing whatever to do with believers.

Nowadays, it appears that most evangelicals are practical antinomians. They think they are free from the law in every sense. Their greatest fear seems not to be of sinning but of possibly being thought legalistic. On the other hand there are others who emphasize the law so much in salvation, sanctification, and service that they have actually adopted a name that means something very similar to *legalistic,* the name *theonomist.* To coin a phrase, theonomists are *God's lawists.* A pair of theonomist writers have stated, "Whatever they may call themselves, all who are not keeping the ten commandments of God can be certain that God does not love them. Anything contrary is a lie. The sinning Christian has been repeatedly told that God loves you and has a wonderful plan for your life. Sadly nothing could be further from the truth for their end shall be eternal destruction. Can we despise God's grace by flouting His law and be loved?" These writers make it plain that being an object of God's love depends on our personal observance of the law. The same writers go on to say, "God's love is not unconditional." This is the opinion of an important and voluble section of the Reformed church in reaction to the practical antinomianism of much of modern evangelicalism.

So the battle lines are drawn and the controversy about the believer's relationship to the law still rages. The issue is not a small one. Indeed, it is so great that it touches the very essence of salvation and Christian living. How are we to be saved? And as Christians how are we to live? What is the God-given standard for the Christian's life? What part, if any, does God's law have to play in the lives of justified believers in Christ?

Under the influence of dispensationalism many Christians shrug off the obligations of God's law. When one seeks to bring the plain commands of God's word to bear upon their manner of life, these people facilely reply, "We are not under law. It does not apply to us." The statement of James 1:25 directly addresses this attitude: "Whoso looketh into the perfect law of liberty, and continueth therein, he being not a forgetful hearer, but a doer of the work, this man shall be blessed in his deed." James describes the law as every Christian should view it: "the perfect law, the one of liberty." True believers look into God's law. They do not ignore it or shrug it off by saying, "That belongs to the Old Testament." No, looking into this perfect law of liberty they continue in it by yielding blessed obedience to it. That is the proper attitude of Christians to the law of God.

In the light of James 1:25, the relationship of the believer to the law appears so clear as to be beyond controversy. However, there are other statements in the New Testament that appear to say something else. *Appear* is the operative word. In this study I hope to make it clear that the outline just given of James' teaching is in fact the teaching of the whole Bible on the subject. The point to be proved is that Christians are called to continual obedience to the moral law of God and thereby to blessing and liberty.

No Salvation by Law-keeping

First of all, one truth must be emphasized: No one can be saved by keeping the law of God. God offered life on the basis of keeping the law once and only once, and that was in the Garden of Eden. When Adam fell, such was the devastating result of the entrance of sin into humanity that from that point onwards it was totally impossible for men to fulfil God's law. By any attempt at personal obedience, it was impossible for them to remove the guilt and stain of the sin of which they were already guilty. It was impossible for them to establish a perfect righteousness before God.

When the rich young ruler came to the Lord Jesus Christ, he asked Him what good thing he might do to inherit eternal life. The Lord Jesus answered him, "If thou wilt enter into life, keep the commandments" (Matthew 19:17). Some imagine that the Saviour was offering the young man eternal life on the basis of law-keeping. The Lord Jesus would not have been so cruel. We are told that He looked on this young man and loved him. Thus we are certain that He was not dealing with him in irony or in judgment, but in kindness. But there would have been no kindness in saying to a man who was a sinner by nature and practice, "If you provide yourself a perfect obedience to the law you will have eternal life." That would have been a cruel mockery. To see what the Lord meant, consider the story of the rich young ruler. Here was a very upright young man who could not imagine that he was a sinner. As he came before the Saviour he said, "I have kept the entire law." Anyone who thinks or speaks like this has no conception of sin or of the absolute holiness of God. So the Lord Jesus met the young man on his own ground. In effect He said to him, "You wish to gain eternal life by your obedience to the law. But the standard of the law is one of perfect righteousness. If you cannot meet that standard you can never enter into life." The Saviour's treatment of the young ruler left him in no doubt (a) that he loved his wealth more than he loved God; and (b) that he was unwilling to become a disciple of Christ. If the young man had little doubt about his goodness when he approached the Lord Jesus, he could have had no doubt about his sinfulness as he went away—a sorrowful, money-worshipping Christ rejector.

It is always difficult to get men to see their sin. All too often preachers compound the difficulty. In their desire to be "relevant" to people today they adopt the slang of the streets. One preacher recently thought he had a better way of showing men their sin than by quoting or expounding any statement of Scripture. He told his audience that God had said, "You really goofed up." Not only did that preacher have no right to attribute such language to the Lord, but his definition of sin was extremely deficient. That became alarmingly clear as he went on to speak of sin as a lack in man that hindered his living up to his potential and as something that hurt his neighbours. In his entire treatment of sin, the preacher made no reference to the absolute holiness of God or to the absolute righteous standard of His law.

Nowadays, it is common for men to claim that they are "not too bad." The absence of any real consciousness of deep and terrible guilt is attributable, at least in part, to the fact that the Christian pulpit has been largely silent on the holiness of God, holiness so awesome that the very angels of heaven cover their faces in God's presence and cry, "Holy! Holy! Holy!" Let a sinner get just a glimpse of the holiness of God and he will never again claim that he is not too bad or that he is doing his best to work his way to heaven.

In His treatment of the rich young ruler, the Lord Jesus clearly teaches us to see the sinfulness of the best of men and to recognize their inability to do anything to merit eternal life. Unless a man has a holiness as perfect as that of the purest archangel from the moment of his conception until the moment of his death, he can never gain salvation by keeping the law.

The word of God uses the law to make men see their lost state so that, with God's judgment hanging over them, they will be driven to seek salvation where God has revealed it, namely in the person and work of the Lord Jesus Christ. Paul gave the Christians at Rome this clear exposition of the way of salvation: "Now we know that what things soever the law saith, it saith to them who are under the law: that every mouth may be stopped, and all the world may become guilty before God. Therefore by the deeds of the law there shall no flesh be justified in his sight: for by the law is the knowledge of sin. But now the righteousness of God without the law is manifested, being witnessed by the law and the prophets; even the righteousness of God which is by faith of Jesus Christ unto all and upon all them that believe: for there is no difference: for all have sinned, and come short of the glory of God; being justified freely by his grace through the redemption that is in Christ Jesus: whom God hath set forth to be a propitiation through faith in his blood, to declare his righteousness for the remission of sins that are past, through the forbearance of God; to declare, I say, at this time his righteousness: that he might be just, and the justifier of him which believeth in Jesus" (Romans 3:19–26).

In other words, pointing condemned sinners to His Son in whom His law is perfectly fulfilled and in whose blood its sentence has been fully satisfied, God says, "I will forgive your sin. I will put to your account the immaculate righteousness of Christ. You stand before me invested with all the merit of His sinless life and atoning death. I made Him to be sin for you that you might be made the righteousness of God in Him." This is God's answer to the all-important question, "What must I do to be saved?" There is no other answer.

The Christian's Duty to Obey the Law

No man can become a Christian by keeping the law, but once he is saved by grace through faith in Christ it is his continuing duty to observe God's holy law. James 1:25 makes that abundantly clear, and many other Scriptures confirm it.

When God gave the Ten Commandments to the Israelites gathered at the foot of Mount Sinai, He did something unique in the history of the world. Most people seem to have the idea that the Lord took Moses up into the mount and that there He wrote the commandments on the tables of stone with His own finger. That is true as far as it goes, but it misses a vital point. When He gave His law the Lord personally spoke the Ten Commandments in the hearing of all the gathered nation of Israel. They actually heard the voice of God. "God spake all these words, saying, I am the Lord thy God, which have brought thee out of the land of Egypt, out of the house of bondage. Thou shalt have no other gods before me" (Exodus 20:1–3; see Deuteronomy 4:33, 36; 5:4, 22). No wonder the people feared and quaked! That was the only time in recorded history that God spoke to such a company in such a way—and He did it to impress on them the duty of redeemed people to receive and obey His moral law.

This is the thrust of the preface to the Ten Commandments: "I am the Lord thy God, which have brought thee out of the land of Egypt, out of the house of bondage." In other words, "I have redeemed you; therefore, keep my commandments." The New Testament confirms this message and makes the keeping of God's law the mark of true believers. We are saved by faith, but as James tells us, faith that saves, works. It produces fruit. This is what distinguishes real faith from dead faith. "Hereby we do know that we know him, if we keep his commandments. He that saith, I know him, and keepeth not his commandments, is a liar, and the truth is not in him" (1 John 2:3–4). The plain meaning of this statement is that anyone who professes to be a Christian and disregards God's law is a liar and, worse still, "the truth is not in him." He is not a Christian at all.

Grace does not lessen a believer's obligation to keep God's law; it increases it. The New Testament believer should have a greater regard for God's law than the Old Testament believer. Paul asks, "Do we then make void [abolish, do away with] the law through faith? God forbid: yea, we establish the law" (Romans 3:31). Does the gospel do away with the law as far as a Christian is concerned? Paul assures us that nothing could be further from the truth: "God forbid!" Or as the Greek text actually puts it, "May it not be!" Rather, we who preach grace alone for salvation establish the law.

All this is clear enough, but it raises a question. How are we to understand some of Paul's other statements? "Wherefore, my brethren, ye also are become dead to the law by the body of Christ; that ye should be married to another, even to him who is raised from the dead, that we should bring forth fruit unto God. . . . But now we are delivered from the law, that being dead [or, we being dead to that] wherein we were held; that we should serve in newness of spirit, and not in the oldness of the letter" (Romans 7:4, 6); "I through the law am dead to the law, that I might live unto God" (Galatians 2:19); and "Ye are not under the law, but under grace" (Romans 6:14).

In Romans 7, Paul likens the sinner who is under the law—and all sinners are—to a woman married to a husband. As long as her husband lives, she is bound to him. If she marries another man while her first husband lives she is an adulteress, whatever human law may say to the contrary. But if her husband dies and she marries again she is not an adulteress. Why? Because death has ended the hold of the law of marriage over her. A sinner is like one who is married to the law. Following his analogy, Paul may be expected to say, "Your first husband—the law—died, and you are free to be married to Christ." However, that is not what the apostle says. Rather, he says, "Ye also are become dead [literally, were slain] to the law by [in] the body of Christ; that ye should be married to another" (Romans 7:4). His meaning is, "In the realm of the flesh you were married to the law, but Christ satisfied the law and has set you free from its condemnation. You are no longer on a fleshly level and—this is the key—in a higher sphere you are married to Christ. In the sphere of the spirit and not of the flesh you are united to Christ who by His death has satisfied the law for you and wiped out its condemnation."

Thus the passages that describe a Christian as being dead to the law or not under the law teach us that he is free from the *condemnation* of the law. It no longer holds him in bondage. He is Christ's free man—free, that is, from the law's condemnation, not from its regulative authority. Christ did not slay the law, He satisfied it (Matthew 5:17).

That is what Paul means in Romans 6:14: "Sin shall not have dominion over you: for ye are not under the law, but under grace." This is a promise of the utmost importance to every Christian. It is a promise about experiencing real holiness in this present evil world. "Sin shall not have dominion over you." Paul's basis for this sweeping statement is the truth that Christians "are not under law, but under grace." Here is the key to Christian victory over sin. It starts with the assurance that the law cannot condemn a believer in Christ, for Christ has satisfied the law on his behalf and set him free to serve God in newness of life.

Puritan preachers liked to make a distinction between the law as a covenant and the law as a commandment. That is a sound and scriptural distinction. As a covenant, the law is finished for every believer in Christ for He has perfectly fulfilled the covenant for all His people. This is glorious news. Because Christ fulfilled the covenant for us, we do not have to work to get to heaven, or to make God love and accept us. His love is not conditioned upon how well we perform, but flows freely to us because of how perfectly Christ performed in our place. For all who are in Christ, the law as a *covenant* has been abrogated forever.

However, the law as a *commandment* has not been abrogated. The commandment still stands. This is clear from the manner in which Paul continues the argument of Romans 6. In verse 15 he proceeds: "What then? shall we sin, because we are not under the law, but under grace? God forbid." If by not being under the law he means that the commandment of the law has been abrogated for believers, this verse makes no sense. Sin is the breach of the law (1 John 3:4), and if the law does not exist for Christians, then Christians cannot sin no matter what they do. Where there is no law, there can be no sin.

But if Paul means that the law as a covenant has been abrogated for believers, Romans 6:15 has a clear and powerful argument: As a means of gaining eternal life, the law is removed. We are now dependent solely on Christ for the merit necessary to enter heaven. Shall we, because we have been freed from the necessity of working our way to heaven by law-keeping, conclude that we have no obligation to obey the call of the law to holiness of life? "God forbid!" says the apostle. The commandment of the law lives on.

In considering the unlawful use of the law in our last chapter, we noted Paul's words in 1 Timothy 1:9–10 (one of antinomianism's favourite verses): "The law is not made for a righteous man, but for the lawless and disobedient, for the ungodly and for sinners, for unholy and profane, for murderers of fathers and murderers of mothers, for manslayers, for whoremongers, for them that defile themselves with mankind, for menstealers, for liars, for perjured persons, and if there be any other thing that is contrary to sound doctrine." Most commentators interpret this to mean that God did not enact His law for righteous men but for sinners. We may safely say that this is most assuredly not the meaning of the passage. God first gave His law to Adam when He placed him under the covenant of works. Was Adam then a righteous man? He certainly was (Ecclesiastes 7:29). God first gave His law to a righteous man—so the popular interpretation of Paul's words to Timothy is in error.

The fact is that God enacted His law for both the righteous and the unrighteous. Indeed, for rational creatures, the words *righteous* and *unrighteous* have no meaning apart from the law. (We must be careful not to try to apply the same rule to God. To us creatures, the word *righteousness* has meaning only because of the prior existence of law. This is not true of God who is inherently and eternally perfect and whose nature defines righteousness. For there to be any law, there must be a righteous lawgiver. Thus law is possible only because God is eternally what He is.) The word translated "made" in 1 Timothy 1:9—"the law is not made for a righteous man"—has various applications. Literally, it means "to lie upon." Paul is saying that the law does not lie upon justified people as a burden, particularly as a burden of condemnation.

Most of the Puritans took this text to mean that the law was not given to condemn the righteous as sinners. To do so was to misuse the law. However, the Puritans never denied that Christians should heartily obey God's law. In 1 Corinthians 9:21, Paul makes obedience to the law the duty of Christians: "To them that are without law, [I became] as without law, (being not without law to God, but under the law to Christ,) that I might gain them that are without law." This is a far-reaching statement. Paul clearly means to distinguish between his attitude to the Mosaic ceremonial laws—to which the Jews were in bondage and which he felt free to ignore in the interest of winning Gentiles for Christ—and the moral law, which he continually observed. Alford's *New Testament for English Readers* renders the apostle's words, "Not being an outlaw from God, but a subject-of-the-law of Christ." Alford adds, "The words seem inserted . . . to put before the reader the true position of a Christian with regard to God's law revealed by Christ." A Christian is neither *antinomian,* "against law," nor *anomian*, "without law," but *ennomos Christo*, as the Greek text has it, "in law to or for Christ."

Christians are "in law," not outside law. God's moral law is their rule and direction. They obey it "for Christ," and that is what makes it a perfect law of liberty. Christians are not lawless people and lawless people are not Christians, but godless, Christless, and enslaved. An old Puritan saying goes to the heart of true liberty for a Christian: "The liberty of a Christian man is not liberty from the obedience of the law but from the disobedience of the law." It is a Christian's duty to obey God's law.

The Christian's Delight in Obeying God's Law

To a true Christian, obedience to God's law is more than a duty—it is a delight. "The law of his God is in his heart" (Psalm 37:31). With God's law written in his heart, it is the mark of a regenerate man that he can say with Paul, "I delight in the law of God after the inward man" (Romans 7:22). David said of God's commandments, "More to be desired are they than gold, yea, than much fine gold: sweeter also than honey and the honeycomb" (Psalm 19:10).

The apostle John makes the same point in 1 John 5:3: "This is the love of God, that we keep his commandments: and his commandments are not grievous." Anyone who does not love God is lost (1 Corinthians 16:22) because to love Him is the first and great commandment of the law (Matthew 22:37–38). The proof of the reality of our love for God is our hearty obedience to His commandments. The man who finds the will and commandment of God a burden from which he longs to be free and who lives in rebellion against it, bears witness against himself that he is still in his sins. By his hatred of God's law he testifies to his unregenerate state. Christians reflect the heart of their Saviour who said, "I delight to do thy will, O my God: yea, thy law is within my heart" (Psalm 40:8).

The Christian's Motivation and Power to Obey God's Law

Delighting in God's law is one thing, actually doing it is quite another. The question of how a Christian obtains the power to obey God's law is urgently important. A wrong answer here can lead to a lifetime of legalistic bondage. The truth we must never forget is that the motivation and the power to keep God's law do not come from the law but solely by grace through faith in Jesus Christ. Sanctification is conformity to the likeness of Christ in obedience to God. Thus, it involves keeping God's moral law. We could make the case that every command to the New Testament church is an exposition of some part of the Ten Commandments, an elaboration of the moral enactments of the Lord at Sinai. Therefore, sanctification is a working out of the law of God into every part of our lives. This is the Christian's standard of living.

But where does he obtain the power to live up to this standard? Certainly not in the law. The law may tell us what to do and what not to do, but it can never empower us to do it. R. J. Rushdooney, the father of the Reconstruction/Theonomy movement, said, "Man's justification is by the grace of God in Jesus Christ; man's sanctification is by means of the law of God" (*Institutes of Biblical Law,* p. 4). As far as sanctification goes, this is one hundred percent wrong. Sanctification fulfils the law, but it is accomplished by grace through faith in Christ just as certainly as justification is. In 2 Corinthians 3:18 Paul describes the process of sanctification: "We all, with open [unveiled] face beholding as in a glass the glory of the Lord, are changed into the same image from glory to glory, even as by the Spirit of the Lord." Christians are transformed into the image of their Saviour as they behold His glory. That is, as the Holy Spirit reveals Christ's person and work to them in Scripture and enables them to lay hold of what He is to them, and to grasp what they are and have in Him, He will progressively create the image of Christ in them.

The law has no power to accomplish this transformation. Thus, in dealing with the place and function of the law in the life of a believer (Romans 7), Paul speaks of our serving "in newness of the spirit, and not in the oldness of the letter" (verse 6). Here is a familiar phrase that few people understand. In context, Paul is arguing that believers serve God, not merely by outward conformity to some rule, but as those who are married to Christ. Our relationship with Christ clearly dictates what we should do and provides us with the motivation and power to do it. He has written His law in our hearts (Hebrews 8:10) and His love constrains us to obedient service (2 Corinthians 5:14). This is service in the newness of the spirit and it springs from Christ, not from the law.

The Christian's Imperfect Obedience Accepted by God Through Christ's Perfect Obedience

Some of the statements in this chapter will have caused concern to many Christians. We acknowledge that we have a duty to obey God's moral law but we lament that we do such an imperfect job of fulfilling that duty. At best, our law-keeping and obedience fall far short of perfection. But here is good news: Though our obedience is imperfect, the Lord accepts it and rewards it for the sake and on the merits of the Lord Jesus Christ. "The kingdom of God is not meat and drink; but righteousness, and peace, and joy in the Holy Ghost. For *he that in these things serveth Christ is acceptable to God,* and approved of men" (Romans 14:17–18). Philippians 4:18 tells us that our service is "an odour of a sweet smell, a sacrifice acceptable, wellpleasing to God."

We may wonder how our lives and service, imperfect as they are, can be acceptable and well pleasing to God. Peter supplies the answer: "Ye also, as lively stones, are built up a spiritual house, an holy priesthood, to offer up spiritual sacrifices, *acceptable to God by Jesus Christ"* (1 Peter 2:5). Christ is our perfect righteousness and sanctification (1 Corinthians 1:30). He is our sole merit before God. Our lives and service are under the blood, and God receives our imperfect obedience because Christ covers it with His perfect righteousness. This is not an excuse for sin but is the measure of the grace of God to His people. The Father adds the sweet incense of the Saviour's merits to our service and rewards us for Jesus' sake.

Isn't this how we pray, pleading for God to bless us "in Jesus' name," or "for Jesus' sake"? This is how our prayers are acceptable to God. The same is true of every aspect of Christian service. God applies Christ's merits to our imperfect labours, thereby making them acceptable and rewardable.

Here then is the believer's relationship to God's law. He is not justified by the law, nor is he sanctified by it. But he delights in God's law and does not despise it or cast it off as something belonging to the Old Testament. Every single one of the Ten Commandments is repeated in the New Testament (including the fourth, contrary to the assertions of some misinformed preachers). A true believer does not despise these commandments but delights to obey them because he has his eye on Christ and acts in response to His redeeming love.

Were the whole realm of nature mine,
That were an offering far too small;
Love so amazing, so divine,
Demands my soul, my life, my all.

CHAPTER SEVEN

CHRIST THE END OF THE LAW

"Christ is the end of the law for righteousness to every one that believeth."
Romans 10:4

In many ways Romans 10:1–4 is an alarming passage of Scripture. No one who understands it will ever again rest comfortably on the mere fact that he is sincere in his religion. Here Paul speaks of people who were sincere in their religious beliefs and exceedingly zealous toward God in implementing those beliefs. They were even diligent in their works to gain God's salvation. They were really trying to get to heaven. But Paul says they were utterly ignorant of the Lord's way of making sinners righteous and acceptable before Him. By depending upon their own obedience to the law of God, they rejected the gospel message of righteousness by faith in Jesus without any additional works of man. It is obvious that their sincerity and zeal did not save them from the guilt of rejecting Christ. Thus they remained in their sin, unsaved, away from God, with the doom of a lost eternity hanging over their heads. Their tragic folly lay in the fact that they strove to achieve salvation by personal obedience to God's law, all the while ignoring the truth that Paul spells out for us in the fourth verse of this passage: "Christ is the end of the law for righteousness to everyone that believeth." The Jews are not alone in that folly. There are millions sitting in churches around the world who are guilty of the same sin, striving to establish their own righteousness before God. They are culpably ignorant of God's righteousness provided for sinners in the Lord Jesus Christ. Thus the words of verse 4 are vital for us to grasp: "Christ is the end of the law for righteousness to everyone who believeth."

This is a difficult text. At first sight the terms *law* and *end* appear to be easy to understand. On closer examination, however, it is apparent that they raise deep and far-reaching questions.

What is this law of which Christ is the end? Some believe that it is the Levitical ceremonial law, which the Lord Jesus brought to an end by His life and death. At first sight this appears to be the simplest interpretation: The Jews were wedded to the types and shadows of the old economy and were ignorant of the fact that Christ had abrogated them by fulfilling all of them in His own person and work. Thus they missed God's salvation in Christ. While this is a perfectly true statement it cannot stand as an exegesis of Paul's words. This is clear from what follows in Romans 10. In verse 5 the apostle quotes the words of Moses recorded in Leviticus 18:5 where the entire emphasis is on a detailed application of the *moral* law, not the ceremonial. It is clear then that Paul's meaning cannot be limited to the ceremonial law.

Recognizing this, some commentators contend that the law mentioned is the *moral law considered as a covenant of works.* Others insist that this does not go far enough and hold that Paul is referring to the moral law considered not only as a covenant but also as a *commandment.* So the first question we must answer is what the word *law* means in Romans 10:4.

Equally important is the question of what *end* means: "Christ is the end [Greek, *telos*] of the law." According to many interpreters the word *end* simply means "termination." Christ has put an end to the law. Those who see the law in the text as ceremonial law take the meaning to be simply that Christ has abrogated all the types and shadows of the Mosaic economy by fulfilling them in His person and work. Those who take the law to refer to a covenant, use this text as proof that Christ has replaced a covenant of salvation by works with a covenant of salvation by grace through faith. Those who believe that the apostle Paul intended to include the idea of commandment as well as covenant are confident that Romans 10:4 establishes their antinomian position that Christ has completely finished the law in every sense of the term as far as Christians are concerned. The fatal weakness in all these views is that the law was never given to fallen man as a way of salvation. Throughout Scripture, salvation is always by grace. Christ could not terminate what was never commenced. So *termination* is not the idea in Paul's statement.

Some take the *end* of the law to mean its aim—that to which it inclines and the purpose for which God appointed it. For example, when the *Shorter Catechism* says, "Man's chief *end* is to glorify God," it means that the supreme purpose for which he was created is to glorify God. In Romans 7:10 we read, "The commandment, which was ordained to life, I found to be unto death." That is, the aim or purpose for which God ordained the law was life.

Another suggested meaning of *end of the law* is the idea of fulfilment, so that the meaning of the text would be that Christ fulfilled the law. This interpretation of the word *end* is well established in Scripture. "The end of the commandment is charity out of a pure heart" (1 Timothy 1:5). Love is the fulfilment of the law (Galatians 5:14; Romans 13:8–9). Jesus used the word with this meaning of fulfilment in Luke 22:37, "This that is written must yet be accomplished [Greek, *teleo*] in me, and he was reckoned among the transgressors: for the things concerning me have an end [Greek, *telos*]." The context makes his meaning clear: "The things Isaiah 53 records of me must be fulfilled and the time for this fulfilment is at hand." The precise significance of Christ's being the *end* of the law is obviously vital to a proper understanding of the text.

In addition, we have a question of translation to concern us. In the Greek text the order of the words is significantly different from that in the English translation. The Greek text reads, "For the end of the law is Christ for righteousness to every believing one." There is a grammatical question to settle. What is the subject of the sentence? Is it *Christ* or is it *end*? The Authorised Version takes *Christ* to be the subject and so translates, "For Christ is the end of the law for righteousness to every one that believeth." While this is perfectly admissible, there does not appear to be any overpowering reason to depart from Paul's original order of words which yields a beautifully simple but sublime statement of gospel truth: "The end of the law is Christ for righteousness to every believer." *Christ-for-righteousness-to-every-believer* may be viewed as a single expression.

The end of the law is Christ for believers' righteousness. That settles the meaning of the term *end.* It is not the termination but the aim and fulfilment of the law that Paul has in mind. What is the aim and fulfilment of the law? The answer is plain: Christ for our righteousness. Not only does this make good sense but it is the very heart of the message that Paul expounds throughout the book of Romans. Indeed, it is the message he expounds in every epistle. This message consumed the heart of the apostle. Everywhere he went, in every situation, this was his message: Christ is our righteousness. When he confronted the Jews' view of the law his argument was always the same: The law has its aim and fulfilment in Christ for the righteousness of all who believe in Him.

Here then is the doctrine of Romans 10:4: *The aim of God's law is eternal life on the ground of a perfect righteousness in man, which is achieved in the Lord Jesus Christ who fulfilled the law and established a perfect legal righteousness which God imputes to all His believing people.* This is Paul's great statement. Here is the truth that the Jews rejected and stumbled over to their destruction, the truth that men still reject and stumble over to their destruction. Here is the truth that we must grasp by faith if ever we are to be saved.

The Law's Fundamental Aim

The fundamental aim of the law is to stir men up to seek Christ. To use the law as a way of salvation is to *abuse* it. To use it as an excuse to reject Christ is to *pervert* it. To feel no need for the Lord Jesus Christ as Saviour is to *ignore* it. He who feels no need of Christ has never faced the full rigour of the law of God. He has never viewed the absolute holiness and righteousness of God his Judge. He has never grasped the reality of the terrible wrath of a sin-hating God.

The law aims to make sinners feel their sinfulness. That is why the modern self-esteem movement is such a danger to souls. To make people who live in arrogant rebellion against God feel good about themselves is a hateful and heinous crime. While sinners remain depraved, sinful, corrupted, and wicked in the sight of God, while God's wrath hangs over their heads and hell looms before them, they have little cause to feel good about themselves. God's law does not aim to boost the ego of sinners.

Rather it seeks to convict them in order to drive them outside of themselves for hope. Under that conviction, feeling their utter and absolute hopelessness, they will be ready to receive the revelation of saving grace in the Lord Jesus Christ. The aim of the law is to make every sinner know that only in Christ can he ever be made righteous and acceptable to God.

The aim of the law remains the same for Christians. It consistently points believers to Christ. God's law reminds us that He demands a perfect righteousness from any man who would enter heaven and that apart from Christ we have no righteousness. Thus it establishes our assurance not in ourselves but in the merit of the Lord Jesus Christ. It directs us to Christ as the ground of our acceptance and as our example in holiness. It also directs us to Christ to receive from Him the motivation and power to obey its commandments. God can use His law to point us to Christ, for He who satisfied the law can satisfy our need of a righteousness that satisfies the law.

Christ's Obedience to the Law in His Life

The second thing we must remark is that Christ perfectly kept the law of God in His life. *He came into the world as one subject to the law:* "But when the fulness of the time was come, God sent forth his Son, made of a woman, made under the law" (Galatians 4:4). *His purpose in coming into the world was to fulfil all the law's righteous standards:* "Think not that I am come to destroy the law, or the prophets: I am not come to destroy, but to fulfil" (Matthew 5:17). He said to John the Baptist when John demurred at baptizing Him, "Suffer it to be so now: for thus it becometh us to fulfil all righteousness. . . . And lo a voice from heaven, saying, This is my beloved Son, in whom I am well pleased" (Matthew 3:15, 17).

In Romans chapter 5, Paul contrasts Christ's righteousness with Adam's sin, and Christ's obedience with Adam's disobedience. Neither God nor devil, neither friend nor foe, could find any fault in Him. In Him the moral law found its absolute fulfilment. He could declare with complete honesty, "I do always those things that please Him [the Father]" (John 8:29). He evidenced perfect love for God and for His neighbour, thereby perfectly fulfilling the law. Attacked by all the fury of hell, He never suffered one shadow of sin or impurity to soil His soul. In mind, in body, in motive, and in action, the Lord Jesus was always the sinless servant of God, the perfect fulfiller of God's law throughout His life on earth.

Christ's Satisfaction of the Law in His Death

Further, the Lord Jesus Christ perfectly satisfied the law of God in His death. First, *He died as a sacrifice to satisfy divine justice.* He said, "The Son of man came not to be ministered unto, but to minister, and to give his life a ransom for many" (Matthew 20:28). Centuries earlier the prophet Isaiah had predicted Christ's sacrificial death: "It pleased the Lord to bruise him; he hath put him to grief: when thou shalt make his soul an offering for sin, he shall see his seed, he shall prolong his days, and the pleasure of the Lord shall prosper in his hand" (Isaiah 53:10). He laid down His life (Hebrew *nephesh,* meaning "life" or "soul") as a trespass offering (*'asham*), a sacrifice for sin to satisfy divine justice. As Paul expressed it, God "made him who knew no sin to be sin for us" (2 Corinthians 5:21).

Second, in His atoning death *Christ drank the cup of God's wrath against sin.* In rebuking Peter's attempt to rescue Him from arrest in Gethsemane He asked, "The cup which my Father hath given me, shall I not drink it?" (John 18:11). What was that cup? It was the cup of sacrificial suffering, the endurance of God's wrath against our sin.

Third, *He suffered the full penalty of God's law against sin.* According to Galatians 3:13, "Christ hath redeemed us from the curse of the law, being made a curse for us: for it is written, Cursed is every one that hangeth on a tree." It is evident from these words that Christ bore the curse of the broken law in our place. Thus He satisfied both the precept and the penalty of the law.

Christ's Righteousness Imputed to Believers

In the light of all this we can say that God imputes the righteousness of Christ to every believer. Christ kept the law in His life and satisfied it in His death. By so doing He set before God a perfect righteousness in which the divine law finds no fault. This is the only case in the history of the world of a man fulfilling God's law and earning its acceptance. If ever we are to enter heaven we must somehow come to possess that righteousness, for only perfect human righteousness can gain any human being a place in heaven ("Since by man came death, by man came also the resurrection of the dead" [1 Corinthians 15:21]).

If we have that righteousness, we will be saved. If we do not, we cannot be saved. Here is the genius of the gospel: God fulfils the great purpose of the law to make us legally righteous by imputing Christ's righteousness to us through faith.

This is the grand theme of Scripture. Paul said that Christ "is made unto us . . . righteousness" (1 Corinthians 1:30). He expounded this theme again in 2 Corinthians 5:21: "He hath made him to be sin for us, who knew no sin; that we might be made the righteousness of God in him." Hugh Martin, a leading nineteenth-century Scottish theologian, beautifully paraphrased this divine description of counter imputation: "God made Him, who knew no sin, to be sin for us, who knew no righteousness, that we might be made the righteousness of God in Him." All our sin was imputed to Christ; all His righteousness is imputed to us. The Lord Jesus Christ did not become morally corrupt—there was no *moral* change in His character—when God made Him to be sin for us. It was a *legal* transaction. God laid all the legal liability of our sins upon the Lord Jesus in order that He might lay upon us all the legal merits of His righteousness. All that we deserved was laid on Jesus and all that Jesus deserved is laid on His believing people.

That is the gospel. What a glorious gospel it is! Well did Jeremiah call the Saviour *Jehovah Tsidkenu,* "The Lord our Righteousness" (Jeremiah 23:6). In Christ, God confers an absolutely perfect righteousness upon His people. His law is therefore satisfied with them. Instead of being a clamorous witness for their prosecution and destruction, it is now an advocate for their salvation. Thus with Isaiah every believer exults, "I will greatly rejoice in the Lord, my soul shall be joyful in my God; for he hath clothed me with the garments of salvation, he hath covered me with the robe of righteousness" (Isaiah 61:10).

Paul gives us a glorious summation of this central gospel truth in Romans 5:19–21: "As by one man's disobedience many were made [legally constituted] sinners, so by the obedience of one shall many be made [legally constituted] righteous. Moreover the law entered, that the offence might abound. But where sin abounded, grace did much more abound: that as sin hath reigned unto death, even so might grace reign through righteousness unto eternal life by Jesus Christ our Lord." Saving grace cannot operate apart from perfect righteousness. Grace cannot save sinners by ignoring the law, but His grace reigns through righteousness to eternal life. Peter plainly stated the same truth in 2 Peter 1:1: "Simon Peter, a servant and an apostle of Jesus Christ, to them that have obtained like precious faith with us *through the righteousness of God and our Saviour Jesus Christ.*" What a statement! We obtain saving faith, with all the benefits it brings, through (or on the merit of) the righteousness of our great God and Saviour Jesus Christ. It is in this way that "the end of the law is Christ for righteousness to every believer."

This is the righteousness to which the Jews refused to submit themselves (Romans 10:3). Literally, they would not place themselves under it. The pride of man naturally wants to adopt the lie of the *Humanist Manifesto*—that man's salvation can never come from outside of himself, but must be by his own efforts. Many who do not consider themselves secular humanists have adopted a humanistic view of salvation: Man is not a hopelessly depraved sinner, but a creature who, whatever his limitations, can do what is necessary to save his own soul, or at least to contribute to his salvation. By contrast God's word calls on us to submit to a righteousness that is outside of ourselves, to place ourselves under that righteousness, confessing our own demerit, and to take by faith God's promise of salvation by the free imputation of the righteousness of Christ.

There is no other way of salvation. There is no place in heaven for *our* righteousness. There is no place in hell for the righteousness of *Christ*. Submitted to this righteousness, we cannot perish. God can never deny His own law, and "the end [aim, fulfilment] of the law is Christ for righteousness to every believing one."

CHAPTER EIGHT

LOVE FOR GOD

"Jesus said unto him, Thou shalt love the Lord thy God with all thy heart, and with all thy soul, and with all thy mind."
Matthew 22:37

The Lord summarized the entire moral duty of man in what the Hebrew Scriptures call "The Ten Words," what we know as the Ten Commandments. Then He further summarized those ten words in one word, *love*. "Love is the fulfilling of the law" (Romans 13:10). The Lord Jesus Christ clarified the meaning of that statement in His reply to the lawyer who asked Him which of the commandments was the greatest: "Thou shalt love the Lord thy God with all thy heart, and with all thy soul, and with all thy mind" (Matthew 22:37).

We tend to think of the Ten Commandments as a list of prohibitions. Certainly eight of the ten are couched in those terms. The Lord had good reason to issue most of the commandments in the negative because He knew the innate wickedness of fallen man. He recognized his inclination to break every boundary. He also knew that sinners are quite capable of claiming the loftiest moral justification for their wicked acts. We have abundant evidence of that propensity all around us. Many sodomites, especially those who wish to pass themselves off as Christians, claim to glorify God and to give expression to His love and justice by the pursuit of their perversion. Many adulterers try to justify their immorality by perversely calling their lust *love.* Since love is of God, they reason, their actions cannot be considered evil. The simple reason for such high-sounding justification of sin is that all too many people have forgotten the law of God and have conveniently ignored the fact that He has laid down a set of far-reaching prohibitions that remove any semblance of an excuse for sin. So the Lord had good reason to express the Ten Commandments as prohibitions.

However, having said that, we fail to understand the Ten Commandments if we see only their prohibitions. They are more than that. The Lord may have stated many of the commandments in a negative form but He intended us to understand the full scope of their meaning affirmatively as well as negatively. That is why Paul says, "Love is the fulfilling of the law."

The meaning of law is expressed by love. The Ten Commandments come down to this: "Thou shalt love the Lord thy God. . . . Thou shalt love thy neighbour." The Lord never intended true religion to be a tedious list of do's and don'ts but a matter of the heart. The power of all true religion lies in love for God and man. That is the obvious meaning of the great New Testament love chapter, 1 Corinthians 13: "Though I speak with the tongues of men and of angels, and have not charity, I am become as sounding brass, or a tinkling cymbal. And though I have the gift of prophecy, and understand all mysteries, and all knowledge; and though I have all faith, so that I could remove mountains, and have not charity, I am nothing. And though I bestow all my goods to feed the poor, and though I give my body to be burned, and have not charity, it profiteth me nothing" (vv. 1–3).

The meaning of love is defined by the law. This is a truth that many people ignore. Ecumenical apostates and new evangelical compromisers cite love as the motive for their betrayals of biblical truth, but a love that ignores truth is not what God's word means by love. The biblical meaning of love is clearly defined by the law of God. Love is a hearty obedience to the Lord's commandments. Love never disregards the law of God. "This is the love of God, that we keep his commandments: and his commandments are not grievous" (1 John 5:3). "Whoso keepeth his word, in him verily is the love of God perfected: hereby know we that we are in him" (1 John 2:5). The carnal man looks on God's law as a curtailment of his liberty. He cannot understand how anyone can willingly and joyfully embrace its commandments. He is still in his sins and knows nothing of love for God. If he did love God, he would love God's law. Far from curtailing our liberty, the law guides the expression of our love. Certainly then, love can never be an excuse for breaking God's law.

With these thoughts in mind let us consider this royal law of love. It has two main thrusts, love for God and love for man. The whole duty of man is to love the Lord with his whole being and consequently to love his neighbour as himself. From this we gather that the law of God commands us to love God, ourselves, and our neighbour. In this chapter we will concentrate on the first of these commands: We should love the Lord with our entire being. As we examine this love for God we will note its *elements,* its *exercise,* and its *effects.*

The Elements in Love for God

Love for God consists of four elements: a knowledge of Him, a delight in Him, a desire for Him, and a confiding trust in Him. Given the vital importance of loving God, we must examine each of these elements in some detail.

The first element in loving God is a knowledge of Him. Thomas Boston, the great eighteenth-century Scottish preacher and theologian, said, "An unseen but not an unknown God can be loved with all the heart, soul, strength, and mind. Ignorant souls cannot love God." Since we can love only what we know, our love for God will be in direct proportion to our knowledge of God. Thus the primary means of producing a love for God is to create a knowledge of God. Every Christian and every Christian church struggles with the difficulty of motivation. We know we should love God and man, but how do we do so? How do we maintain our love at the level we know it should be? All too often churches subject their people to the emotional manipulation of some motivational speaker or scheme. But if our love does not spring from our knowledge of God it is false and fleshly. Such motivational methods will leave us worse off than before. The primary means of producing true love for God is to gain a true knowledge of God. How may we do that?

The *Scriptures* are the most obvious source of the knowledge of God. The bride in the Song of Solomon spoke of "the voice of my beloved" (Song of Solomon 2:8). That is what the Bible is to a Christian. God's word is not primarily a textbook for establishing a series of doctrines—

though it certainly fills that role—but it is the self-revelation of God. In every part God speaks to us about Himself. Wherever we may be reading in Scripture we should always ask ourselves, "What does this passage teach me about God? What does it teach about Christ? What does it say about the Holy Spirit?" A scriptural knowledge of God begets a true love for Him.

The *gospel* provides a particularly clear knowledge of God. Paul says, "The light of the knowledge of the glory of God [shines] in the face of Jesus Christ" (2 Corinthians 4:6). The full light of God's glory shines in the face of His Son. He is the full and final revelation of the Father (Hebrews 1:1–3). He is the central theme of all Scripture (Luke 24:27, 44–45; Acts 10:43). Thus in all our Bible reading we must be careful to search out the good news of the gospel, the glorious message of the covenant of God's grace through Jesus Christ our Mediator and Saviour. It is by the gospel of the person and work of Christ that we know God and therefore love Him.

Ultimately, *saving faith* in the Lord Jesus Christ is the sure way to know and love the Lord. The law commands, "Thou shalt love the Lord *thy* God." He must be *our* God before we can love Him. The law does not propose to sinners that they should love God in order that He may love them. It does not teach sinners that there is some possibility of salvation by works. On the contrary, it is only as we lay hold of Christ and believe that in Christ God loves us, that we will ever truly love Him. "We love him, because he first loved us" (1 John 4:19). The first element in loving God is knowing God.

The second element in loving God is a delight in Him. The Bible defines God's love for us in terms of the delight He takes in us. "He brought me forth also into a large place; he delivered me, because he delighted in me" (Psalm 18:19). To His people the Lord says, "Thou shalt no more be termed Forsaken; neither shall thy land any more be termed Desolate: but thou shalt be called Hephzibah [*my delight is in her*], and thy land Beulah [*married*]: for the Lord delighteth in thee, and thy land shall be married" (Isaiah 62:4). The essence of love is a delight in the object of the love. And that is how we are to love God. Psalm 37:4 says, "Delight thyself . . . in the Lord." The bride in the Song of Solomon describes her bridegroom as "the apple tree among the trees of the wood" and expresses her love for him as follows: "I sat down under his shadow with great delight, and his fruit was sweet to my taste" (Song of Solomon 2:3).

God's people find Him pleasing. They take pleasure in Him. *They delight in His person,* rejoicing to learn more and more about Him—His perfections, His purposes, and His promises. *They delight to draw near to Him.* With the Psalmist they say, "One thing have I desired of the Lord, that will I seek after; that I may dwell in the house of the Lord all the days of my life, to behold the beauty of the Lord, and to enquire in his temple" (Psalm 27:4). *They delight to praise Him.* They have a spirit of gratitude and thankfulness. It is natural for God's redeemed people to praise Him. "O give thanks unto the Lord, for he is good: for his mercy endureth for ever. Let the redeemed of the Lord say so, whom he hath redeemed from the hand of the enemy" (Psalm 107:1–2). *God's people also delight to serve Him.* David expressed the feelings of every lover of God: "I delight to do thy will, O my God: yea, thy law is within my heart" (Psalm 40:8). The second element in love for God is delight in Him.

The third element in loving God is a desire for Him. The soul that loves the Lord sees in Him all that satisfies; apart from Him, it sees nothing that is necessary to its good or happiness. "Whom have I in heaven but thee? and there is none upon earth that I desire beside thee" (Psalm 73:25). The well-known gospel hymn expresses this desire admirably:

Now none but Christ can satisfy,
None other name for me;
There's love, and life, and lasting joy,
Lord Jesus, found in Thee.

In the Song of Solomon the bride's yearning for her beloved gives voice to the believer's desire for Christ: "I sought him whom my soul loveth. . . . I will seek him whom my soul loveth. . . . Saw ye him whom my soul loveth? I found him whom my soul loveth; I held him, and would not let him go" (Song of Solomon 3:1–4). The soul that has no desire for Christ does not know Him.

The fourth element in loving God is a confiding trust in Him. Even in human relationships, true love is marked by a trusting spirit. Love "believeth all things, hopeth all things" (1 Corinthians 13:7). Paul taught Timothy that "God hath not given us the spirit of fear; but of power, and of love, and of a sound mind" (2 Timothy 1:7). How may we know that we love God? Because we trust Him. The apostle John wrote, "There is no fear in love; but perfect love casteth out fear: because fear hath torment. He that feareth is not made perfect in love" (1 John 4:18). John's main focus in this text is God's love for us—the more we grasp God's love for us the less we will suffer from slavish fear, especially fear of judgment (v. 17). But it is also true that the more we love the Lord the more we will trust Him and not be bound by fear and dread.

The Exercise of Love for God

The Lord Jesus Christ commanded us to exercise love for God: "Thou shalt love the Lord thy God with all thy heart, and with all thy soul, and with all thy might" (Matthew 22:37; see Deuteronomy 6:5; Mark 12:30; Luke 10:27). From all these texts we gather that we are to love the Lord with all our *heart, soul, mind,* and *strength.* Taken together these terms instruct us to love the Lord with everything that is in us. What that means will become clear if we look at each term separately.

We must love the Lord affectionately: "Thou shalt love the Lord thy God with all thy heart." In certain circles there is a disdain for emotion in religion. It is looked on as ignorant fanaticism. There is plenty of emotion that is both ignorant and fanatical. That kind of emotion is wrong. Emotion that is produced by a mere play upon the feelings, by psychological pressures, or by mass hysteria is not genuine spiritual affection. It is all wrong. But there is a deep emotion in religion that is all right. Isaiah experienced powerful emotions when he saw the glory of God (Isaiah 6). John felt deep emotion when he received the vision of the glorified Saviour and fell at His feet as one dead (Revelation 1). Paul was evidently deeply moved by his visions and revelations from God when he felt himself "caught up into paradise" (2 Corinthians 12:4). The early Christians were openly emotional when the Holy Ghost fell upon them (Acts 2:13–17; 5:41). The Lord Jesus Christ must have experienced unspeakably deep emotions in Gethsemane when His sweat was like blood oozing through His skin. According to Scripture, then, there is emotion that is deep, real, and spiritual, produced by God's revelation to us of His greatness, grandeur, power, and glory. Only people who see little or nothing of the beauty of Jesus, can be without emotion in their religion. The testimony of true believers to their Saviour is ever the same: "Yea, he is altogether lovely" (Song of Solomon 5:16). They love Him affectionately.

We must love the Lord spiritually: "Thou shalt love the Lord thy God with all thy soul." Love for God is not just a warm, fuzzy feeling. It is a powerful inclination of the will and a firm dedication of all our faculties to promote the glory of God. Jesus said, "If ye love me, keep my commandments" (John 14:15). Thus a spiritual love for God seeks to obey and glorify Him: "Whatsoever ye do in word or deed, do all in the name of the Lord Jesus, giving thanks to God and the Father by him. . . . And whatsoever ye do, do it heartily, as to the Lord, and not unto men" (Colossians 3:17, 23).

We must love the Lord reasonably: "Thou shalt love the Lord thy God with all thy mind." Love for God may produce ecstasy but it will never suspend the functions of the mind. It is not uncommon for certain types of preachers, professedly seeking to lead their audiences into the experience of the fulness of the Holy Spirit, to invite them to let their minds go blank and allow their feelings to take control. That is the very opposite to what the word of God teaches. Those who are carried away in unthinking swoons may claim deep emotion, but it is not biblical love for God.

Those who love the Lord *think* of Him. According to Psalm 10:4, the great crime of the wicked is that "God is not in all his thoughts." God's people think upon their God. They love to *remember* His grace and His power. Peter told the young Christians to whom he wrote, "I think it meet . . . to stir you up [which must include arousing the emotions] by putting you in remembrance" (2 Peter 1:13). God's people love to remember. For example, they remember Calvary. Is that not why they meet around the Lord's Table, fulfilling Christ's command, "This do in remembrance of me"? Daily, in prayer and in praise, they feed their souls with the remembrance of all their Saviour did for them. They constantly remember their conversion to Christ. With David they celebrate God's saving grace: "He brought me up also out of an horrible pit, out of the miry clay, and set my feet upon a rock, and established my goings. And he hath put a new song in my mouth, even praise unto our God: many shall see it, and fear, and shall trust in the Lord" (Psalm 40:2–3). God's people also call to mind the past blessings with which the Lord has enriched their lives. With the Psalmist they cry, "I love the Lord, because he hath heard my voice and my supplications" (Psalm 116:1). Christians love to think; they love to remember.

Most important of all, God's people love to *reason* their way biblically through the implications of the gospel. The New Testament epistles are full of this logic of love. For example, Paul wrote, "The love of Christ constraineth us; because we thus judge, that if one died for all, then were all dead [rather, then all died]" (2 Corinthians 5:14). Notice carefully Paul's message: From the fact that Christ died for all, we deduce that all for whom He died, died in Him—that is, we logically think through the implications of the gospel. Paul loved to follow this course. In Romans 8:18 he speaks of "the glory which shall be revealed in us" and reckons that in the light of that glorious future the sufferings of the present are bearable. In Romans 8:32–39 he ponders the consequences of the fact that God "spared not his own Son, but delivered him up for us all." From that fundamental gospel truth he deduces that since God has given us the greatest possible gift, He will not fail to give us every lesser gift in Christ. Thus, nothing can possibly bring us under condemnation or separate us from His everlasting love. This is how we ought to think. Such spiritual reasoning will lead us to the joy of full assurance and will fill us with genuine love for the Lord. The more deeply we pursue the implications of the gospel, the more deeply we will know and love our great God and Saviour.

We must love the Lord energetically: "Thou shalt love the Lord thy God with all thy strength." Love leads to action. It cannot be satisfied with mere theory or empty profession. It can never be inactive. It must serve selflessly and give unstintingly. Someone has very wisely observed, "You may give without loving, but you can never love without giving." How then can professing Christians offer their Saviour the burnt-out ends of their lives? All too many exhaust themselves in the pursuits of this present evil age and seek to placate the demands of their consciences by giving the Lord what is left over of their time, money, or energy. But this command teaches us that we should love the Lord with all our strength. Whatever we do, we should do it as unto Him. Wherever we work and whatever our jobs, we should work as witnesses for Christ. The work and worship of His church should never be a matter of secondary importance. He loved us and gave Himself for us and we should therefore love Him energetically.

Finally, *we should love Him preeminently:* "Thou shalt love the Lord thy God with *all* thy heart, *all* thy soul, *all* thy mind, *all* thy strength." As Thomas Boston taught, if we do not love the Lord *above all,* we do not truly love Him *at all.* Love for God can never take second place to any other love. That is what Jesus meant when He said: "If any man come to me, and hate not his father, and mother, and wife, and children, and brethren, and sisters, yea, and his own life also, he cannot be my disciple" (Luke 14:26). Our love for God should be such that when the choice is between Him and any earthly object of our love—even one related to us by the nearest and dearest bonds of kinship—we must love and cleave to Him. If we love our God at all we love Him preeminently.

The Effects of Love for God

The effects of our love for God will extend to every aspect of our lives. *The first aspect to be affected will be our devotional life.* Love for God will shed a holy lustre over our Bible study and our times of private prayer.

The second aspect of our lives to be affected by our love for God will be our church life. We cannot love God without loving His people (1 John 3:16–17). He who loves God will not think lightly of His church or treat its ministry as something low on his list of priorities. Nor will he be content to be either a spectator of the work or a critic of the efforts of others to do it. As we have seen, he who loves God feels the necessity to serve Him, to fulfil his role as a member of the church, the body of Christ.

The third aspect of life to be affected by our love for God is our relationship with the world. Love for God demands that we use the world, not abuse it (1 Corinthians 7:31). Thus the apostle John bluntly states, "Love not the world, neither the things that are in the world. If any man love the world, the love of the Father is not in him" (1 John 2:15). "Holiness unto the Lord" will be the watchword of those who love God in all their dealings with the world.

Last, speaking generally, Christ's words in Matthew 22:37–39 teach us that *the effect of our love for God will be a proper regard for ourselves and others.* Thus we must proceed to consider the subjects of loving ourselves and loving others. Before we do, let us seriously ponder this solemn fact: God commands us to love Him. When faced with the demands of His law, many seek to excuse themselves by parading before Him their imagined righteousness. They are quick to remind Him of the sins they do not commit, sins of which many others are guilty. This is as ridiculous as a murderer standing before a judge and trying to excuse himself with the plea that he had not stolen candies! The command to love God is the first and greatest of all God's commandments. To break it is the worst of all sins. Thus the Scripture teaches us, "If any man love not the Lord Jesus Christ, let him be Anathema [accursed]" (1 Corinthians 16:22).

We cannot manufacture love for God. We must come to know Him if we are to love Him. We can know Him only in Christ. Love for God is the product of saving faith in Jesus Christ. It is only by faith in Him that sinners can escape the curse of breaking the first and great commandment of the law. And it is only by continuing to look by faith unto "Jesus the author and finisher of our faith" (Hebrews 12:2) that believers will love their God affectionately, spiritually, reasonably, energetically, and preeminently.

CHAPTER NINE

LOVING OURSELVES

"Jesus said unto him, Thou shalt love the Lord thy God with all thy heart, and with all thy soul, and with all thy mind. This is the first and great commandment. And the second is like unto it, Thou shalt love thy neighbour as thyself. On these two commandments hang all the law and the prophets."
Matthew 22:37–40

This passage of Scripture requires us to love God and men. Having given some thought to love for God we must consider the subject of love for men. Something lies on the very surface of this text that rarely obtains any scriptural attention in the Christian pulpit: In teaching us that we must love our fellow men, the Lord Jesus Christ asserts that God's law commands us to love ourselves. We cannot love our neighbours as ourselves if we do not love ourselves. That is God's law.

Instinctively we think of self-love as something base and unworthy of a Christian, a display of pride and arrogance. This instinct is absolutely right. It is difficult to imagine anything less in keeping with the Lord Jesus Christ's description of the blessed man as "meek" and "poor in spirit" than what the world thinks of as self-love. The law of God most assuredly does not command us to engage in self-confidence, self-expression, self-indulgence, self-promotion, and self-interest. In fact, far from commanding these as virtues, the Scriptures condemn them as vices. When the law of God calls us to self-love, it means love in its biblical purity. From our Lord's words in Matthew 22:37–40, it is clear that by self-love He means the attitude and care we should take for ourselves because we love the Lord with a love that is begotten by His love for us.

This self-love includes proper care of our bodies. Paul said, "No man ever yet hated his own flesh; but nourisheth and cherisheth it, even as the Lord the church" (Ephesians 5:29). Contextually, the apostle is teaching that every Christian husband should love his wife as he loves his own body. He makes this argument in these terms because no man who obeys the law of God will destroy his own flesh. He who loves the Lord and obeys His law will nourish and cherish his physical body, even as the Lord Jesus cares for His mystical body, the church.

Self-love also includes care for the welfare of our souls. In the book of Proverbs the attainment of wisdom signifies the spiritual use of the means God has provided for the good of our souls. This is the highest form of self-love: "He that getteth wisdom loveth his own soul" (Proverbs 19:8). By using the metaphor of a soldier protecting himself Paul exhorts us to employ this wisdom: "Let us, who are of the day, be sober, putting on the breastplate of faith and love; and for an helmet, the hope of salvation" (1 Thessalonians 5:8). These are all protective coverings for our souls. Just as we protect the body, we should protect the soul. Just as we feed the body, we should feed the soul. Self-love includes care for the welfare and the spiritual development of our souls. As Peter says, we should "grow in grace, and in the knowledge of our Lord and Saviour Jesus Christ" (2 Peter 3:18).

The aim is to present both body and soul to the Lord as useful instruments in His service. That is the deduction the apostle Paul draws from his exposition of the gospel. Having taken the first eleven chapters of Romans to expound the glories of sovereign, justifying grace he concludes: "I beseech you therefore, brethren, by the mercies of God, that ye present your bodies a living sacrifice, holy, acceptable unto God, which is your reasonable service [i.e., make your bodies the Lord's servants]. And be not conformed to this world: but be ye transformed by the renewing of your mind, that ye may prove what is that good, and acceptable, and perfect, will of God [i.e., make your souls the Lord's servants]" (Romans 12:1–2).

All this brings us back to the fundamental observation of our last study: A proper attitude toward ourselves and others is the result of a true love for God. Let us first consider the initial idea in that statement—a proper attitude toward ourselves.

No Man Can Have a Proper Regard for Himself Without a True Love for God

He who disregards God has a totally false view of himself. He forgets or ignores the fact that he is God's creature and that he is answerable and accountable to God. He mocks the very idea of his giving account to God, either in so many words or by works that loudly proclaim his boast that he will never stand before God for judgment. In Psalm 94:3 the Psalmist described such people as wicked, or lawless: "Lord, how long shall the wicked, how long shall the wicked triumph?" A few verses later he lets us see right into the mind of the lawless: "They say, The Lord shall not see, neither shall the God of Jacob regard it" (Psalm 94:7).

A man who disregards God acts as if he were an independent being, but actually he is dependent on the Lord for everything he needs, even for life itself. Belshazzar the Chaldean king had no fear of God or of His judgment. He took pride in his own power and glory. While he was in the very act of blaspheming the Lord, surrounded by his like-minded friends in a pagan orgy of drunken idolatry, God reminded him of his utter dependence on the one he so openly despised. "[Thou] hast lifted up thyself against the Lord of heaven; and they have brought the vessels of his house before thee, and thou, and thy lords, thy wives, and thy concubines, have drunk wine in them; and thou hast praised the gods of silver, and gold, of brass, iron, wood, and stone, which see not, nor hear, nor know: and the God in whose hand thy breath is, and whose are all thy ways, hast thou not glorified" (Daniel 5:23). *God in whose hand thy breath is.* What a statement, not only of Belshazzar's dependence on the Lord, but of ours also! Belshazzar imagined himself in an impregnable position. Even God could not shake him, or so he thought. He could not have been more wrong. All it took to remove him from the face of the earth was for God to shut His hand and cut off from him the breath of life. And He did: "In that night was Belshazzar the king of the Chaldeans slain" (Daniel 5:30).

The man who has no regard for God embraces insanity and proclaims it good. He binds himself to sin, Satan, sorrow, and destruction, and cries, "I am free!" Jesus said, "Verily, verily, I say unto you, Whosoever committeth sin is the servant [slave] of sin" (John 8:34). But this fool says,

"Nonsense! I commit what you call sin and find it to be perfect liberty. I am doing what I please—isn't that liberty? And I can walk away from it whenever I want—isn't that liberty?" He binds himself to Satan, the great dominator and destroyer of souls, and proclaims him a loving master. He exalts the lusts of his lowest nature to the throne of his being, ignoring the fact that his lust is like a fire that will consume him. He laughs at the warning of Scripture, "When lust hath conceived, it bringeth forth sin: and sin, when it is finished, bringeth forth death" (James 1:15). Indeed, he lives as if there were no God, no heaven, and no hell. Such a man is a fool, because God is real, heaven is real, and hell is real—a burning lake of fire that will consume sinners in endless punishment as long as the eternal God exists.

Thus, *the man who disregards God betrays and destroys himself.* The man who hates God, truly hates himself. The man who rejects God rejects his own good. The man who makes God his enemy is the enemy of his own soul. Think of what it means for a man to have God as his enemy. It means that he sets up the full authority of God's throne against him. He engages the full might of God's power for his own destruction. He even makes God's love and mercy plead against him: "Thus saith the Lord God; Behold, I, even I, am against thee" (Ezekiel 5:8). It is a terrible thing to make God an enemy. "It is a fearful thing to fall into the hands of the living God. . . . For our God is a consuming fire" (Hebrews 10:31; 12:29). The man who has no love for God invokes God's judgment against his own soul. Is this self-love? Is it true self-regard that calls down the wrath of God? No! It is suicidal to disregard and reject the Lord of heaven.

A man cannot love himself until he loves God. He may enrol in every available seminar for self-help and self-esteem, but he will never regard himself in a true light until he loves God. Until he casts aside every notion of his own goodness and greatness and falls before the Lord Jesus Christ to embrace Him as Saviour and Lord, he will remain on a course of self-destruction. He must, therefore, get to the cross, see the love of God in Christ crucified, and receive Him as his Saviour and Lord. Then he will begin to love the Lord and as a result, will begin to love himself.

That leads us to consider something of vital importance to every Christian. How is a Christian to maintain true humility and yet love himself?

How is he to avoid the twin evils of grovelling in the mire of self-inflicted gloom and of glorying in the mist of self-imagined goodness? The gospel has the answer.

A Thorough Understanding of God's Love for Us Produces Proper Regard for Ourselves

Nowadays there is an avid interest in self-esteem, self-image, and self-acceptance. This interest highlights a deep problem. Hope is one of the most fundamental revelations of the gospel. It is impossible to believe the gospel and have no hope. Yet many people, even Christians, live in a fog of hopelessness. They suffer deeply from feelings of abject failure and utter personal worthlessness. The result is often total despair. Focusing on themselves, such people can see no ray of light to pierce their darkness. Some of them develop a hatred for their bodies and either feed or starve them to death. Some hate their circumstances and live in bitterness against God and those around them. Some hate their very lives and, bereft of hope, plunge blindly into the abyss of suicide.

All this is sin. God commands us to love ourselves, not to loathe ourselves, or to incapacitate ourselves, or to destroy ourselves. He commands us to love ourselves in the glow of His love for us and our love for Him. Lawless self-destruction betrays not only a lack of love for self, but a lack of trust in and love for the Lord.

That is the problem. What is the answer? It is certainly not any of the psychological theories behind the positive self-image techniques that are so popular today. These techniques typically emphasize being positive about ourselves, our abilities, our worth, and our capacity for getting on top of our circumstances without any reference whatsoever to loving God as our Creator and Redeemer in Christ. They teach self-reliance and try to bolster it by the example of others to motivate us to a better acceptance of ourselves as we are.

What is wrong with such techniques? Simply this: They replace one godless view of ourselves with another. Remember the fundamental point in Christ's words in Matthew 22:37–40: All true love for self flows from love for God—which means it flows from knowing God in Christ as Saviour. The great need of the millions who are vainly thronging the offices and seminars of psychologists and therapists is to know Christ. That need runs deeper than any unsaved therapist can know. The answer is more wonderful than any worldly psychologist can supply. What people bound in darkness need is not a therapist who is in even greater darkness, but Christ who said, "I am the light of the world: he that followeth me shall not walk in darkness, but shall have the light of life" (John 8:12). Then, as Christians loved by God and loving Him, they will develop a true regard for themselves by grasping the fulness of the gospel's description of what they are and what they have in Christ.

This is how the Bible deals with the issue of a person's proper regard for himself. First, he must be saved. Then, once he is saved he must enter into an ever deepening understanding of the gospel revelation of the fulness of Christ. This is what is missing for so many Christian people today. They come to Christ and trust Him for the salvation of their souls. So far so good, but then their churches feed them the husks of second-hand psychology. By contrast, the Bible never treats the gospel as something whose sole use is to show us the way to heaven, leaving us to live our lives by a complex set of psychological rules (with or without a Bible verse tagged on to them). For example, in the first chapter of 1 Peter the apostle addresses a people who today would be termed a challenged and vulnerable people. Verse 1 describes them as "strangers scattered abroad" in places far from their home environment. They had been uprooted from their homeland. Today we would call them refugees. They had lost all they ever lived for in the world. They had to bid farewell to the scenes of youth and every happy memory. They were alienated from loved ones, probably never to meet them again in this world. Besides this they were "in heaviness through manifold temptations [trials]" (verse 6). The word *heaviness* carries the idea of deep oppression and distress of mind. They were depressed. Who could blame them? But they didn't need a psychologist, or a therapist, or a self-esteem seminar, for despite their mental distress, they were rejoicing. That seems a contradiction in terms. How does a person rejoice when he is in such a situation? The opening words of verse 6 supply the answer: "Wherein ye greatly rejoice." *Wherein* refers to the great salvation expounded in verses 2–5. They were rejoicing in the truth of the gospel. That truth had so gripped their hearts that their joy in it survived even the natural feeling of distress at their difficult circumstances.

They rejoiced to know they were the elect of God—"elect according to the foreknowledge of God" (v. 2). That is always a great source of strength and joy to a Christian. He can rest in the realization that from before the beginning of time God predestinated him to eternal life. He is not an accident or an afterthought, but the object of God's eternal, electing purpose. That lies at the heart of how a Christian should regard himself.

They rejoiced that God the Holy Spirit had regenerated them—"through sanctification of the Spirit" (v. 2). God's eternal purpose toward them had been executed by the Holy Spirit. He had set them apart unto God. Though they were currently suffering they knew the blessedness of the assurance that He would not fail to complete the work He had begun. A work in progress under the personal supervision of the Holy Spirit—that is how a Christian should look upon himself. Following John Newton he should say, "I am not what I should be; I am not what I desire to be; I am not what I am going to be; but, bless God, I am not what I was. The Spirit is doing His good work in me."

They rejoiced that Christ had shed His precious blood for them and that it had been applied to their hearts—"unto sprinkling of the blood of Jesus Christ" (v. 2). They knew that the blood could never be overcome by any power of man or devil. They rejoiced to know that no blood-washed souls could ever perish. However deep their present suffering, they knew they would never suffer the torments of hell. They were redeemed unto God, sprinkled with the blood of His Son. A brand plucked out of the fire by the hand of God—that is how a Christian should think of himself.

They rejoiced that God provided grace and peace to fortify their hearts in every trying time—"grace unto you, and peace, be multiplied" (v. 2). They had learned that in every deep valley they must lift their eyes beyond their circumstances and see in the gospel how God described their true state. With God as their Father, Christ as their redeemer, the Holy Spirit as their sanctifier, divine election as their guarantee of security, and the blood of Christ as their atonement for sin, they had every right to be happy however much their "light affliction, which is but for a moment" (2 Corinthians 4:17) might burden them. A child with all his heavenly

Father's resources promised to him—that is how a Christian should regard himself.

They also rejoiced that they had a living hope. They had the joy of knowing that their hope of immortal bliss was present and well founded—"God . . . according to his abundant mercy hath begotten us again unto a lively hope by the resurrection of Jesus Christ from the dead" (verse 3). By rising again from the dead Christ assured them of "an inheritance incorruptible, and undefiled, and that fadeth not away, reserved in heaven" for them (verse 4). In the depths of their suffering and weariness they had something to look forward to: God had reserved heaven for them. And His power was standing guard over them to ensure that they reached heaven, as the Greek verb *phroureo* (verse 5) indicates. *Saved,* not only *from* hell but *for* heaven, and secure in that salvation—that is how a Christian should consider himself.

Meditating on these benefits of the gospel is how early Christians maintained a happy and proper regard for themselves. Time has not altered God's method of keeping His people in perfect peace. He directs us to ponder the great truths of His salvation with its description of what we are and what we have in Christ. Even when our earthly circumstances are bleak we may rejoice in the Lord. A thorough grasp of what God says about us in Christ is the key to a happy and proper regard for ourselves.

This is the uniform message of Scripture. Ephesians 1 also presents us with a list of unchanging gospel truths that describe the glories of being "in Christ." Indeed, throughout all the epistles the apostles constantly establish the position of the justified in Christ and then proceed to direct them how to live effective and fulfilled lives. Faith's strong grasp of the doctrine of justification and the imputed righteousness of Christ—the central point of New Testament soteriology—is the surest way for a Christian to regard himself in a true and positive light. The worldly dogma of self-esteem is an empty counterfeit of this divine revelation. It is depraved man's way of trying to feel good about himself while he continues in rebellion against his Maker. Christians need no such mental trickery. They have solid truth upon which to stand. In 2 Corinthians 5:21 Paul shows us this sure foundation of a Christian's peace about his state: "He [God] hath made him [Christ] to be sin for us, who knew no sin; that we might be made the righteousness of God in him." Just as surely as God laid our sins to Christ's account He now lays Christ's righteousness to our account. However Satan tempts and taunts us, or however the world scorns or persecutes us, we can rejoice that in God's eyes we stand complete in Christ (Colossians 2:10). As the apostle John puts it, "Behold, what manner of love the Father hath bestowed upon us, that we should be called the sons of God: therefore the world knoweth us not, because it knew him not. Beloved, now are we the sons of God, and it doth not yet appear what we shall be: but we know that, when he shall appear, we shall be like him; for we shall see him as he is" (1 John 3:1–2). What a statement of our present dignity ("now are we the sons of God") and our future destiny ("we shall be like him")! This passage enables us to look at ourselves as our God does, rather than making ourselves miserable by looking at ourselves as the devil and his minions would have us do.

What God says about us is true. Dare we despise one who is so dear to the Lord, one whom the Lord Jesus purchased with his own precious blood? We must answer with a firm negative. If we believe the gospel and understand what it says about us, we must regard ourselves in its light. But there are situations that seem to go from bad to worse and under the strain they impose, many Christians are tempted to lose the sight, or at least the joy, of their standing in Christ. This lends special significance to our third observation on this matter of loving and accepting ourselves:

Loving God Will Enable Us to Maintain a Proper Regard for Ourselves, and Not Despair, Even When Circumstances Grow Bleak

We have to recognize the reality of a problem many people face. They say, "I believe the gospel but there are very practical questions to which I need an answer." These are not easy questions and they are often asked out of a sense of deep agony and near despair. For example: How do you maintain a proper regard for yourself when your health is continually deteriorating? Or when your pain is intractable, or when persecution is persistent, or when your problems multiply and there is apparently no escape from them in this world?

We must face the fact that sometimes it is not God's will to heal our bodies, or to remove our pain, or to lift us out of our problems. That is difficult for any of us to accept. Satan is without mercy and will exploit such times of suffering and anguish. He whispers his lies in our ears and tempts us to imagine that God does not love us at all, or that He is angry with us. This was his tactic with Job and it has never varied throughout history. As in Job's case, Satan tries to get us to "curse God and die" (Job 2:9). He wants us to despair and to regard ourselves in a light very different from the gospel's description of us. So how do we as Christians maintain a proper regard for ourselves in such situations?

The word of God addresses this problem directly. Hebrews 12:3 tells us, "Consider him that endured such contradiction of sinners against himself, lest ye be wearied and faint in your minds [enfeebled in your souls]." Christ suffered more than any of us and glorified His Father in doing so. Therefore, as we consider Christ we understand that sometimes it is our sufferings that glorify God, not their removal. In Hebrews 11:33–38 the Holy Spirit makes this very plain. In verses 33–35, he records great deliverances some saints experienced through faith. But others possessed of the same faith were not delivered from their troubles but had to endure them for the glory of God, with their eye on the resurrection day: "Others were tortured, not accepting deliverance; that they might obtain a better resurrection: and others had trial of cruel mockings and scourgings, yea, moreover of bonds and imprisonment: they were stoned, they were sawn asunder, were tempted, were slain with the sword: they wandered about in sheepskins and goatskins; being destitute, afflicted, tormented; (of whom the world was not worthy:) they wandered in deserts, and in mountains, and in dens and caves of the earth" (Hebrews 11:35–38). From this passage it is evident that some of these servants of God had miraculous answers to prayer, while others apparently received no answer and had to suffer indescribably. Yet both companies lived by such great faith that God includes them in His gallery of the heroes of faith. The second group were just as triumphant as the first. The first were triumphant in their deliverance; the second were triumphant in their suffering. Some had to learn that they could glorify God more by suffering than by being delivered. And because they loved the Lord more than they loved themselves, they joyfully accepted His will and endured for His sake. They did not conclude that they were worthless or useless. In fact, the scripture specifically draws attention to their worth: "Of whom the world was not worthy." What they bore, they bore out of love for Christ. And that enabled them to maintain a true regard for themselves in life's darkest passages. So, a true love for God will enable us to maintain a true regard for ourselves, even in dire situations. The converse is also true.

A True Love for Ourselves Will Move Us, Irrespective of Our Circumstances, to Maintain a Loving Fellowship with the Lord

Carnal ease often leads Christians to neglect the word of God, private and public worship, and a life of service for Christ. But a true love for our bodies and souls will never allow such neglect. Cosseting the flesh is not true self-love. Self-love would become master over destructive lusts, not their victim. But it is only in walking with God that we find relief from sin's pollution and power: "If we walk in the light, as he is in the light, we [God and his people] have fellowship one with another, and the blood of Jesus Christ his Son cleanseth us from all sin" (1 John 1:7). Self-love would seek joy, not misery, and it is only in walking with God that our souls are refreshed and made joyful. Every Christian wants to be happy but it is a mark of a true Christian that he cannot be happy except as he walks in fellowship with His Lord. To those who walk in the Spirit and not after the flesh God's promise is, "The fruit of the Spirit is . . . joy" (Galatians 5:16, 22). A Christian cannot be happy if he feels that his life is empty and useless to God. But how may we serve Him? Only as we walk in fellowship with Him. He still gives the Holy Ghost (and therefore power for service) to those who obey Him (Acts 5:32). So a true love for ourselves will lead us to "walk with the Lord in the light of His word," as John H. Sammis puts it in his famous hymn "Trust and Obey."

We must love ourselves—not our sins, or our follies—but our own bodies and souls. God commands us to love ourselves with a love that expresses a true knowledge of Him, a simple trust in Him, and a deep delight in Him. Even this command to love ourselves is one we cannot keep except by faith in Christ. As always, God's law drives us to Christ. When our faith is in Him as our Saviour and Lord we will love God. As a result, we will love ourselves in Him and because of Him.

CHAPTER TEN

LOVING OUR NEIGHBOUR

"Thou shalt love the Lord thy God with all thy heart, and with all thy soul, and with all thy strength, and with all thy mind; and thy neighbour as thyself."
Luke 10:27

Seven times in the New Testament the Holy Spirit records the divine law, "Thou shalt love thy neighbour as thyself." The Lord Jesus Christ plainly stated this commandment. The apostle Paul used it to summarize the entire second table of the law. James termed it "the royal law according to the scripture" (James 2:8) and said, "Ye do well," if you fulfil it.

The first mention of this law is in Leviticus 19:18. While that is the only occurrence of the actual words *Thou shalt love thy neighbour as thyself* in the Old Testament, the law of Moses and the message of the prophets were founded on this precept and were an exposition of it. The law's strict standards of honesty and integrity in our dealings with others, its protection of the most vulnerable members of society (for example, the poor, servants, strangers, and hired help), and even its care that no one should ever be regarded as vile and loathsome (not even the condemned criminal who must be lashed) are applications of the theme, "Thou shalt love thy neighbour as thyself."

So the Lord Jesus Christ was not teaching something new when He stated that this was the second great commandment of God's law. He set it in a clear, new light, however, for He made a true love for our neighbour dependent on and subject to a true love for God. Matthew 22:39 records this precept and Luke 10:30–37 illustrates it with the parable of the Good Samaritan, which the Saviour used to show the precept put into action.

"A certain man went down from Jerusalem to Jericho, and fell among thieves, which stripped him of his raiment, and wounded him, and departed, leaving him half dead. And by chance there came down a certain priest that way: and when he saw him, he passed by on the other side. And likewise a Levite, when he was at the place, came and looked on him, and passed by on the other side. But a certain Samaritan, as he journeyed, came where he was: and when he saw him, he had compassion on him, And went to him, and bound up his wounds, pouring in oil and wine, and set him on his own beast, and brought him to an inn, and took care of him. And on the morrow when he departed, he took out two pence, and gave them to the host, and said unto him, Take care of him; and whatsoever thou spendest more, when I come again, I will repay thee. Which now of these three, thinkest thou, was neighbour unto him that fell among the thieves? And he said, He that shewed mercy on him. Then said Jesus unto him, Go, and do thou likewise" (Luke 10:30–37).

Christians must learn an important lesson from this parable: We express our love for God, at least in part, by our love for our fellow men, and we measure our love for them by comparing it with our love for ourselves. This is the true meaning of the biblical command to love our neighbours. The precept is not difficult to understand but it has far-reaching implications.

The Precept

Love for God Comes First

He who would best serve his fellow men must first love God. Anyone who wants to do all the good he possibly can in this needy world must not be an enemy of God, a despiser of Christ, or a rejecter of the gospel. Wherever he goes, a hater of God spreads rebellion against God with all the bitter results it produces. He may be liberal with his time, energy, and fortune, but by his actions and attitude toward God he uses his beneficence to blind men to their need of Christ. The man who would do his best for his fellow men must first love the Lord his God.

This an invigorating truth for God's people. Those who are in the best position to do the greatest amount of good in the world are Christians. Sometimes Christians feel inadequate for the task God has set before them, lamenting that they do not have the talents or the financial resources needed to do all they would like to do for others. While talents and money are useful, a saving knowledge of the Lord Jesus Christ is far more important. A saved man has the love of God shed abroad in his heart (Romans 5:5) and is therefore well equipped to do good wherever he goes. The history of missions and Christian philanthropy bears eloquent witness to this truth: Livingstone gave his life for the good of Africa; Brainerd pushed his dying frame beyond endurance to do good to the despised American Indians; Carey yielded himself to plant the gospel in heathen India; Barnardo and Mueller spent their lives rescuing orphan children; William Booth established a Salvation Army of soldiers of love to seek and to win the poor and the outcast; Gladys Aylward exposed herself to disease, imprisonment, and constant danger to adopt Chinese children doomed to die and to find a way to lead them to safety. The list could be extended indefinitely. All these outstanding Christians were ordinary sinners saved by grace and fired to serve men by a mighty love for God.

This is the only kind of humanitarian service that is worthy of the name Christian. Any other kind will quickly degenerate into some form of humanism. Lacking the motivation of divine love, it will also lack the goal of divine love, which ultimately is not the comfort or happiness of man but the glory of God. People who love and serve men out of a genuine love for God will continue to do all the good they can because their Saviour is worthy of their efforts, not because the objects of their love are worthy or thankful.

Lovers of God Love Men

It is clear that if we love God, we should love our fellow men. We cannot love God and be indifferent to men. The apostle John says, "He that loveth not knoweth not God; for God is love. . . . If a man say, I love God, and hateth his brother, he is a liar: for he that loveth not his brother whom he hath seen, how can he love God whom he hath not seen?" (1 John 4:8, 20).

More specifically, *if we love the law of God we must love our fellow men.* All too often Christians make their professed love for God's law an excuse to despise flagrant lawbreakers. We are particularly prone to adopt this attitude toward those of a different religious or political persuasion. This is as far from the teachings of Christ as anything we may condemn in others! The wickedness of sinners is all the more reason we should love them with the love of the Lord Jesus Christ who came not "to call the righteous, but sinners to repentance" (Mark 2:17).

There is an observation we must make as we consider our attitude toward others: In all our dealings with unsaved people we must never expect to do any good without showing the love of Christ to them. This is a lesson Christian parents especially need to learn. If they deal with their children by a law that excludes the love of Christ, they will fail to teach them either law or gospel. "Love is the fulfilling of the law" (Romans 13:10).

We do not magnify God's law by hating sinners. If love is the fulfilment of the law, hatred and hatefulness are marks of the world and sin. "For we ourselves also were sometimes foolish, disobedient, deceived, serving divers lusts and pleasures, living in malice and envy, hateful, and hating one another" (Titus 3:3). This describes our state while we were without Christ. But grace changed that state. Thus if hating and being hateful were characteristic of our unconverted days, *loving and being lovable should be characteristic of our new lives in Christ.* And these marks of grace should be clearly in evidence wherever we go, in the home, in the work place, and in the church.

Love Reaches to All Men

We must not limit this love to a few, but bestow it generally on all men. The Lord Jesus commands us, "Love thy neighbour." He even tells us to love our enemies (Matthew 5:44). Paul calls on us to pray for all men (1 Timothy 2:1), while Peter warns servants whose masters were difficult and unfair, "Servants, be subject to your masters with all fear; not only to the good and gentle, but also to the froward [crooked, perverse]" (1 Peter 2:18). We must show this love to all with whom we share humanity, because all who share our nature may, by God's grace, be brought to enjoy

His salvation by faith in Christ. We all tend to love those who love us. We give to those who may give back to us and we cut off the rest as somehow unworthy of the embrace of our love. Jesus warned against this very attitude: "Then said he also to him that bade him, When thou makest a dinner or a supper, call not thy friends, nor thy brethren, neither thy kinsmen, nor thy rich neighbours; lest they also bid thee again, and a recompence be made thee. But when thou makest a feast, call the poor, the maimed, the lame, the blind: and thou shalt be blessed; for they cannot recompense thee: for thou shalt be recompensed at the resurrection of the just" (Luke 14:12–14). Obviously this is not an absolute prohibition of serving a supper for family or friends (otherwise Christ Himself would have been in breach of it for conducting the Last Supper). The Lord is attacking the practice of limiting our love and hospitality to those from whom we feel we may benefit, while excluding the poor who can never make us a penny richer. He commands us to employ the logic of grace and seek the rewards of eternity, not of the world: "Thou shalt be blessed; for they cannot recompense thee: for thou shalt be recompensed at the resurrection of the just."

Love Thy Neighbour as Thyself—Not as God

While love for men flows from and expresses our love for God, it must never replace it. We are commanded, "Thou shalt love thy neighbour as thyself," *never as thy God.* We must never elevate any person to the place that belongs uniquely to the Lord. This will govern *how* we love and *why* we love our fellowman.

We must not accord any creature the adoration that belongs only to God. Love for God is the essence of worship. "Worship God" is the clear command of Scripture (Revelation 22:9). Jesus repelled the temptation of Satan to worship him with the statement, "It is written, Thou shalt worship the Lord thy God, and him only shalt thou serve" (Matthew 4:10). This leaves no room for the worship of Mary and the saints and angels, as practised by the Roman Catholic and Orthodox churches. It is vain to draw impractical distinctions between *latria,* the worship accorded to God, *dulia,* the devotion accorded to the saints, and *hyperdulia,* the devotion accorded to Mary. The minds of the worshippers are incapable of maintaining such distinctions. Furthermore, the ingredients of the devotion to Mary and the saints includes the necessary elements of the worship of God, namely praise and prayer. When even Pope John Paul II prostrates himself before Mary and adopts the motto *Totus Tuus,* which may be translated "I am entirely yours," it is evident that Mariolatry and saint worship transgress the law of God by giving His glory to a creature. We must reserve our adoration for Him alone.

We must not give to any man the affection that belongs alone to God. Jesus said, "If any man come to me, and hate not his father, and mother, and wife, and children, and brethren, and sisters, yea, and his own life also, he cannot be my disciple" (Luke 14:26). There is a sense in which we should love ourselves and our neighbours, but there is another sense in which we should hate ourselves and our neighbours. There is no contradiction here. According to Christ, there is a love and devotion that belongs solely to God. We must allow no one to steal or share that devotion. In dealing with others, not only should we seek always to apply God's law to them with biblical love, but we should also always express our love according to God's law. We must allow no earthly love to keep us from Christ or to make us disobey God. We must put no earthly relationship before the Saviour or permit any man to come between us and doing God's will. To fail in these matters is idolatry.

We must not attribute to any man the authority that belongs to God alone. This will save us from the vices of the personality cult. Too often we fail to hold our leaders to the authoritative standards of the word of God. For example, they may ignore its commands, amend its standards of personal or ecclesiastical separation, or establish unscriptural methods of their own devising, but because of their prominent position or their apparent success we do not judge their actions as we ought. To make matters worse, we often pass off this dereliction of duty as the exercise of Christian love. It is not. It is rather a betrayal of that love, and it is the elevation of man to a place of authority above that of the word of God. We must love men with a love that is due to creatures, never with the love that is due only to the Creator.

Love Meets Physical Needs

Loving men includes meeting their physical needs. We have already noted that self-love includes the nourishment of our bodies. Similarly, love for others includes helping with their physical needs. By His illustration of this point in the parable of the Good Samaritan, the Lord Jesus does not teach the socialist philosophy of state intervention but the scriptural philosophy of Christian intervention.

In recent years a wholly spurious argument has arisen as to whether the only duty of the church to the world is evangelism, or whether it should also engage in some forms of social action to help the poor and needy. When modernists and liberals espoused the social gospel and its various offshoots, they replaced the biblical message of redemption from sin with a social message of earthly amelioration. Predictably, the evangelicals' response tended to emphasize the spiritual message of salvation to the exclusion of any of the social implications of the gospel. However understandable such a response, it ignores both history and Scripture. The true social advances of the western world have been the result of the preaching of the gospel. Christians instituted hospitals for the care of the sick. Christians battled both industrialists and politicians during the industrial revolution to gain a better life for working men and for the urchins and orphans who thronged England's cities. Christians made heroic efforts to feed the poor, care for the widow, and visit the afflicted, especially during times of plague or epidemic. Historically, God's people have taken Moses' words seriously: "If thy brother be waxen poor, and fallen in decay with thee; then thou shalt relieve him: yea, though he be a stranger, or a sojourner; that he may live with thee" (Leviticus 25:35).

This kind of love is really doing unto others what we hope others would do for us if we were in need. "Whoso hath this world's good, and seeth his brother have need, and shutteth up his bowels of compassion from him, how dwelleth the love of God in him?" (1 John 3:17). Perhaps repeated television and press coverage of major disasters has inured us to the everyday sufferings of others. Also, frequent reports that many charities use most of what we give not to relieve the needy but to pay professional fund raisers may make us sceptical about giving. Such excuses for disengagement from the needs of our fellow men are empty, however. There are always dependable channels through which we can "do good unto all men, especially unto them who are of the household of faith" (Galatians 6:10).

Love will always find a way to serve. The book *God's Ravens Still Fly* illustrates this beautifully. It is the story of an Ulster minister who read of the exodus of thousands of Jews from Russia. He discovered that while they awaited clearance to settle in the United States and other western countries, they were trapped for long periods in Italy under very difficult conditions. They needed food and clothing and someone to care for their souls. The minister felt stirred to bring them relief. With the support of thousands of Christians who gave sacrificially to help those needy exiles he was able to bring them much-needed physical help as well as personal copies of the word of God. Only eternity will reveal how much good was accomplished. Wonderful as the story is, it is far from unique. Indeed, it is normal for Christians to react in such a manner to those in need.

Love Addresses Spiritual Needs

Christian love labours to bring men to Christ. Indeed, its work to meet men's temporal needs is a means toward addressing their spiritual needs. William Booth taught the early Salvationists that it was of little use speaking to starving men about the gospel of God's redeeming love before they had given the men a meal. But he would never have thought that once his soldiers had provided food they had accomplished their task. No, their great aim was to point sinners to Christ.

When John the Baptist sent to enquire from the Lord Jesus whether He was indeed the Christ, Jesus included in His reply the statement, "The poor have the gospel preached to them" (Matthew 11:5). If that was part of the proof of the genuineness of Christ's messianic mission it surely must be part of the proof of the validity of any church's ministry. Christians cannot be unmoved by the need of the poor to hear the gospel. They cannot be careless about the spiritual plight of the populations of our inner cities where millions sink ever deeper not only into poverty but into hopeless darkness without much gospel light. Recognizing the Saviour's imperative demand that His gospel be preached to the poor will save our churches from becoming middle-class social clubs for believers. The fact that the middle classes have fled to suburbia should not mean that the gospel is no longer presented to the poor and needy with all available resources of spiritual love and power. A love that labours for the salvation of souls will lead us to pray earnestly, give generously, and labour fervently in an effort to win men for Christ and make them His mature disciples.

Here then is the Saviour's precept: "Love thy neighbour as thyself." In John Wesley's words, "Do all the good you can by all the means you can to all the people you can." That is how we should love our neighbours.

The Parable

The Lord Jesus illustrated this precept with the parable of the Good Samaritan. This parable is more than a heart-warming story. It is is our Saviour's explanation of loving our neighbour.

The Parable Identifies Our Neighbour

When a lawyer asked Christ, "Master, what shall I do to inherit eternal life?" (Luke 10:25), the Saviour set before him the perfect standard of God's law: "Thou shalt love the Lord thy God with all thy heart, and with all thy soul, and with all thy strength, and with all thy mind; and thy neighbour as thyself." The lawyer evidently felt Christ's reply deflating to his self-righteousness for, "he, willing to justify himself, said unto Jesus, And who is my neighbour?" Christ's answer was the parable of the Good Samaritan.

By replying in this way the Lord Jesus said in effect, "If you were the man lying on the Jericho road, robbed, wounded, and near death, you would have no trouble in recognizing your neighbour. He is the one who comes to your aid." Who is my neighbour? The question can be asked only by a complacent, hard-hearted, self-centred man, who knows little or nothing of real love for God or men. Anyone to whom we can be a neighbour, is our neighbour. A few years ago there was serious rioting in Los Angeles following the announcement of the verdict of "not guilty" on the four police officers who had been accused of beating Rodney King.

In the midst of widespread violence and looting, the news cameras of the world's television networks captured an enthralling scene. A white truck driver, Reginald Denny, was driving through the troubled area. Suddenly a hostile crowd surrounded his truck and forced it to a stop. Reaching into the cab and pulling him to the ground, a mob of young black men started kicking him to death. The cameras rolled, but no one did anything to help the innocent driver. Just around the corner a young black woman was watching all this on television. Immediately she ran from her home saying, "I can't let this happen." She pushed through the crowd and fought furiously to pull the attackers off Denny. Somehow she succeeded. A young black man who also was a witness to the horrifying attack decided he must do something. Seeing his chance, he bundled Denny back into the cab of the truck and, risking his own life, began to drive the truck and its injured driver to safety.

Would Reginald Denny have the slightest difficulty in answering the question, "Who was your neighbour on that near-fatal day?" Who was his neighbour? The two out of the hundreds present and the thousands watching nearby television sets—the two who came to his aid—they were his neighbours. Denny could certainly identify his neighbours. Equally, the two courageous people who braved the wrath of the mob to save his life had no difficulty recognizing that Denny was their neighbour. In the light of the parable of the Good Samaritan, can any Christian be in doubt about who his neighbour is?

The Parable Exemplifies Our Duty

A priest and a Levite saw the man lying at the point of death on the Jericho road but passed by on the other side. We are not told exactly why they did so. They may have had religious reasons. Or they may have been afraid that the robbers were still in the vicinity. Whatever their reasons, the priest and the Levite passed by on the other side.

This is precisely what Christians must not do. No matter how many other people do so, we must not ignore need where we see it. We must not put our own comfort before the needs of others. We must not allow prejudice to harden our hearts, as many do. The answer of the lawyer to Jesus' question, "Which now of these three, thinkest thou, was neighbour unto him that fell among the thieves?" shows the power of prejudice. The lawyer replied, "He that shewed mercy on him." He could not even bring himself to utter the word *Samaritan.* Clearly, if he had travelled the Jericho road and found a Samaritan robbed and beaten he would not have gone to his assistance. The Jews had no dealings with the Samaritans. They hated each other. But by His parable the Lord Jesus commands us not to allow prejudice to harden our hearts. Instead, we must look with compassion on the needy. We must get involved and not leave the work of love to others. We must pay whatever price is necessary to be faithful to God in our service to men.

We must also make loving others an ongoing thing. The Samaritan not only tended the man by the roadside, put him on his own beast, and brought him to the inn for treatment, but also paid for his keep, and said he would return to make sure nothing was left undone that needed to be done. In other words, he completed the job. Too often our compassion has little endurance. We want to do good but we want to see immediate results for our efforts. If the response does not come quickly enough we lose interest. Sometimes that can have dreadful consequences. No man had a bigger heart than Martin Luther. Unlike most people of his day, Luther had a great love for the Jewish people and an ardent zeal to see them saved. He saw the Protestant Reformation as a glorious opportunity for the Jews to be brought into the Kingdom, and he set out to win them. But they did not respond—at least not quickly enough or in large enough numbers. At that point Luther turned against them. His love was replaced with bitterness and while it is a travesty of history to blame him for the Nazi holocaust, it is true that Jew haters have constantly appealed to his crude anti-Semitic outbursts. What was wrong with Luther? He had a big heart, but as far as the Jews were concerned, he didn't stay the course. We are all prone to fall into the same error. Winning Jews or Gentiles for Christ is not quick or easy work. We must never give up in our labour of love to make disciples of all men (Matthew 28:19).

The Parable Typifies Our Saviour

Christ treated us as the Good Samaritan treated the stricken man on the Jericho road. We were lying at the gate of death. Religion passed us by and could do nothing to save us. Then Jesus came. He stopped, He looked, He loved, and He lifted us. In love He paid the price for our deliverance. "God commendeth his love toward us, in that, while we were yet sinners, Christ died for us" (Romans 5:8). That's how our Saviour treated us.

Can we treat others any other way? If God loved us, can we deal with others without reference to His love? Paul commands us, "Be ye kind one to another, tenderhearted, forgiving one another, even as God for Christ's sake hath forgiven you" (Ephesians 4:32).

So we come full circle. God has loved us. His love has begotten in us a love for Him. Loving Him is the key to loving ourselves and others. His law requires that we live our lives in love—this triple love for God, ourselves, and others. This is true love. This is true obedience. This is true holiness. Indeed, this is true life.

CHAPTER ELEVEN

THE FULL FORCE OF THE LAW

"Be ye therefore perfect, even as your Father which is in heaven is perfect."
Matthew 5:48

Nothing is better calculated to puncture the pride of man than a clear understanding of the Ten Commandments. In them God summarizes man's entire moral duty. In them He shows us Himself and ourselves. This message of God's holiness and our sinfulness is not one we really wish to hear. Even the most self-confessed sinner wants to find some evidence of goodness in himself. We listen to the law of God, and, while we acknowledge that we do not meet its standards, we try to evade its full force.

The Pharisees did that. They had so restricted the meaning and application of God's law that they could comfortably persuade themselves that they kept it. They even boasted of their obedience and appealed to it as the basis of their justification. They could see no reason that God should not receive them because they were such good keepers of His law. But the Lord Jesus Christ would not allow them to comfort themselves with such a delusion. In order to make all men feel the full force of the Ten Commandments, He devoted a major part of the Sermon on the Mount to the subject of God's law (Matthew 5:17–48).

A true understanding of the full force of the Ten Commandments will save us from the damning delusion of self-righteousness and will confirm us in the faith of the gospel of Christ's imputed righteousness.

The Ten Commandments Have a Surface Meaning

Matthew chapter 5 clearly teaches that the Ten Commandments have a simplicity no one can misinterpret. The vocabulary is plain and down to earth. God has not cloaked these fundamental commandments in the language of philosophy or difficult theology. God has set them forth in such a way that we may teach them to little children, who may grasp the surface meaning of the Ten Commandments.

The *first* commandment teaches that there is only one God who demands that we worship Him. This commandment undermines a popular modern theory, that we worship the God with whom we feel comfortable—that is, a God after our own imagining. There is but one God, the living and true God, and He commands us to worship Him. The *second* commandment commands us to worship God in spirit and in truth, not according to our opinions, imaginations, feelings, or intuitions, but according to the revelation that He has given in His word. He forbids any physical representations of Himself in worship. The *third* commandment condemns all who use the Lord's name profanely. To profane His name is to use it in any way other than in genuine worship. The *fourth* commandment celebrates the fact that He has given us a weekly sabbath to observe.

The *fifth* commandment ordains that children should honor their parents. The *sixth* tells us that murder is a crime against God, and, according to the *seventh* and *eighth,* so are adultery and theft. The *ninth* commandment commands us that we are each to speak truth with our neighbour, and the *tenth* prohibits us from covetousness. These are the plain, simple standards of the law of God. Its surface message is wide-ranging and heart-searching. The first four commandments deal with our duty to God—His worship, His honor, and His day. The next six deal with our duty to man—his person, his station in life, his safety, his property, and his reputation.

The Ten Commandments Have a Spiritual Meaning

But the meaning of the Ten Commandments goes deeper. They clearly have a spiritual meaning also. Frequently, in referring to the law during the Sermon on the Mount, the Lord Jesus employed this or an equivalent formula: "Ye have heard that it was said . . . but I say unto you" (Matthew 5:21–22, 27–28, 31–32, 33–34, 38–39, 43–44). He was not changing the law or raising a superior standard of morality. Rather He was expounding the true meaning and scope of the Ten Commandments. The Psalmist said, "Thy commandment is exceeding broad" (Psalm 119:96), and in Matthew 5 the Lord Jesus shows us just how broad. Let us remember what we have already established in chapter three:

- Each commandment has a positive and negative aspect to it. Each precept implies a prohibition and each prohibition implies a precept.
- Each sin prohibited and each virtue commanded includes all actions of the same kind or nature, with all the means that lead to those actions. Thus murder includes unjust wrath and hatred, and adultery includes fantasizing lust.
- The Ten Commandments not only regulate outward behaviour, but reach to the heart, binding all the powers of the soul to complete obedience in word, thought, and deed. They command our understanding to *know* the will of God, our memory to *retain* it, our will to *choose* it, and our affections to *love* it.
- God's law is not only the *rule* for our obedience, but should also be the *reason* for it. In another words, we must obey it by faith in Christ and out of love for Him. "Whatsoever is not of faith is sin" (Romans 14:23). If faith does not inform our obedience our attempted righteousnesses will be "as filthy rags" (Isaiah 64:6).
- The law demands that our obedience be for the glory of God. The Lord Jesus showed by His obedience that this is the motive of all true submission to God's law: "I have glorified thee on the earth" (John 17:4). We must never lose sight of this supreme aim in all we say and do: "Whether therefore ye eat, or drink, or whatsoever ye do, do all to the glory of God" (1 Corinthians 10:31).

The Full Scope of the Ten Commandments

When we consider the Ten Commandments we must keep in mind the full scope of the statutes and not hide behind some truncated version of them. As we do so we will find that the full force of each commandment accomplishes five important goals.

The Holiness of God

The full force of the Ten Commandments *expresses the holiness of God.* The Puritans loved to point out that the law is a transcript of the nature of God. We have already considered the difference between God's positive (arbitrary) commands and His moral commands. He does not base His moral requirements on the mere sovereignty of His will, though that is always good enough reason for any creature to obey Him. If God commands it, we should obey for that reason. But His moral law reveals His very nature. The standard of holiness He requires reflects His own holy being.

God does not accommodate the standard of His law to the powers of fallen man. He never says, "Fallen man cannot perform this; therefore I will not require it." John Calvin correctly commented, "In the commandments of the law, God does not look at what men can do, but at what they ought to do" (*Commentaries,* 17.59). The Ten Commandments, therefore, are a great corrective to the fatal habit sinners have of casting God in their own image. Heathen men always make gods according to their own vain imaginations. Primitive heathens produce works of wood or stone in the likeness of men or beasts (Romans 1:23); more sophisticated heathens sometimes dispense with the idols but still make their gods no more than projections of their own thoughts. It is not too much to say that everyone who worships God other than according to His self-revelation in Christ (Hebrews 1:1–3) worships an extension of himself or an invention of others. Invariably, fallen man's reason for abandoning God's self-revelation for his own imagination of deity is to make accommodation for his sin. It is to evade the full force of God's commandments by inventing a god whose standards may be attainable, or whose wrath may be appeased, by human effort.

This is folly. God does not accommodate His standards to the ideas or abilities of fallen man. He is infinitely holy, as His law plainly declares. Again and again in giving the law, He states His reason for the statute as "I am the Lord" (Exodus 20:2; see Leviticus chapters 18 and 19). In giving His law, God is true to His own nature. The law comes with a "thus saith the high and lofty One that inhabiteth eternity, whose name is Holy" (Isaiah 57:15).

God is true to His own nature not only in *giving* the law, but also in *administering* it. God is not unrighteous in applying His law. In dealing with men, God will always be entirely true to His own holiness. What a withering rebuke of the facile notions men entertain that God will wink at their sin or adopt their depraved standards of judging their sin! The law expresses the holiness of God.

The Goodness of God

The full force of the Ten Commandments *exalts the goodness of God.* God revealed His law not in wrath, but in love. He revealed it first to Adam before the fall and that was clearly a revelation made in love. He revealed it again to fallen man, especially through Moses at Mount Sinai. When God gave the Ten Commandments, He revealed them as part of His statement of the covenant of grace. He says in effect, "I am the Lord who redeemed you; therefore, here are the Ten Commandments for you to obey." In Hosea 8:12, He lists the giving of the law as a proof of His grace: "I have written to him the great things of my law, but they were counted as a strange thing." In love He reveals His own perfection, the acceptable way to worship Him, the things that constitute true religion, and the standards that make for social justice (all of which expose the folly of all national policies aimed at promoting racial and social harmony that exclude God and His law). Even the biblical revelation of the impossibility of our keeping the law is given in grace. Thomas Boston aptly says, "The commandments require perfection. No partial obedience can be admitted or sustained. The least defect is fatal, and exposes to the curse. This ought to be seriously considered, that we may see our need of Christ's blood and righteousness to cover and atone for our obedience and all its defects" (*Works,* 1.70).

To summarize, it is kindness in God that will not allow men to wallow in sin or self-righteousness but will make them face the reality of their need and the only possible provision for meeting it.

The Wickedness of Man

The full force of the Ten Commandments *exposes the wickedness of man*. Who can hold up his head before the law of God? Who can endure Mt. Sinai's fiery thunders? Who can look into the face of God as He gives the Ten Commandments and congratulate himself on his righteousness? Men may compare themselves with others and come to the conclusion that they are not such bad people after all. But God doesn't compare us with others. He brings us to the standard of His law, a standard that rips off the façade of decency with which we cloak our sin. As we stand under Mt. Sinai, we all stand condemned as lawbreakers, indeed as violators of each commandment of the ten:

1. We have not worshipped God with a pure and constant devotion.
2. We must confess that our worship has not always been scriptural, pure, hearty, and spiritual.
3. We have lacked a deep fear and reverence of the holy name of the Lord and have even used it lightly, not only in conversation, but even in our praying.
4. We have not counted His sabbath a delight, but have profaned it, even while we pride ourselves in keeping it.
5. We have not guided and guarded our family relations with biblical faith and humility, nor have we demonstrated a Christ-like attitude to lawful authority in our homes, in the church, and in the state.
6. We have come under God's description of a murderer by our carnal anger and hatred of others, especially of our brethren in Christ.
7. We have defiled our souls with wicked uncleanness not only by the physical actions of immorality, but by indulging the lusts of the flesh in those thoughts which we too easily excuse as innocent fantasies.

8. We have indicted ourselves as thieves before God, not only by our disregard for the rights of others but even by our refusal to give ourselves and our substance to God.

9. We have proved ourselves to be liars before God. How often have we cast off our obligations to men! Worse still, we have thoughtlessly ignored our obligations to God Himself. Some have lied to Him by promising to repent and receive the Lord Jesus Christ as Saviour when, like the young man in the parable in Matthew 21, they have no intention of keeping their promise. Even Christians frequently vow to the Lord and fail to pay their vows—which is lying.

10. We have trampled the tenth commandment under our feet with all kinds of selfishness, covetousness, and greed, as well as by our faithless, carnal murmuring against God's sovereign disposition of our affairs.

We have not even begun to plumb the depths of the wickedness of the human heart. It is a veritable pit of iniquity, uncleanness, rebellion, and wickedness. Not much wonder Paul said, "What things soever the law saith, it saith to them who are under the law: that every mouth may be stopped, and all the world become guilty before God" (Romans 3:19).

Guilty! That is the law's verdict on every son of Adam's fallen race. Its fierce light lays bare every hidden recess of the soul and exposes its unspeakable depravity.

The Sinlessness of Christ

The full force of the Ten Commandments does something else: *It extols the sinlessness of Christ.* What a joy to turn from bemoaning sinners' breaches of the law to beholding Christ's perfect obedience. The very recital of our wickedness highlights the beauty of His sinlessness.

The word of God testifies repeatedly to the Saviour's sinlessness. "[He] did no sin, neither was guile found in his mouth" (1 Peter 2:22); "[He] knew no sin" (2 Corinthians 5:21); "In him is no sin" (1 John 3:5); "[He] is holy, harmless, undefiled, separate from sinners" (Hebrews 7:26). God the Father spoke from heaven saying, "This is my beloved Son, in whom

I am well pleased" (Matthew 3:17). When each commandment of God confronts us, it cries, "Guilty!" When those same commandments confront Christ, they each cry, "I find no fault in Him at all! In Him I find perfect righteousness." *The first table of the law confronts the Lord Jesus Christ* and testifies, "Here I find a perfect love for God, for His worship, His name, His day, and His service. In Christ, I find no tardiness in obeying His Father, but rather a constant zeal for His glory, untarnished by any inferior motive." *The second table of the law confronts Christ* and testifies, "Here I find a perfect love for man, such a love as neither angels nor men can comprehend—a love that feels no sacrifice too great and no suffering too painful to save sinners from their sin."

The law of God examines our blessed Saviour and says, "*Here I find a body* free from every taint of inbred sin, a body that is the perfect temple of the Holy Ghost and that has never been the home of any unrighteous word or deed. *Here I find a mind* unstained by any wicked lust or by any thought that is in the slightest degree unworthy of God. *Here I find a will* inflexible in its disposition to all good, a will whose affections are invariably godly and whose decisions are unfailingly right." The law extols the sinlessness of Christ.

Any lesser righteousness would leave the Lord Jesus Christ a debtor to the law and unable to save anyone. But His was no lesser righteousness! Such perfection as His defies man's puny comprehension, but it is what the law of God demands. Voluntarily, the great Lawgiver made Himself subject to the law. He who owed nothing to the law—indeed who was the very ground of its existence—became a debtor to do the whole law as our substitute. Where we had broken the law, He fulfilled it. Where we had earned its sentence, He earned its reward of righteousness. This is the reward He freely confers on the people whom He has united to Himself in the covenant of redemption.

The Righteousness of Believers

The full force of the Ten Commandments not only expresses the holiness of God, exalts the goodness of God, exposes the wickedness of man, and extols the sinlessness of Christ, but it also *expounds the righteousness of believers.* In Romans 5:17–19 Paul describes the perfect righteousness in which believers in Christ stand before God and His law: "If by one man's offence death reigned by one; much more they which receive abundance of grace and of the gift of righteousness shall reign in life by one, Jesus Christ.) Therefore as by the offence of one judgment came upon all men to condemnation; even *so by the righteousness of one the free gift came upon all men unto justification of life. For as by one man's disobedience many were made sinners, so by the obedience of one shall many be made righteous.*" The expression *made righteous* means *constituted righteous.* It refers to the legal standing believers have in Christ. In other words, the law's verdict on them is, "Righteous!" How can that be? Why does the law, once a voice raised to condemn us, now cry aloud for our acceptance as perfectly righteous? The answer of Scripture is unambiguous: It is solely on the basis of the righteousness of Christ imputed to us. "Christ Jesus . . . is made unto us . . . righteousness" (1 Corinthians 1:30). Jeremiah 23:6 actually calls the Saviour "the Lord our righteousness." Here is the perfection believers enjoy. "Their righteousness is of me, saith the Lord" (Isaiah 54:17). The imputed righteousness of Christ is their passport to glory, for "whom he justified, them he also glorified" (Romans 8:30). Well may we exclaim with Paul, "O the depth of the riches both of the wisdom and knowledge of God! how unsearchable are his judgments, and his ways past finding out!" (Romans 11:33). That the very law that thundered its anathemas on our hell-deserving heads should now pronounce us righteous and worthy of heaven—while we performed no meritorious work either to expiate our past guilt or to earn our future glory—is a miracle of wisdom, love, and grace that is entirely worthy of our God.

What a God! And what a gospel!

Part II

The Ten Commandments

CHAPTER TWELVE

THE FOUNDATION OF THE TEN COMMANDMENTS

"I am the Lord thy God, which have brought thee out of the land of Egypt, out of the house of bondage."
Exodus 20:2

There are many good reasons for us to obey God's law. The Ten Commandments themselves suggest that there is great personal benefit for those who observe them. They also bear eloquent testimony that there is a peculiar blessing for the family in observing God's commandments. At least five, possibly six, of the ten carry a reference to the family, from which we can conclude only that family welfare is a major object of the Lord in giving us His law. It would therefore be quite scriptural to say that we should obey the law of God because of the benefit it will bring to us, to our families, and to society in general. The law "was ordained to life" (Romans 7:10). Jesus said, "Keep the commandments" (Matthew 19:17) and "This do, and thou shalt live." (Luke 10:28). We must not make the mistake of denying the plain meaning of these words because they sound as if they teach works-religion and works-righteousness. The Bible states two important truths in regard to the law. First, the law teaches a man how to obtain righteousness by works (perfect obedience will be rewarded with eternal life); second, it teaches that no man can obtain righteousness by works. Is that a contradiction? "These two statements are perfectly consistent with each other . . . because the fault lies not in the doctrine of the law, but in man" (John Calvin, *Commentaries,* 17.60). The law was ordained unto life and there is therefore a blessing in observing it. Once we are justified by grace through faith in the Lord Jesus Christ without works, obedience to the law of God will strengthen and support our new life and it will enable us to enjoy the peculiar holiness of believers in Christ.

However, having said all that, and freely admitting that these are good reasons for obeying the law of God, we must recognize that there are much more fundamental reasons for doing so. Exodus 20:1–2 clearly makes this point: "God spake all these words, saying, I am the Lord thy God, which have brought thee out of the land of Egypt, out of the house of bondage." The doctrine is unmistakable: The Lord's person and His relationship with us establish His authority to command us and our obligation to obey Him. This is the real foundation of the Ten Commandments.

God Commands Us

God *commands* us. The Ten Commandments are just that—commands. In them God does not advise, cajole, or coax us. He does not give us His opinion or set His law before us as an option. He gives us commands. The law of God is *imperative,* carrying ultimate authority. It is *directive,* coming to us as a royal decree from the throne of glory. It is *regulative,* setting the proper standards for our behaviour and character. And it is *vindictive,* or more properly, *vindicative,* that is, vindicating its righteous standard by pronouncing a sentence for breaking it.

In Genesis 26:5 God says, "Abraham obeyed my voice, and kept my charge, my commandments, my statutes, and my laws." While the terms *voice, charge, commandments, statutes,* and *laws* are synonymous in that they all describe God's command to Abraham, they each carry a peculiar emphasis. God's law is His *voice,* to be heard and believed; His *charge,* to be observed; His *commandment,* to be obeyed; His *statute* or *decree,* to be acknowledged; and His *laws* or *instruction,* to be followed.

God Has a Perfect Right to Command Us

God has the right to command us. He says, "I am the Lord." His authority is not an assumed or usurped authority. It is not merely an authority of superior might or power. It is both natural and essential, belonging to His very Being. Both who God is and what God is establish His authority. He emphasizes this truth constantly in His word. For example, in Leviticus 18–26, almost fifty times He states the ground of His authority to command in the words, "I am the Lord," or "I am the Lord your God," or "I am the Lord their God." The *Larger Catechism* (Question 101) comments on Exodus 20:1–2: "[Here] God manifests his sovereignty, as being JEHOVAH, the eternal, immutable, and almighty God; having his being in and of himself, and giving being to all his words and works." If only we could grasp the immensity of the statement "I am the Lord," we would fall before Him and acknowledge His right to command us.

He is absolutely independent of all. He is the great "I AM," "the first and the last," "the alpha and omega," "the beginning and the ending." Nothing caused or contributes to His being. God is not upheld, enriched, or strengthened by any.

Not only is God absolutely independent, but *every other being derives its existence from Him and is dependent upon Him.* As Paul informed the Athenians, "In him we live, and move, and have our being" (Acts 17:28). "By [in] him all things consist [cohere, hang together]" (Colossians 1:17). He holds in being everything that exists. He rules over all and sustains all, so that even a sparrow cannot fall to the ground without Him.

His will and word are essential to our very life. The Psalmist says, "By the word of the Lord were the heavens made; and all the host of them by the breath of his mouth" (Psalms 33:6). Paul added that He upholds all things by the word of His power (Hebrews 1:3).

In the light of these truths it is undeniable that God has the right to command us. The Scriptures testify, "The statutes of the Lord are right" (Psalm 19:8). His "judgments are right" (Psalm 119:75). He declares only "things that are right" (Isaiah 45:19). Only fools contend with such obvious truth. "Who is wise, and he shall understand these things? prudent, and he shall know them? for the ways of the Lord are right, and the just shall walk in them: but the transgressors shall fall therein" (Hosea 14:9).

Every Man Has the Inescapable Obligation to Obey God's Commands

Every man has the inescapable obligation to obey God's command. *As His creatures, we have all received good at His hand.* He "giveth food to all flesh" (Psalm 136:25). "Every good gift and every perfect gift is from above, and cometh down from the Father of lights, with whom is no variableness, neither shadow of turning" (James 1:17). The Lord Jesus reminds us that even the blessings we take for granted as being merely natural occurrences, such as sunrise and rainfall, are in reality the gifts of God (Matthew 5:45). Shall we bite the hand that feeds us and sustains us in being?

As God's creatures we exist for His pleasure (that is, to fulfil His purpose) and His glory. "The Lord hath made all things for himself" (Proverbs 16:4). In Colossians 1:16 Paul asserts, "By him were all things created, that are in heaven, and that are in earth, visible and invisible, whether they be thrones, or dominions, or principalities, or powers: all things were created by him, and for him." Thus, "of him, and through him, and to him [for His glory], are all things" (Romans 11:36). The glorified saints in heaven rejoice in this truth. The more heavenly minded we are the more we will echo their testimony: "Thou art worthy, O Lord, to receive glory and honour and power: for thou hast created all things, and for thy pleasure they are [exist] and were created" (Revelation 4:11). Here is the answer to questions that we must all face: Why am I here? What is the purpose and meaning of life? Evolutionists want us to believe that we are merely parts of an ongoing cosmic accident. Nothing could be further from the truth. We are here by the creative fiat of God and are sustained in being to do His will and to bring glory to His name. That is why He created us.

As God's creatures and as moral agents we will give an account to Him. "Every one of us shall give account of himself to God" (Romans 14:12); therefore we should obey Him. God is the great *I AM*. That is ultimate reality. He is the one "with whom we have to do" (Hebrews 4:13), and His standard of judgment will be obedience to His will. Jesus said, "Not every one that saith unto me, Lord, Lord, shall enter into the kingdom of heaven; but he that doeth the will of my Father which is in heaven" (Matthew 7:21).

Our Obligation to Obey God Is Reinforced by Special Blessings

This universal obligation to obey the Lord is strengthened for many of us by the special blessings we have received from Him. He says, "I am the

Lord thy God." *All who profess to acknowledge Jehovah as the true God have a special obligation to obey Him.* He has given us special light and has surrounded us with blessings that only the gospel of grace can bring. "Unto whomsoever much is given, of him shall be much required" (Luke 12:48). Great blessings—the word of God in our mother tongue, the preaching of the gospel, the liberty the gospel brings to a nation and its people, the strivings of the Spirit, to name a few—bring increased obligation.

This increased obligation belongs even more to those who have been redeemed by the blood of Christ. The preamble to the Ten Commandments states, "I am the Lord thy God, which have brought thee out of the land of Egypt, out of the house of bondage" (Exodus 20:2). In Psalm 105:43 and 45 we learn God's reason for saving His people: "He brought forth his people with joy, and his chosen with gladness . . . that they might observe his statutes, and keep his laws." The preamble to the Ten Commandments belongs to each commandment. To appreciate its force we should read it before each one of the ten.

- Because the Lord redeemed you by His grace and power, *you should acknowledge Him and no other as your God.*
- Because the Lord redeemed you and brought you out of Egypt by signs and wonders, but with no visible or physical manifestations of Himself, *you must never pollute His worship with any images or representations of deity or of any other device intended to incite thoughts of Him.*
- Because the Lord has redeemed you with a mighty demonstration of His holiness and power, *you must never profane His holy name.*
- Because the Lord has delivered you from bondage *you must observe his sabbath rest.*
- Because the Lord has redeemed you and has spared your firstborn on that terrible night when the angel of death passed through the land of Egypt, *you should count the bond between parents and children as part of God's sacred covenant.*
- Because the Lord has brought you out of bondage and has given you life, *you shall not unlawfully take the life of another.*

- Because the Lord has brought you out of slavery and made you His servants in holiness, *you shall not pollute or enslave yourselves by lust and immorality.*
- Because the Lord has redeemed you and endowed you as His people, making rich provision for you, *you shall not steal the property of another.*
- Because in redeeming you, the Lord has sealed His grace with an oath, "I am the Lord," swearing by Himself because He could swear by none greater (Hebrews 6:13, 17), *you shall make His truth the sentinel of all your words and witness-bearing.*
- Because the Lord has redeemed you and has covenanted to bring you into a land flowing with milk and honey, *you shall be content with such things as are lawfully yours and shall not covet what belongs to another.*

This tenfold obligation rests on this foundation, "I am the Lord thy God, which have brought thee out of the land of Egypt, out of the house of bondage." When He redeems His people, He writes His law in their hearts (Hebrews 8:10). Antinomianism falls before this plain statement that God has redeemed us to observe His statutes and keep His law. When we sing, "Free from the law, O happy condition," we should remember that we are free from its condemnation, not from all obligation to obey it. We who have received the greatest blessing, God's gracious redemption, have the greatest reason to obey His law.

Failure to Obey God Is a Vicious Crime

Failure to obey the Lord is the greatest possible crime. "I have written to him the great things of my law, but they were counted as a strange thing" (Hosea 8:12). What a crime! And it carries an appropriate condemnation: "They would none of my counsel: they despised all my reproof. Therefore shall they eat of the fruit of their own way, and be filled with their own devices" (Proverbs 1:30–31). Those who sow contempt for God's law will reap its eternal condemnation.

What shall a sinner do? He must obey God's law. Yet he fails to obey it. Indeed, he cannot obey it. And even if suddenly he could, it would not remove the guilt of the life of sin he has lived until now. So what will a sinner do? Is there no hope? Must he perish forever? The gospel declares that there is hope. "We must needs die, and are as water spilt on the ground, which cannot be gathered up again; neither doth God respect any person: yet doth he devise means, that his banished be not expelled from him" (2 Samuel 14:14). God has devised means whereby those banished from Him by sin may not be expelled from Him forever. Romans 3:21 reveals what those means are: "But now the righteousness of God without [our keeping] the law is manifested, being witnessed by the law and the prophets; even the righteousness of God which is by faith of Jesus Christ unto all and upon all them that believe: for there is no difference: for all have sinned, and come short of the glory of God; being justified freely by his grace through the redemption that is in Christ Jesus: whom God hath set forth to be a propitiation through faith in his blood."

Here is God's answer to the crimes of lawbreakers. He saves them without any law-keeping on their part, solely on the merit of Christ's obedience unto death. And in doing so He makes them lovers of His law, people who obey it, not in order to be accepted as righteous in His sight, but as those who have been justified freely through the redeeming blood of Christ.

CHAPTER THIRTEEN

WHY TEN COMMANDMENTS?

"He declared unto you his covenant, which he commanded you to perform, even ten commandments; and he wrote them upon two tables of stone."
Deuteronomy 4:13

Why did God give *ten* commandments? According to the Lord Jesus Christ there are two great commandments upon which hang all the law and the prophets: "Thou shalt love the Lord thy God with all thy heart, and with all thy soul, and with all thy mind. This is the first and great commandment. And the second is like unto it, Thou shalt love thy neighbour as thyself. On these two commandments hang all the law and the prophets" (Matthew 22:37–40). If two commandments comprehend our entire moral duty, would it not be sufficient for God to command us to love Him and our neighbour? We acknowledge that to do so would fulfil the whole law (Romans 13:10), but we remember that love tends to do what is good and right toward its object. But what is good? What is right? Professing love as their motive, people often do wrong. The image-worship of the church of Rome and of the Orthodox churches is a case in point. So strong is their belief that their images express their love for God that they refuse to consider the implications of the second commandment. The message is clear: Love needs divine law to instruct the understanding. In one sense, we may say that love is enough, but in another sense we must confess that it is not. Love requires the guidance of God's law.

A child may love his parents and may have a sincere desire to please them. Yet through lack of understanding and discernment he may do the opposite of what is right and pleasing to them. So his parents, while rejoicing in his love, must give him a plain statement of their will. The same thing is true in our relation to God. The Ten Commandments are a necessary revelation of the will of God to instruct our understanding and to direct the expression of our love for Him. They are all the more necessary when we consider that they are addressed to sinful creatures with a natural bias towards evil, and with minds and wills set towards sin. So the Ten Commandments are necessary and must be preached.

But they must be preached in the right way. There is a wrong way to preach them and all to often preachers choose the wrong way. In the early stages of his ministry Thomas Chalmers illustrated the wrong way of preaching the commandments. The parishoners in the Scottish parish of Killmany were greatly excited at the thought of a new and brilliant young minister as their pastor. Few men in nineteenth-century Europe could compare to him for intellect and oratory. But soon the people were as perplexed as they were impressed because Sabbath after Sabbath Chalmers expounded the Ten Commandments and related themes, and excoriated his congregation for great sins, some of which his rustic audience had never heard of, much less committed. For eight years Chalmers continued in this vein, plainly preaching a gospel of works, "Do this and live." Then he came to a personal knowledge of Christ as Saviour and understood the place of the law in the revelation of grace. Only then could he preach the law of God as he ought—first, to convict sinners of their sin and to show them the perfect righteousness available to them in Christ, not by their own works, but by His; and second, to direct believers in the paths of faithful obedience to God, out of love for Christ. That is the right way to preach the Ten Commandments.

The proper use of any or all of the Ten Commandments must lead us to faith in the Lord Jesus Christ. Jesus said to the scribes and Pharisees, "[Ye] have omitted the weightier matters of the law, judgment, mercy, and faith" (Matthew 23:23). Judgment, mercy, and faith are the truly weighty matters of the law. We must keep these three words in mind as we study the Ten Commandments. It is obvious that they teach us our duty.

The first term Christ uses to show us our duty according to God's law is *judgment,* or *justice*—justice for all men, especially for the weak and oppressed. In recent church history—for this certainly was not so in earlier times—fundamental Bible-believers have allowed liberals to claim the theme of justice as their peculiar property and to redefine it in humanistic rather than biblical terms. They have permitted liberals to caricature it, sever it from the central message of the gospel, and then present their defective views as the whole gospel. Because liberals have misused the concept of justice, Bible-believers have all but dropped it from their vocabulary and preaching. Frequently our political philosophy or ideology has inured us to the cry of the oppressed and has influenced us to treat the idea of justice for them as something that has no place in the programme of those who labour to spread the gospel.

Why do we give so little thought to the concept of justice? Christ's words leave us in no doubt as to the importance He places upon it. They clearly declare that if we are to fulfil our duty to God we must stand for justice among men. That means more than crying out for law and order. It does includes law and order (something liberals usually leave out of their notions of justice), but it also transcends it and takes an interest in the weak, the vulnerable, and the downtrodden (witness the frequent references to injustice practised upon the widow, the fatherless, and the oppressed as in Deuteronomy 24:17; 27:19; Proverbs 22:22–23; 23:10–11; Jeremiah 22:13; Malachi 3:5; Matthew 23:14; James 5:4–6).

The second term Christ uses to show us our duty according to God's law is *mercy* for the needy and even for the guilty. Mercy is one of the weighty duties imposed on us by the command of God. Our God desires His people to be just *and* merciful, a people marked by their Master's lovingkindness, treating others as He has treated them (Ephesians 4:32).

The third term Christ uses to show us our duty according to God's law is *faith*—faith in God and His Son, faith in His Word and His gospel, faith that will guide us in the exercise of both justice and mercy. In other words, all our dealings with men must reflect a right attitude to God and His truth and must demonstrate a living faith in the gospel of His Son. In examining the Ten Commandments we must not fail to pay attention to these duties. In the context of Matthew 23 the Lord Jesus warns against a Pharisaic observance of the law that takes pride in minutiæ but ignores justice, mercy, and faith. Any purported obedience to God's law that does not do justly and love mercy because of the faith of the gospel is entirely bogus. These are the things on which the law lays heavy emphasis.

But the words *judgment, mercy,* and *faith* teach us our duty only because the Ten Commandments first teach us three great truths about God. First, *the Ten Commandments present us with God's judgment.* The Commandments are just. They make us feel our sin and face our condemnation. Each of the Ten Commandments cries out "Judgment!" against every one of us.

Further, *these same commandments also reveal God's mercy.* They teach us that the holy and almighty God is approachable (first three commandments). He will receive spiritual worship (third and fourth commandments). He has made provision for our rest (fourth commandment). He has set before us a rich provision and a rich inheritance (fifth commandment). The prohibitions of His law and the precepts of His law are for our good (fifth through tenth commandments). By the very perfection of their standards, the Ten Commandments show us the impossibility of salvation by works and suggest God's free provision of a righteousness earned for us by another. We know that this message is in the law if it is properly understood, for Paul testified, "The righteousness of God without the law is manifested, being witnessed by the law and the prophets" (Romans 3:21). John Calvin saw that clearly. In his summary of the Ten Commandments he said that from the law we learn that God is our Father and ruler who delights in righteousness and justice and to whom we should render righteous obedience. From the law we also learn our inability to attain to righteousness by our attempts at obeying God's commandments, and come to understand that we therefore must seek righteousness outside of ourselves. Under the burden of sin and the terror of wrath we flee to the only righteousness that *does* fulfil the law and that God freely offers us. We should never forget that with the Ten Commandments God gave the entire sacrificial system of the Old Testament, every detail of which cries, "Mercy for sinners!" and points to the sacrifice of Christ.

Finally, therefore, *the Ten Commandments call us to faith.* They bid us to believe God's judgment on our sin and to cast ourselves upon His mercy, believing His promise in His Son. This is the biblical use of the law of God. In chapter 11, "The Full Force of the Ten Commandments," we saw that the commandments showed five great truths: the holiness of God, the goodness of God, the wickedness of man, the sinlessness of Christ, and the righteousness of believers.

We must diligently keep these things before us as we study the Ten Commandments, remembering God's triple purpose in giving them: first, to instruct us as to the meaning of love and to direct us in its ministry; second, to expound the exercise of justice, mercy, and faith; and third, to make us feel the utter failure of all our efforts to establish our righteousness by law-keeping, thereby driving us to look for the ground of acceptance with God in the vicarious merit of another.

If we learn these important truths by our consideration of the Ten Commandments, our study will be eternally beneficial.

CHAPTER FOURTEEN

ONE GOD AND ONLY ONE
THE FIRST COMMANDMENT

"Thou shalt have no other gods before me."
Exodus 20:3

The *Shorter Catechism* catches the depths of the meaning of the first commandment. Its three-part statement first deals with what the commandment requires, then states what it forbids, and finally expounds the phrase "before me":

> *The first commandment requireth us to know and acknowledge God to be the only true God, and our God; and to worship and glorify Him accordingly.*
>
> *The first commandment forbiddeth the denying, or not worshipping and glorifying the true God as God, and our God; and the giving of that worship and glory to any other, which is due to him alone.*
>
> *These words* before me *in the first commandment teach us, That God, who seeth all things, taketh notice of, and is much displeased with, the sin of having any other God.*
>
> (Questions 46, 47, 48)

To summarize, *the Lord commands our exclusive worship and condemns every form of idolatry.* In establishing this proposition we will note three truths that the first commandment teaches us.

The Exclusive Dignity of Jehovah

The first commandment teaches us the exclusive dignity of Jehovah. With the words, "Thou shalt have no other gods before me," the Lord claims the worship of all His creatures. In effect He states, "I am God, and there is none else" (Isaiah 45:22). This is the constant testimony of the Old Testament: "Hear, O Israel: The Lord our God is one Lord" (Deuteronomy 6:4—teaching not only the unity of the Godhead, but that Jehovah is the one and only true God). In Exodus 15:11 Moses sang, "Who is like unto thee, O Lord, among the gods? who is like thee, glorious in holiness, fearful in praises, doing wonders?" The Lord made sure the Israelites learned that truth: "See now that I, even I, am he, and there is no god with me: I kill, and I make alive; I wound, and I heal: neither is there any that can deliver out of my hand" (Deuteronomy 32:39). The prophet Isaiah repeatedly addressed this subject. "O Lord of hosts, God of Israel, that dwellest between the cherubims, thou art the God, even thou alone, of all the kingdoms of the earth: thou hast made heaven and earth" (Isaiah 37:16; see 45:6, 22). Again and again the Lord testified through His prophets, "Beside me there is no God" (Isaiah 44:6; see Deuteronomy 4:39; Isaiah 37:20; 43:10–11; 44:8; 45:21).

The New Testament continues the same witness. In Ephesians 4:6 Paul speaks of "One God and Father of all, who is above all, and through all, and in you all." To Timothy he sounds out his great ascription of praise "unto the King eternal, immortal, invisible, the only wise God" (1 Timothy 1:17). In the next chapter he states, "There is one God" (1 Timothy 2:5). Jude finishes his epistle with another outburst of praise "to the only wise God our Saviour" (Jude 25).

Here then is the united testimony of Scripture. There is but one God, who is the only creator, upholder, ruler, and Saviour. In contrast, other gods are mere creations of men: "We know that an idol is nothing in the world, and that there is none other God but one" (1 Corinthians 8:4). As Psalm 115:4 says, "Their idols are silver and gold, the work of men's hands."

Since gods other than Jehovah do not exist, idols are proof of the insanity of the sinners who worship them. Isaiah 44:16–17 is an ironic passage that describes the madness of idolatry: "[A man cuts down a tree:] he burneth part thereof in the fire; with part thereof he eateth flesh; he roasteth roast, and is satisfied: yea, he warmeth himself, and saith, Aha, I am warm, I have seen the fire: and the residue thereof he maketh a god, even his graven image: he falleth down unto it, and worshippeth it, and prayeth unto it, and saith, Deliver me; for thou art my god." What utter folly! What absolute lunacy!

Idolatry bestializes men: "Every man is brutish by his knowledge; every founder is confounded by the graven image: for his molten image is falsehood, and there is no breath in them. They are vanity, the work of errors: in the time of their visitation they shall perish" (Jeremiah 51:17–18).

The Bible declares that idols have eyes that see not, ears that hear not, hands that work not, and feet that walk not. Idols are nothing. Other gods do not exist. That raises a question. If false gods have no real existence, why does the Bible take them so seriously? Does the first commandment chase spectres? No, the word of God takes idols seriously with good reason, for idols and idolatry have a baneful effect on all associated with them. J. Douma, a modern Dutch theologian, explained, "People worship powerful forces within creation as if these were deities. They are not gods, but only called gods (1 Corinthians 8:4); still they are very real powers, and able to enslave a person totally."

For example, the sun, the moon, the stars, the Earth, rain, thunder, fertility, are all real, but they are not gods. But that does not stop people from *treating* them as gods. Again, the Old Testament Scriptures have a lot to say about Baal. From Hosea 2: 2, 8, and 12, we gather that this idol was looked upon as the author of the fertility of the land. As a god, Baal did not exist; the fertility he was associated with was God's creation. But imaginary as Baal was, the effects of Baal worship were evil beyond description. Included in its rituals were prostitution, sodomy, and child sacrifices.

Idolatry continued to curse men in New Testament times. Paul described idolaters as depraved men, alienated from their Creator, refusing to give glory to God, and revelling in their own wisdom. These idolaters "changed the glory of the uncorruptible God into an image made like to corruptible man, and to birds, and fourfooted beasts, and creeping things.

[They] changed the truth of God into a lie, and worshipped and served the creature more than the Creator, who is blessed for ever" (Romans 1:23, 25). The results of such idol worship were terrible and far-reaching: "For this cause God gave them up unto vile affections [homosexuality] . . . and even as they did not like to retain God in their knowledge, God gave them over to a reprobate mind, . . . [they] being filled with all unrighteousness . . . [knowing] that they which commit such things are worthy of death (Romans 1:26, 28, 29, 32). Vice, enslavement, and the judgment of God always accompany idol worship.

Idolatry is serious, not because the gods men worship have any objective reality, but because of the lie that inheres in their worship. The real father of that lie is Satan. In 1 Corinthians 10:20, Paul says of idolatry, "The things which the Gentiles sacrifice, they sacrifice to devils, and not to God: and I would not that ye should have fellowship with devils." Sacrifices to idols are sacrifices to devils. Behind every idol lurks the Devil himself. That is what gives idolatry its awful grip. "In whom the god of this world hath blinded the minds of them which believe not, lest the light of the glorious gospel of Christ, who is the image of God, should shine unto them" (2 Corinthians 4:4). While other gods do not exist, Satan exists and Satanism exists. These are dreadful realities that wreak havoc across the world.

Nonetheless, Satan is God's creature and he lives under all the limitations of a creature. The Lord governs him. The Lord has broken his head at Calvary. The Lord will soon cast him bound into a bottomless pit and then into the lake of fire forever. Jehovah alone is God. This is His exclusive dignity. He says in Isaiah 43:10, "Understand that I am he: before me there was no God formed, neither shall there be after me." Here is the Lord's exclusive dignity. He is our Creator and He alone can be our Saviour: "Look unto me, and be ye saved, all the ends of the earth: for I am God, and there is none else" (Isaiah 45:22).

The Essential Duty of Man

The first commandment teaches the essential duty of man. What is that duty? "Thou shalt have no other gods before me." This is the basis for the *Shorter Catechism*'s statement that we must acknowledge Jehovah as the only true God, and our God, worshipping Him and repudiating every other god. That is the duty of every man. It is not the duty of only Jews and Christians, but of all men. No man or nation has any excuse for ignorance of the Lord: "That which may be known of God is manifest in them; for God hath shewed it unto them. For the invisible things of him from the creation of the world are clearly seen, being understood by the things that are made, even his eternal power and Godhead; so that they are without excuse" (Romans 1:19–20). Every individual and every nation on earth owes worship to the Lord Jehovah.

Because the Lord claims worship from every man, He holds the entire world to the standard of His law. "We know that what things soever the law saith, it saith to them who are under the law: that every mouth may be stopped, and all the world may become guilty before God" (Romans 3:19). But the Lord especially claims the worship of His covenant people: "I am the Lord thy God, which have brought thee out of the land of Egypt, out of the house of bondage. Thou shalt have no other gods before me" (Exodus 20:2–3). In other words, redeemed people have particular reason to worship the Lord.

Worship is a comprehensive word. It includes every duty that we owe to the Lord.

- We must *know* Him. "This is life eternal, that they might know thee the only true God, and Jesus Christ, whom thou hast sent" (John 17:3). Knowing Him we must take care to receive His word and to refuse all that opposes it.
- We must *adore* Him, that is, do homage to His majesty. "Ye that are near, acknowledge my might" (Isaiah 33:13).
- We must *trust* Him. As we have seen (Chapter 13), faith is one of the weighty matters of the law.
- We must *confess* Him. "Ye shall be witnesses unto me both in Jerusalem, and in all Judaea, and in Samaria, and unto the uttermost part of the earth" (Acts 1:8). So important is an open confession of Christ in true religion that Paul makes it essential to salvation (Romans 10:9), while the Lord Jesus warned, "Whosoever therefore shall be ashamed

of me and of my words in this adulterous and sinful generation; of him also shall the Son of man be ashamed, when he cometh in the glory of his Father with the holy angels" (Mark 8:38).

- We must *love* Him. Jesus said, "Thou shalt love the Lord thy God with all thy heart, and with all thy soul, and with all thy mind" (Matthew 22:37). Without love all religion is vain (1 Corinthians 13:1–3).
- We must *fear* Him. "Fear God" (1 Peter 2:17). This is the "beginning of wisdom" (Proverbs 9:10).
- We must *pray* to Him. "My house shall be called the house of prayer" (Matthew 21:13). He commands us to pray (Psalm 27:8) and promises to hear us when we seek Him wholeheartedly (Jeremiah 29:13). So essential is prayer to worship that the Lord says, "I will go and return to my place, till they acknowledge their offence, and seek my face" (Hosea 5:15).
- We must *praise* Him. "Give thanks unto the Lord" is a constant command to worshippers (Psalm 105:1; 106:1; 107:1; 118:1, 29).
- We must *obey* Him. "Hath the Lord as great delight in burnt offerings and sacrifices, as in obeying the voice of the Lord? Behold, to obey is better than sacrifice, and to hearken than the fat of rams" (1 Samuel 15:22).

The duty of man is clear. He should worship the Lord. "He hath shewed thee, O man, what is good; and what doth the Lord require of thee, but to do justly, and to love mercy, and to walk humbly with thy God?" (Micah 6:8). But in spite of that clear command, most of mankind follows the practice of the foreigners whom the king of Assyria planted in Samaria: "Every nation made gods of their own" (2 Kings 17:29). Men are still busy in that same pursuit. Idolatry is rampant. Pagan idolatry still abounds, not only in foreign countries, but in what were once considered Christian lands in Europe and America. In addition to heathen temples and heathen gods all around us, we now have the worship of man and his technological and scientific accomplishments. Men call this secular humanism, or atheism, but in reality it is idolatry. Then we have the "yuppie" religion of earth worship. New Agers are forever speaking of "Mother Earth." They call her *Gaia,* from the Greek word for earth. That was the name of the ancient Greek goddess worshipped as the mother of all the living. Some self-styled "Christian feminists" worship a goddess they call *Sophia*. At a 1993 conference in Minneapolis they announced to the world their rejection of the God of the Bible and of the Christ of the Bible—especially His blood atonement—in favour of this goddess, Sophia. Idolatry is on every hand.

There are also many other idols. Some are so popular that they are welcomed by Christians into their lives, homes, and churches. According to Colossians 3:5, *covetousness is a form of idolatry*. Given such a definition of idolatry, who can plead innocent to the charge of being an idolater? *Rebellion and stubbornness are forms of idolatry.* "Rebellion is as the sin of witchcraft, and stubbornness is as iniquity and idolatry" (1 Samuel 15:23). A stubborn pursuit of our own way, rejecting the wisdom, word, and will of God is idolatry. *Sensuality is a form of idolatry.* "Many walk, of whom I have told you often, and now tell you even weeping, that they are the enemies of the cross of Christ: whose end is destruction, whose God is their belly, and whose glory is in their shame, who mind earthly things" (Philippians 3:18–19). We live in such a sensuous age. People dress sensually, talk sensually, and act sensually. Sensuality is not only the breach of the commandments that deal with personal and social behaviour, but it is the rejection of God Himself. It is the worship of the human body. It is idolatry.

In fact, *ungodliness of every kind is idolatry.* To ignore or neglect God and His word, to resist the workings of the Holy Spirit, and to reject the Lord Jesus Christ are all idolatrous actions. So is every hypocritical pretence to worship. What shall we say of those who outwardly profess to worship God in Spirit and in truth by faith in His Son, while all the time they reject Him in their hearts? Jesus recognized such people and condemned their deceit: "This people draweth nigh unto me with their mouth, and honoureth me with their lips; but their heart is far from me" (Matthew 15:8). Such hypocrites compound their ungodliness by their pretence. Samuel Hopkins justly charged, "The hypocrite calls on God to be an accomplice and partaker with him in his crimes."

Such sins are heinous enough in themselves, but according to the first commandment they are committed in the very face of God. He says, "Thou shalt have no other gods before me" or, *before my face,* or *in my presence.* Every sin is committed in the Lord's face, under the Lord's eye, but especially the sin of idolatry. Therefore He says, "Will ye steal, murder, and commit adultery, and swear falsely, and burn incense unto Baal, and walk after other gods whom ye know not; and come and stand before me in this house, which is called by my name, and say, We are delivered to do all these abominations? Is this house, which is called by my name, become a den of robbers in your eyes? Behold, even I have seen it, saith the Lord" (Jeremiah 7:9–11).

The first commandment reveals the duty of man and condemns every one of us as an idolater, a criminal at the judgment bar of God. Ought we not to tremble to think of our breach of it? Exposing our idolatry, it calls on us to do what the Thessalonians did when they heard Paul's preaching—turn from idols to serve the living and the true God (1 Thessalonians 1:9). But it does more than expose our sin and command our obedience, it holds out a message of hope and grace, for it points us to Christ.

The Eternal Deity of Christ

The first commandment teaches the eternal deity of Christ. Worship belongs only to Jehovah. "I am the Lord: that is my name: and my glory will I not give to another, neither my praise to graven images" (Isaiah 42:8). Worship offered to any other is idolatry. Yet, God the Father commands even the angels of heaven to worship Christ: "When he bringeth in the firstbegotten into the world, he saith, And let all the angels of God worship him" (Hebrews 1:6). By the express command of God worship is given to the Lord Jesus Christ. We must not fail to grasp the plain logic of the word of God here. We may put it in the form of a syllogism.

Major premise:	Worship belongs exclusively to Jehovah, the only true God;
Minor premise:	God commands worship to be given to Jesus Christ;
Conclusion:	Therefore Jesus Christ is the true God and Jehovah.

The first commandment, therefore, should be read in the light of the gospel. When it says, "Thou shalt have no other gods before me," it commands us to acknowledge and confess the Lord Jesus Christ to be the true God and our God and Saviour. Jesus Himself said this: "Ye believe in God, believe also in me" (John 14:1). That is the full significance of the first commandment. It condemns our sin, but it points us to Christ. To obey it is to join with Thomas as he exclaimed of Christ, "My Lord and my God" (John 20:28).

The dearest idol I have known,
Whate'er that idol be,
Help me to tear it from Thy throne
And worship only Thee.

CHAPTER FIFTEEN

IDOLS, IMAGES, AND ICONS
THE SECOND COMMANDMENT

"Thou shalt not make unto thee any graven image, or any likeness of any thing that is in heaven above, or that is in the earth beneath, or that is in the water under the earth: Thou shalt not bow down thyself to them, nor serve them: for I the Lord thy God am a jealous God, visiting the iniquity of the fathers upon the children unto the third and fourth generation of them that hate me; and shewing mercy unto thousands of them that love me, and keep my commandments."
Exodus 20:4–6

The language of the second commandment is intentionally very solemn. Its terms are deliberately blunt and uncompromising. There can be no doubt about its meaning. Yet it is almost universally unacceptable to men. There is something in man's heart that resents this commandment. Despite all the Lord has said, image production and veneration are as prevalent in Christendom as in heathendom. This is a dangerous act of disobedience. The Lord has attached terrible sanctions to this commandment—indeed, the heaviest of any that accompany the commandments. His justice has severe punishments for all who make images or who bow down before them. Hence, we do well to take heed to this commandment.

For a Christian, however, there is a much stronger reason for obeying the second commandment. *Here we learn how to worship the Lord acceptably.* This is the fundamental difference between the first and second commandments. The first commands us not to worship false gods. The second commands us not to worship the true God in a false way. This distinction is sufficiently plain to render the action of the Roman Catholic Church of combining both as the first commandment (and dividing the tenth so as to retain ten commandments) inexcusable. By this device, Rome conveniently omits the second commandment with its strong denunciation of images from many of her catechisms.

The central message of the second commandment is as follows: The Lord has blessed His people by revealing to them how He desires to be worshipped. He limits legitimate worship to His prescribed way and threatens terrible judgment upon all idolatrous departures from His law. He bans images, icons, and idols from His worship. Human imagery, imagination, and ingenuity have no place in the solemn business of man's approach to God.

A Sweeping Prohibition

The subject of the prohibition in the second commandment *is not sculpture or art generally.* The prohibition of "graven images" (works of carving or sculpture) and of "any likeness [artistic representation] of any thing that is in heaven above, or that is in the earth beneath" is limited to the sphere of public and private worship. This is obvious from the words that immediately follow the prohibition: "Thou shalt not bow down thyself to them, nor serve them: for I the Lord thy God am a jealous God" (Exodus 20:5).

The second commandment deals with *the unauthorized use of images, indeed of any unauthorized use of art in the worship of God.* In that connection it prohibits the making of any image or any likeness of anything in heaven, in earth, or under the earth. It prohibits venerating, bowing down before, praying to, or serving the cause of, any image.

The law of God is very clear on this issue. The Scriptures reiterate the prohibition frequently and forcefully. Both the Old and New Testaments denounce all use of images in worship as idolatrous. "Ye shall make you no idols nor graven image, neither rear you up a standing image, neither shall ye set up any image of stone in your land, to bow down unto it: for I am the Lord your God. Ye shall keep my sabbaths, and reverence my sanctuary: I am the Lord" (Leviticus 26:1–2). "Turn ye not unto idols, nor make to yourselves molten gods: I am the Lord your God" (Leviticus 19:4).

In Deuteronomy 4:15–19 the Lord reminds us that when He revealed Himself on Mount Sinai He did not appear in any physical or material form or shape that the art of man could replicate. The lesson He intends us to learn from this fact is that we must not countenance any artistic impression or representation of God. "Take ye therefore good heed unto yourselves; for ye saw no manner of similitude on the day that the Lord spake unto you in Horeb out of the midst of the fire: Lest ye corrupt yourselves, and make you a graven image, the similitude of any figure, the likeness of male or female, the likeness of any beast that is on the earth, the likeness of any winged fowl that flieth in the air, the likeness of any thing that creepeth on the ground, the likeness of any fish that is in the waters beneath the earth: and lest thou lift up thine eyes unto heaven, and when thou seest the sun, and the moon, and the stars, even all the host of heaven, shouldest be driven to worship them, and serve them, which the Lord thy God hath divided unto all nations under the whole heaven."

Not only does the Lord forbid the use of images in His worship, He also forbids all use of human art to modify the biblically revealed forms of worship: "Ye shall not make with me gods of silver, neither shall ye make unto you gods of gold. An altar of earth thou shalt make unto me, and shalt sacrifice thereon thy burnt offerings, and thy peace offerings, thy sheep, and thine oxen: in all places where I record my name I will come unto thee, and I will bless thee. And if thou wilt make me an altar of stone, thou shalt not build it of hewn stone: for if thou lift up thy tool upon it, thou hast polluted it. Neither shalt thou go up by steps unto mine altar, that thy nakedness be not discovered thereon" (Exodus 20:23–26). The use of the tool of man on the altar of God—the introduction of human art or skill into our approach to Him—pollutes the worship of Jehovah.

So abominable to God were man-made images that He placed His curse upon their use, in private as much as in public worship: "Cursed be the man that maketh any graven or molten image, an abomination unto the Lord, the work of the hands of the craftsman, and putteth it in a secret place. And all the people shall answer and say, Amen" (Deuteronomy 27:15).

It is against the background of this Old Testament definition and denunciation of idolatry that we must understand the New Testament's parallel commands. Paul warned the mostly Gentile Corinthians, "Neither be ye idolaters, as were some of them; as it is written, The people sat down to eat and drink and rose up to play. . . . Wherefore, my dearly beloved, flee from idolatry"(1 Corinthians 10:7, 14). John had a similar word for his mostly Jewish readers: "Keep yourselves from idols" (1 John 5:21). In context, these Scriptures command believers not to have fellowship with idols by knowingly eating anything sacrificed to them. If even that level of involvement with idols is prohibited, there can be no doubt that the apostles of Christ continued the Old Testament ban on the use of idolatrous images in the worship of the Christian church. Indeed, in Colossians 2:18 and 23 Paul employs the principle of Exodus 20:25 and shows that human art and invention still defile the worship of God. The apostle condemns what he terms "will worship," which includes all methods and forms of worshipping God that originate, not in divine revelation, but in man's self-will. In worship, whatever has its origin in man's inventiveness is idolatry.

So the second commandment makes a sweeping prohibition: No images of false gods or artistic representations of the true God are acceptable in the worship of the Lord.

The Specific Purposes of This Prohibition

The second commandment also reveals the specific purposes of this prohibition. They are first, *to maintain His honor* and second, *to preserve the purity of His worship*. These should be two matters of the greatest importance to any Christian. From the plain statements of God's own word we should humbly recognize that the honour of the Lord and the purity of His worship can never be maintained by the introduction of human inventions into divine worship, no matter how wise or popular they may be.

Depraved man has never liked this divine restriction and has always sought ways to circumvent it. In Christian churches, images, holy pictures, paintings of Christ, actors playing the part of Christ, and all sorts of will worship have been introduced in defiance of the Lord's command. In most cases these idolatrous innovations are welcomed because they appeal to the masses. The logic seems to be that since people do not relate to the severe simplicity and spirituality of biblical worship we must adopt new methods. User-friendly religion is the goal of most churches. Paul's question in Galatians 1:10 seems to elicit an entirely different response from modern preachers than it did from the apostle: "Do I now persuade [conciliate] men, or God? or do I seek to please men? for if I yet pleased men, I should not be the servant of Christ" (Galatians 1:10). Wherever extra-biblical innovations are introduced into divine worship, pleasing men takes precedence over honouring God.

Having accepted that preaching is not popular with the masses, many churches have turned to all sorts of new methods to attract the unchurched and to hold on to the churched. The rationalization is that the church's methods must be *relevant*. So in many worship services troops of actors perform plays about contemporary social problems and introduce the idea that Christ is the solution to them. Or groups of rock musicians replace the Psalms, hymns, and spiritual songs of the heavenly worship revealed in Scripture with the distinctly earthly—and earthy—rhythms of the ungodly rock culture. The mindset that brings such innovation into the church in the name of making Christ and His gospel relevant to modern man is thoroughly Arminian. It displays an abysmal misunderstanding of the spiritual nature and power of the gospel. The gospel of Christ as revealed in Scripture, preached in the power of the Holy Spirit, is always relevant. Anything that does not measure up to God's law and gospel is will worship, and will worship is the ultimate irrelevancy. Worse still, it is idolatry. It is a direct attack on the honour of the Lord. The idols, images, icons, pictures—indeed any inventions of the world are not proper vehicles for Christian worship or fit expressions of Christian piety.

Images replace revelation with imagination. Imagination is relative to the state of the imaginer, in this case fallen man. Because man is fallen and depraved, the products of his imagination effectively blur, or even blot out, the light of revelation. *They strengthen man in his rebellious sense of autonomy.* They reinforce his notion that he can come to God as he wishes, not as God has commanded. They declare man to be the master of God.

That is the basic aim of all image use: to enable the worshippers to handle and control the powers of the gods they worship. So *images usurp the worship that belongs to God*. They breed superstition and transfer the veneration that belongs to Jehovah to some powerless idols or holy pictures.

These are serious charges that emphasize that the Lord has purposes of the utmost importance in establishing the prohibition of all will worship in His church.

The Severe Punishment for Ignoring the Prohibition

The second commandment pronounces severe punishment on those who ignore its prohibition. Nothing provokes God more than defiance of this commandment. He says, "I the Lord thy God am a jealous God." The word "God" is the Hebrew word *'el,* which signifies "strong" or "powerful." Note carefully the conjunction of the ideas of strength and jealousy. Paul repeated this combination of terms in 1 Corinthians 10:22: "Do we provoke the Lord to jealousy? are we stronger than he?" Archbishop Leighton, the only spiritual giant in Scotland to remain an Anglican in the days of the National Covenant, gave the significance of the divine name *'el* in Exodus 20:5: "I am able to right [avenge] Myself on the mightiest and proudest offender." Thus when the Lord says, "I the Lord thy God am a jealous God," He means that He has power to judge all those who provoke Him to jealousy. And that is precisely what breaking the second commandment does. "Thou shalt worship no other god: for the Lord, whose name is Jealous, is a jealous God"(Exodus 34:14). Deuteronomy 4:24 adds, "The Lord thy God is a consuming fire, even a jealous God."

What is jealousy? Some commentators define it as wounded love. The Lord loves His people and is justly jealous when they give their hearts to another. The *Expository Dictionary of Bible Words* adopts this definition: "When applied to God, 'jealousy' communicates the fierce intensity of his commitment to his people, even when they turn from him." However, though *wounded love* is a fair definition of jealousy as far as it goes, jealousy is more than wounded love. It is a reaction against anything or anyone who steals the object of our love and our desire, or who destroys our enjoyment of it. Samuel Hopkins said, "The cause of it [jealousy] is love, but the effect of it is revenge." So the term the Lord uses in describing Himself, "I am a jealous God," carries the idea of His love and commitment, not only to His people, but also to His own name and honour. In Numbers 25:13, *qana'*, the Hebrew word for "jealous" in Exodus 20, is translated "zealous." The meaning of the second commandment is that the Lord is *zealous* for His own honor and glory, and He is *jealous* for them so that He zealously protects them and will avenge Himself on all who insult them. Through the prophet Zephaniah He said, "I will bring distress upon men, that they shall walk like blind men, because they have sinned against the Lord: and their blood shall be poured out as dust, and their flesh as the dung. Neither their silver nor their gold shall be able to deliver them in the day of the Lord's wrath; but the whole land shall be devoured by the fire of his jealousy" (Zephaniah 1:17–18).

The Lord describes His wrath as "visiting the iniquity of the fathers upon the children unto the third and fourth generation of them that hate me." According to this statement, image worship is "hating God." It is a sin that casts a long shadow. It has vast, baneful effects in the family and in society at large. Many question whether it is just of God to visit the iniquity of the fathers upon their children unto the third and fourth generation. Does the Bible not say that the son will not be put to death for the father's sin, or the father for the son's sin, but that "the soul that sinneth, it shall die" (Ezekiel 18:4, 20; Deuteronomy 24:16)? Yes, the Bible makes these statements. Every man is responsible for his own sin before God. But the second commandment teaches another equally demonstrable truth: Idolatry, once introduced, takes deep root and produces tragic fruit for years to come. It drives out the light of the Lord's presence and leaves families and nations to the darkness of their chosen sin and doom (See Romans 1:19–32). Generations yet unborn, as the children of idolatrous and God-forsaken people, come into an inheritance of wrath. The punishments God inflicts for breaking the second commandment are as far-reaching as they are severe.

Stubborn Persistence in Ignoring the Prohibition.

Despite the severity of the threatened punishment, Scripture records man's stubborn persistence in ignoring the prohibition. The Lord issued this law speedily and repeatedly—and with very good reason.

The Golden Calf

How quickly did the children of Israel turn to images! They were hardly out of Egypt when they made their first image (Exodus 32). The golden calf—and it is important to understand the relevance of this to the second commandment—was not an idol as such. It was a representation of Jehovah Himself: "He received them at their hand, and fashioned it with a graving tool, after he had made it a molten calf: and they said, These be thy gods, O Israel, which brought thee up out of the land of Egypt. And when Aaron saw it, he built an altar before it; and Aaron made proclamation, and said, To morrow is a feast to the Lord" (Exodus 32:4–5). In spite of the fact that all the people of Israel had heard the actual voice of God thundering forth the prohibition of all images, they immediately imported the golden calf into the worship of Jehovah as a representation of the power by which He had brought them out of Egyptian bondage.

Gideon's Ephod

The book of Judges shows us that even such a great man as Gideon committed a similar crime: "Gideon made an ephod thereof, and put it in his city, even in Ophrah: and all Israel went thither a whoring after it: which thing became a snare unto Gideon, and to his house" (Judges 8:27).

Micah's Images

In Judges chapter 17 we learn the real intent of most of Jewish image-making: "There was a man of mount Ephraim, whose name was Micah. And he said unto his mother, The eleven hundred shekels of silver that were taken from thee, about which thou cursedst, and spakest of also in mine ears, behold, the silver is with me; I took it. And his mother said, Blessed be thou of the Lord, my son. And when he had restored the eleven hundred shekels of silver to his mother, his mother said, I had wholly dedicated the silver unto the Lord from my hand for my son, to make a graven image and a molten image: now therefore I will restore it unto thee. Yet he restored the money unto his mother; and his mother took two hundred shekels of silver, and gave them to the founder, who made thereof a graven image and a molten image: and they were in the house of Micah. And the man Micah had an house of gods, and made an ephod, and teraphim, and consecrated one of his sons, who became his priest" (Judges 17:1–5). Later Micah climbed the religious social ladder and got a Levite to come and be the priest in his house of God. But despite the clear breach of the second commandment, the worship was professedly the worship of Jehovah. The images were intended to enhance and advance, perhaps to simplify, beautify, or make relevant the worship of Jehovah.

Jeroboam's Golden Calves

The same was true even of the golden calves that Jeroboam erected (1 Kings 12:29–33). Jeroboam ruled the northern tribes of the divided nation of Israel. As a politician, he was afraid of the consequences of his people's visiting Jerusalem for the yearly feasts of the Lord. He thought that they would resume their loyalty to the house of David, with the result that he would lose his kingdom. So "Jeroboam ordained a feast in the eighth month, on the fifteenth day of the month, like unto the feast that is in Judah, and he offered upon the altar. So did he in Bethel, sacrificing unto the calves that he had made: and he placed in Bethel the priests of the high places which he had made" (1 Kings 12:32). Those golden calves were not intended to replace the worship of Jehovah, but to provide an alternate—and unauthorized—place of worship.

The Brazen Serpent

In the days of Hezekiah, the people of Judah even turned the brazen serpent that Moses had raised up in the wilderness into an idol, so that Hezekiah had to destroy it (2 Kings 18:4).

Ezekiel's Vision

In the days of Ezekiel, the leaders of Judah imported all sorts of idolatrous images into the temple in Jerusalem: "I lifted up mine eyes the way toward the north, and behold northward at the gate of the altar this image of jealousy in the entry. . . . So I went in [to the court of the temple] and saw; and behold every form of creeping things, and abominable beasts, and all the idols of the house of Israel, portrayed upon the wall round about. . . . Then he brought me to the door of the gate of the Lord's house which was toward the north; and, behold, there sat women weeping for Tammuz [a heathen idol]. . . . He brought me into the inner court of the Lord's house, and, behold, at the door of the temple of the Lord, between the porch and the altar, were about five and twenty men, with their backs toward the temple of the Lord, and their faces toward the east; and they worshipped the sun toward the east" (Ezekiel 8:5, 10, 14, 16).

"Christian" Image Worship

How quickly the people turned to images and idols! After their Babylonian captivity, the Jews seemed to be comprehensively purged of such idol worship. But idol worship had not really suffered too great a reversal because after a few centuries even so-called Christian churches adopted image worship. In A.D. 787, the Council of Nicea—not to be confused with the council that produced the Nicene creed—made the following pronouncement:

"Like the figure of the precious and life-giving cross, venerable images of our Lord and God and Saviour, Jesus Christ, and inviolate Lady, the holy Mother of God, and the venerable angels, all the saints and the just, whether painted or made of mosaic or another suitable material, are to be exhibited in the holy churches of God, on sacred vessels, and vestments, walls and panels, in houses and on streets" (*Catechism of the Catholic Church,* ¶1161). The Council of Trent, Rome's answer to the Reformation, endorsed the Nicene statement and indeed, went further by cursing all who denied it. Trent went on to say that images were "to be worshipped as if the persons represented thereby were present." Rome's usual reply to criticisms that her veneration of images is idolatrous is that Roman Catholics bowing before images are not actually worshipping or venerating them but the persons they represent. But Trent's authoritative statement, still binding on Roman Catholics today, is that images are to be worshipped as if the persons they represent were actually present. Thus anyone bowing before an image of Christ must devote to it all the worship he would offer Christ if He were physically present. The second Vatican Council endorsed the views of the Councils of Nicea and Trent on the veneration of images. The *Catechism of the Catholic Church*, the latest authoritative product of Vatican theology, quotes both of those ancient councils as its authority for maintaining the worship of images.

Rome's idolatry is on every hand. Her crucifixes, her holy pictures, and her images of saints, of Mary, and most blasphemous of all, even of the blessed Son of God Himself, are breaches of the second commandment. But even Protestants are far from guiltless. What shall we say of all those holy pictures of Jesus all the way from the manger to the Ascension? However wonderful as examples of an artist's skill, such things are sheer, rank, rampant idolatry. Religious art has the freedom to represent many scenes from Scripture. As we have already noted, the second commandment does not prohibit all sculpture or all painting. To depict Moses leading the Israelites out of Egypt, or Elijah confronting the prophets of Baal on Mount Carmel is not a breach of the commandment. But artistic freedom stops at any representation of deity. That is something the word of God denounces in the strongest terms. If Jesus Christ is God—and that is the central truth of Christianity—it is inescapable that Scripture forbids any representation of Him. It matters not whether the medium is painting, sculpture, or dramatic presentation, the prohibition against rendering any likeness of deity is absolute.

The usual response to such a statement by evangelical Protestants who sanction images or pictures of Christ is that the second commandment has reference only to worship and that the representation in question are not objects, or even means, of worship. This is a hollow response. Can a Christian contemplate his Saviour without some sense of worship? Should a Christian ever be invited to think of Christ apart from any thought of worshipping Him? When God brought His Son into the world, He commanded even the angels to worship Him (Hebrews 1:6). Can souls redeemed by His blood do less? Any representation of Jesus Christ is an object that is deliberately intended to lead our minds to certain thoughts of Him. For a Christian, such thoughts must be devotional. To some, such a proposition sounds unobjectionable, but God has said, "Thou shalt not make unto thee any graven image, or any likeness of any thing that is in heaven above, or that is in the earth beneath, or that is in the water under the earth."

The excuses given for the use of these so-called Christian images are the very same excuses given by the heathen for their images. *We are not worshipping the actual image.* Neither did the heathen worship the actual idol they had made. They did not believe that in itself the piece of wood they carved was a god. They believed that it represented a god. The image represented the abstract concept or commemorated some great thing the god had reputedly done for them. Isn't that the same excuse made for Christian usage of images?

The image is a help to devotion. The Roman Catholic theologian, John of Damascus, eulogized images because they helped his devotion. All who support the use of representation of deity make the same claim. It is entirely false. There is a world of difference between the carnal stirrings of fleshly emotion and true spiritual worship. The use of images and the introduction of the art of man to represent God may stir the imaginations and emotions of the flesh, but they cannot assist us to worship "in the beauty of holiness" (Psalm 96:9). Anything that flies in the face of the word of truth cannot aid our worship "in spirit and in truth" (John 4:24).

The worship given belongs properly not to the image but to the deity pictured by the image. The *Catechism of the Catholic Church* defends this position. Quoting Thomas Aquinas it says: "The Christian veneration of images is not contrary to the first commandment [second commandment; Rome combines the first two under the first commandment] which proscribes idols. Indeed, the honour rendered to an image passes to its prototype, and whoever venerates an image venerates the person portrayed in it. The honour paid to sacred images is a respectful veneration, not the adoration due to God alone: religious worship is not directed to images in themselves, considered as mere things, but under their distinctive aspect, as images leading us on to God incarnate. The movement toward an image does not terminate in it as an image, but tends toward that whose image it is" (¶2132). What a convoluted, contradictory statement! If, as both this catechism and the Council of Trent agree, images should be venerated as if the person represented were present, and if the veneration paid to an image passes over to the person it represents, how can the veneration of an image of Christ be anything less than the adoration due to God alone?

The best answer to such papal obfuscation is to quote the second commandment. There it is evident that the Lord rejects all such excuses. He leaves no room for images in His worship, even if church councils decree that they are aids to worship. "We ought to obey God rather than men" (Acts 5:29), even though it means repudiating the use of crosses, crucifixes, little plastic babies representing Jesus or His angels, manger scenes, and depictions of Christ in life or death, whether by artists or actors.

Scriptural Principles Underlying the Prohibition

Certain clear scriptural principles underlie the prohibition in the second commandment. The first is *the authority of divine law*. The Lord has decreed how we must approach Him. Our duty is to worship Him as He has stipulated. Anything else is rebellion. Second, *the adequacy of divine revelation* undergirds this prohibition. The use of images proclaims unambiguously that the word of God is insufficient for the needs of God's worshipping people. But that is blasphemy, a direct contradiction of Paul's assertion that "all scripture is given by inspiration of God, and is profitable for doctrine, for reproof, for correction, for instruction in righteousness: that the man of God may be perfect, throughly furnished unto all good works" (2 Timothy 3:16–17).

The third principle underlying the second commandment is *the spirituality of divine worship*. Deuteronomy 4:15 says, "Take ye therefore good heed unto yourselves; for ye saw no manner of similitude on the day that the Lord spake unto you in Horeb out of the midst of the fire: lest ye corrupt yourselves, and make you a graven image, the similitude of any figure, the likeness of male or female" (Deuteronomy 4:15–16). Jesus taught the Samaritan woman at the well of Sychar the same truth: "God is a

Spirit: and they that worship him must worship him in spirit and in truth" (John 4:24). Though this means more than simply worshipping without images, it certainly excludes the use of images from public or private worship. We need no images of God or of spiritual middle-men or angels, because God has perfectly revealed Himself in Christ. Jesus said, "He that hath seen me hath seen the Father" (John 14:9). He is "the brightness of his [Father's] glory, and the express image of his person" (Hebrews 1:3). "The light of the knowledge of the glory of God [shines] in the face of Jesus Christ" (2 Corinthians 4:6). Where and how do we see the face of Jesus Christ? Not by mental conjuring, for any mental pictures we form of Christ are as untrustworthy as any other images. Led by the Spirit of God, *we see Jesus in the word of God.* All Scripture clearly reveals Him. Jesus said, "Search the scriptures; for in them ye think ye have eternal life: and they are they which testify of me" (John 5:39). John Calvin's central thesis in his *Institutes of the Christian Religion* is that God is fully revealed in Christ, and Christ is fully revealed in Scripture. The blessing of Christ revealed comes to us through the reading and meditation of Scripture, not by the aid of pictures or images, which substitute an artist's imagination for the Holy Spirit's application of His word to our hearts. True worship is Christ-centred. The approach to God is always on His merit, through His power, and according to His word. The only images we need in churches are God's redeemed people bearing the image of Christ: "We all, with open face beholding as in a glass the glory of the Lord, are changed into the same image from glory to glory, even as by the Spirit of the Lord" (2 Corinthians 3:18).

The Spiritual Precept Behind the Prohibition

The second commandment directs us how to worship. From it we gather the following truths: First, *the Lord must be the sole object of religious worship.* The Scriptures know nothing of Rome's invention of various levels of worship for God, Mary, angels, and saints. God alone is the proper object of religious worship. Second, *His word must be our sole guide in worship.* This is what is known as the regulative principle in worship. What is allowable in worship? The Lutherans and the Anglicans have adopted the view that *what is not prohibited in Scripture is allowable* in worship. The

Calvinists have taken the much more scriptural line that *what is not commanded by Scripture, either explicitly or implicitly, is disallowed.* We must have the Bible as our sole guide in worship. Third, *humility* ("bowing down"), *spirituality, and sincerity must mark our worship.* Fourth, *the fear of God* ("I, the Lord thy God am a jealous God") *should guard our worship.* Fifth, *prayer, adoration, and submission must be vital parts of our worship* ("bow down"). Sixth, *worshipping God as He has revealed Himself in Scripture means that we must worship Him through Christ alone, as Mediator.* No image, no saint, no Mary, no mediatrix, none but the Lord Jesus may stand between us and our Father. Seventh, *true worship must be a matter of the heart and will,* as the terms "love," "serve," and "keep my commandments" indicate.

The Special Promise to Those Who Observe This Commandment

The second commandment includes a special promise from God to those who observe it: "shewing mercy unto thousands of them that love me, and keep my commandments" (Exodus 20:6). This is a glorious promise, especially as we give attention to the precise wording of the text. We may translate it as follows: "I the Lord thy God am a jealous God, visiting the iniquity of the fathers upon the children unto the third and fourth [generation] of them that hate me; and showing mercy to a thousand [generations] of them that love me." *To a thousand generations* means "forever." Here is God's covenant promise. As long as His worship is kept pure, He will continue to show His particular favor from one generation to the next. The Psalmist had this in mind in Psalm 145:4 and 13: "One generation shall praise thy works to another, and shall declare thy mighty acts. . . . Thy kingdom is an everlasting kingdom, and thy dominion endureth throughout all generations."

This divine promise is the reason for the sustained attack of Satan on the purity of the church's worship. Nothing can overthrow a people sincerely consecrated to the scriptural worship of their Redeemer. Here is the best protection for us and for our children. And here are the best prospects for us and for our children. In considering which church to attend, most people want to know the extent of the youth programme, or whether there is a singles' group, or if the church provides outings for its senior citizens. These activities may contribute to the well being of souls and to the witness of the church, but they should never become our first consideration. While it would be short-sighted to undervalue wholesome activity among youth and other age groups, it is foolish and well-nigh idolatrous to think that we must depend upon things such as the availability of a gymnasium or a sports programme to save our children from the world. The best protection and prospects we can provide for them and for ourselves is to maintain the purity of our worship both in form (liturgy, or what we allow in our services) and substance (the message we preach and practise).

The second commandment will either seal us for the blessing of God or for His curse. Yet, even with the best of intentions, we cannot fulfil it as we should. That is why we must emphasize the mediation of Christ. He makes believers and their sincere, scriptural worship acceptable to God through His perfect merit.

CHAPTER SIXTEEN

HOLY AND REVEREND IS HIS NAME

THE THIRD COMMANDMENT

"Thou shalt not take the name of the Lord thy God in vain; for the Lord will not hold him guiltless that taketh his name in vain."
Exodus 20:7

Few of God's commands are more frequently, contemptuously, and universally transgressed than the third commandment. Indeed, so hardened are most people to this part of God's law that they hardly recognize what it is to take the Lord's name in vain. The primary meaning of taking the Lord's name in vain is *the speaking of God's name in any ungodly manner*. The Jews so feared the possibility that they might inadvertently abuse the Lord's name that they adopted an interpretation of Leviticus 24:16 that forbade them even to pronounce the name *Jehovah.* Despite that precaution, they did not escape the sin of taking the Lord's name in vain—which goes to show that the commandment involves much more than a careless use of the divine name.

To grasp the meaning of the text, we must first understand its terms. The Hebrew verb *nasa',* "take," also means to bring, bring forth, lift up, employ, or use; *shaw',* "vain," denotes vanity, emptiness, frivolity, nothingness, evil, wickedness, or falsehood (Exodus 23:1; Deuteronomy 5:20; Psalm 31:6; Jonah 2:8). Thus "take in vain" means to lift up, to use falsely or in an evil cause; or to use in an empty, frivolous way that counts the Lord's name as valueless, as a nonentity. The Hebrew noun *shem,* "name," signifies not only all God's proper names (Jehovah, Lord, God, the Most

High, the Almighty), but also His personal titles (Creator, Saviour, Redeemer, Shepherd), His nature (Exodus 23:21), His attributes (Isaiah 57:15; Revelation 15:3–4), and His revelation and reputation (Psalm 8:1). It is evident that taking the Lord's name in vain goes much deeper than merely speaking the word *Jehovah,* as the Jews mistakenly imagined. "Anything relating to the true God, his being, his nature, his will, his works, his worship, anything relating to service rendered to him, or to the doctrine concerning him, all pertains to His *name*" (W. S. Plumer). Thus the Lord defines worship as "calling on His name," and describes His people as those who "are called by my name" (2 Chronicles 7:14) or "upon whom my name is called" (Acts 15:17).

The many shades of meaning in the word *name* impart a much wider scope to the third commandment than most people have ever realized. It is easy to see that the fundamental force of the commandment is that we should honour the Lord's name, and that if we fail to do so the Lord will judge us for our sin. Through the prophet Malachi the Lord said, "If ye will not hear, and if ye will not lay it to heart, to give glory unto my name, saith the Lord of hosts, I will even send a curse upon you" (Malachi 2:2). But many people fail to see the full force of the commandment, which the *Shorter Catechism* (Questions 54, 55) summarizes as follows:

> *The third commandment requireth the holy and reverent use of God's name, titles, attributes, ordinances, word, and works.*
>
> *The third commandment forbiddeth all profaning or abusing of any thing whereby God maketh himself known.*

Any breach of this commandment is a serious matter. Men may think lightly of taking God's name in vain, but God doesn't. He will not hold him guiltless who takes His name in vain. In other words, there is no such thing as innocently taking the Lord's name in vain. Deuteronomy 28:58–59 records the judgment pronounced against those who break this commandment: "If thou wilt not observe to do all the words of this law that are written in this book, that thou mayest fear this glorious and fearful name, THE LORD THY GOD; then the Lord will make thy plagues wonderful, and the plagues of thy seed, even great plagues, and of long continuance, and sore sicknesses, and of long continuance."

The scope and application of the prohibition and the precept of the third commandment should now be clear: The Lord demands that we give Him the glory that is due to His name and threatens judgment on all wicked or frivolous insults to that name.

The Revelation of God's Name

The Lord has been graciously pleased to reveal Himself to us. He has given us His *name*. Of all the gifts of divine revelation this is the greatest, for without it every other revelation would be meaningless. He has not left us in the dark as to who and what He is. He has not abandoned us to human speculation or to the tender mercies of philosophers and theologians. We have a divine revelation, with the result that we know *that* God is and *what* God is—the triune God, Father, Son, and Holy Spirit, who is "infinite, eternal, and unchangeable, in his being, wisdom, power, holiness, justice, goodness, and truth" (*Shorter Catechism*, Question 4).

Divine Names Reveal God

The names the Bible uses for God are vital parts of His self-revelation. They are not human attempts to say something about God, or records of man's evolving views of Him. Man has tried to define God. Our English word *God* means "the Good One," which tells us how our ancestors viewed deity. The equivalent Greek word, *theos,* according to the Greek historian Herodotus, is derived from part of the verb *tithemi,* "to put, place, or set." It expresses the belief that God fixed and disposed all things in the world. Plato, however, derives the word from *theo,* "to run," evidently because the pagan notions of deity arose from observing the motion—the *running*—of the heavenly bodies. The Latin word for God, *deus,* from which we get the English word *deity* and the French *dieu,* probably comes from a root that refers to the sky, especially the idea of a shining light. It is obvious why men chose such terms to describe God, but at best they are only feeble attempts to say something about God and about why they worshipped Him. Any truth in them arises from the vestiges of the original revelation God gave to Adam at his creation. At best they are light mixed with darkness, truth with error. The divine names used in Scripture are of an altogether different nature. They are all light with no darkness, truth with no error, for they are God's statements about Himself.

The Hebrew words *'el, 'elohim,* translated "God," signify "the Strong and Mighty One," or "One who is to be feared or worshipped." *'El shaddai* describes God as the Almighty, the loving provider for all His creatures. *'Adonai* is translated "Lord" (with only an initial capital) and means "master" or "governor." *'Elyon,* "The most high God," teaches that God is the possessor of heaven and earth (Genesis 14:19). *Jehovah,* "LORD," as the Authorized Version prints the translation, signifies the *eternal I AM,* the covenant God of His chosen people (Exodus 3:6, 13–15). The covenant aspect of this name is emphasized throughout the Old Testament, notably in a series of titles that combine *Jehovah* with words that describe the glorious relationship that God sustains toward His people: *Jehovah our Righteousness, our Holiness, our Peace, our Provider, our Shepherd, our Healer,* and *our Companion* (*Jehovah shammah,* "the Lord is there"). The New Testament uses the Greek equivalents of the divine names employed in the Old Testament, revealing the same God but with fuller light on every part of His self-description (John 1:18; Matthew 11:27; Hebrews 1:1–3).

God's Works Reveal Him

God reveals Himself in His works. Asaph wrote, "That thy name is near thy wondrous works declare" (Psalm 75:1). Paul made the same point in Romans 1:19–20: "That which may be known of God is manifest in them; for God hath shewed it unto them. For the invisible things of him from the creation of the world are clearly seen, being understood by the things that are made, even his eternal power and Godhead; so that they are without excuse." Everything God does declares some aspect of His being and nature. If we contemplate any part of His creation aright, we will discern the Creator. When David considered the heavens he called them "Thy heavens, the work of thy fingers" (Psalm 8:3). Men blinded by unbelief may examine God's creation and stand in awe at the wonders of "nature." But those whose minds have been enlightened by the Spirit of God, while marvelling at the wonders of nature, see the presence, power, and wisdom of God. We are surrounded by countless eloquent witnesses, all bearing testimony to their Creator.

God's Word Reveals Him

God has revealed Himself in His word, the Bible, that "more sure word of prophecy" of which Peter spoke (2 Peter 1:19). Immediately before giving this description of God's written revelation, Peter referred to the glorious revelation he, with James and John, saw on the Mount of Transfiguration. What a glorious revelation that was! But Peter declared that "we have a more sure [confirmed] word of prophecy." In other words, the revelation God has given us in Scripture is superior even to such a glorious experience as Peter had, when he saw Christ transfigured and heard God speak from heaven! The Lord Jesus stressed the truth that the written word reveals Him: "Search the scriptures; . . . they are they which testify of me" (John 5:39).

God's Son Reveals Him

God has most fully revealed Himself in His Son. The Son of God is the Word incarnate, the eternal self-expression of God. No finite mind can ever comprehend what that name signifies about the eternal, trinitarian relationship of the Son with the Father. We can say, however, that all that God has ever revealed to any creature has been through His eternal Son. "God, who at sundry times and in divers manners spake in time past unto the fathers by the prophets, hath in these last days spoken unto us by his Son, whom he hath appointed heir of all things, by whom also he made the worlds" (Hebrews 1:1–2).

This revelation of God in His Son cannot be separated from His revelation in Scripture. God has fully revealed Himself in Christ and Christ is fully revealed in Scripture. He is "the truth" (John 14:60), "the Amen, the faithful and true witness" (Revelation 3:14). Christ is the pinnacle of all divine revelation, the fulness of all that God ever intended to reveal of Himself. Therefore, the Father commands us to "hear him" (Luke 9:35).

What a revelation of God we have in Christ! He gave us the law and the prophets, for He was the mediator under the old dispensation as well as under the new (Galatians 3:19–20).[1] Now He has given us the full light of glory: "The Word was made flesh, and dwelt among us, (and we beheld his glory, the glory as of the only begotten of the Father,) full of grace and truth" (John 1:14). Grace and truth! We have every cause to fear *truth,* for by nature we are all falsehood, and truth is divine light that exposes us to the judgment of God. But in Christ God combines *grace* with truth. The Psalmist foresaw this: "Mercy and truth are met together; righteousness and peace have kissed each other" (Psalm 85:10). Only in Christ our Redeemer could this take place. In Him alone, and through His merit, can God be just and yet justify the ungodly who believe in Him (Romans 3:26; 4:5).

A Grave Responsibility

The revelation of God's name imposes a grave responsibility upon us. If the light of nature leaves men "without excuse" (Romans 1:20), what shall we say of those who have received the full revelation of God's grace in Christ? This revelation demands a response and the word of God is clear what it should be: "Give unto the Lord the glory due unto his name; worship the Lord in the beauty of holiness" (Psalm 29:2). Again "Sing forth the honour of his name: make his praise glorious" (Psalm 66:2). That is the responsibility the Lord has laid upon us. In contrast, the Bible forbids all acknowledgment of the names of other gods. In Exodus 23:13 we read, "In all things that I have said unto you be circumspect: and make no mention of the name of other gods, neither let it be heard out of thy mouth." In connection with his great messianic prophecy David said, "Their sorrows shall be multiplied that hasten after another god: their drink offerings of blood will I not offer, nor take up their names into my lips" (Psalms 16:4). It is clear from these texts that taking the name of a god upon the lips is an act of worship. Thus when we take the name of God on our lips, it should be in worship. The only proper use of His

[1] This text has occasioned more proposed interpretations than almost any other in the New Testament. Its use here as a proof text rests on the following translation of verse 20: "The Mediator [Christ] is not a mediator of one [of these, namely of either the law or the promise, but of both], but God is one [and the same under both]."

name is to use it in a worshipful acknowledgment of His person, word, and work. That is how to obey the third commandment.

The Lord Jesus taught as much in the opening words of the Lord's Prayer, "Our Father which art in heaven, hallowed be thy name," words taken from Isaiah 8:13, "Sanctify the Lord of hosts himself; and let him be your fear, and let him be your dread." Peter said, "Sanctify the Lord God in your hearts" (1 Peter 3:15). The only allowable use of the Lord's name is to take it upon our lips in holy awe with the purpose of glorifying Him or of edifying men.

Thus, it is proper for us to use His name in all aspects of worship. We should use it *in prayer*. Prayer is "calling upon His name," and it gains access to God only when it is in the name of the Lord Jesus Christ. But even in prayer we should be careful not to take that holy name in vain, avoiding all thoughtless or meaningless repetitions of it. When we call upon the Lord we must make sure that we use His name reverently and considerately.

In worship, we should use His name *in song,* but we should be careful how we do so. Some of the so-called hymns and Christian songs that are popular nowadays appear to use the Lord's name in a light, thoughtless manner. By contrast, Revelation chapter 5 illustrates how we ought to use the Lord's name in song. The glorified saints, surrounded by angels, lift up the name of Christ and cry, "Thou art worthy." What holiness, what awe, what glory, what joy in that song! There is none of the frivolous use of the name of God that so often passes for "worship songs" today.

It is also proper to use the Lord's name *in doxology.* The Scriptures furnish many examples. Paul prefaced his epistle to the Ephesians with this burst of praise: "Blessed be the God and Father of our Lord Jesus Christ, who hath blessed us with all spiritual blessings in heavenly places in Christ" (Ephesians 1:3). Peter used similar language: "Blessed be the God and Father of our Lord Jesus Christ, which according to his abundant mercy hath begotten us again unto a lively hope by the resurrection of Jesus Christ from the dead"(1 Peter 1:3). Romans 16:25–27 and Jude 24–25 also teach us how to rise up in an ecstasy of spiritual praise to the name of our great God and Saviour. The contemplation and exaltation of the Lord's name form a vital and enriching part of all worship, both private and public.

We may properly use the Lord's name *in benediction*. The New Testament repeatedly uses such expressions as, "Grace be unto you, and peace, from God our Father, and from the Lord Jesus Christ" (1 Corinthians 1:3). A benediction using the Lord's name is really a prayer, an invocation of the Lord's grace and favour, as in Numbers 6:24–26: "The Lord bless thee, and keep thee: the Lord make his face shine upon thee, and be gracious unto thee: the Lord lift up his countenance upon thee, and give thee peace."

It is also proper to use the Lord's name *in witness*. A solemn oath is an appeal to God to confirm the truth of what we say. It is a serious religious exercise and is never to be spoken out of mere passion, anger, or vehemence. The command of Christ in Matthew 5:34, "Swear not at all," forbids all profane use of the Lord's name and warns against the practice of swearing in ordinary conversation for mere emphasis. But the Saviour did not forbid the lawful use of the oath for a solemn witness. It is interesting that one of the texts He used to thwart the temptations of Satan contains a direct reference to the lawful use of oaths: "Thou shalt fear the Lord thy God, and serve him, and shalt swear by his name" (Deuteronomy 6:1; Matthew 4:10). Paul told the Corinthians, "I call God for a record upon my soul" (2 Corinthians 1:23). Writing to the Philippians he said, "God is my record" (Philippians 1:8), while to the Romans he asserted his burden for the Jewish people with one of the most solemn oaths any man has ever taken: "I say the truth in Christ, I lie not, my conscience also bearing me witness in the Holy Ghost, that I have great heaviness and continual sorrow in my heart. For I could wish that myself were accursed from Christ for my brethren, my kinsmen according to the flesh" (Romans 9:1–3). An even stronger oath was that taken by God Himself to assure His people of the inviolability of His covenant grace: "For men verily swear by the greater: and an oath for confirmation is to them an end of all strife. Wherein God, willing more abundantly to shew unto the heirs of promise the immutability of his counsel, confirmed it by an oath: that by two immutable things, in which it was impossible for God to lie, we might have a strong consolation, who have fled for refuge to lay hold upon the hope set before us" (Hebrews 6:16–18). Any use of the Lord's name to make people believe a lie not only breaks the ninth commandment but the third.

A special form of this appeal to God, especially in the Old Testament, but also in the New Testament, was the use of the lot. Lots were cast *before God* to determine a matter of importance concerning which the Lord's will was not discoverable by any other means or where no satisfactory decision could otherwise be reached. Acts chapter one records that after prayer for guidance in choosing a man to fill the place among the apostles left empty by Judas Iscariot, the believers cast lots over two names. This action was an acknowledgment of God's providential control of their affairs, according to the promise of Proverbs 16:33: "The lot is cast into the lap; but the whole disposing thereof is of the Lord." It was in the assurance of this promise that Solomon said, "The lot causeth contentions to cease" (Proverbs 18:18).

Abuses of the lot are ancient. Lotteries are not modern inventions; they date back at least to Roman times. The same arguments were made in their favour then as are advanced today. Lottery advocates argue passionately that lotteries are innocent fun and that they provide a painless way to support desirable public policy, such as financing education or programmes to help the underprivileged. These are the same arguments that were employed in favour of lotteries in ancient times, and they are as empty today as then. Lotteries are always destructive to public and private morals. They are not innocent fun. Not all use of dice is wrong, nor is it necessarily sinful to engage in games of chance. But lotteries are wrong and among the objections to them is one that is rarely mentioned nowadays, even by preachers. The lottery perverts the God-given use of the lot to appeal to His sovereign providence, because it is used to further a breach of the tenth commandment, "Thou shalt not covet." It is a particularly pernicious form of taking the Lord's name in vain.

We all have a responsibility to make good use of God's revelation of Himself to us. We should hear it, heed it, and herald it—and never corrupt it. God has graciously revealed His name to us. His revelation imposes a very grave responsibility on us to glorify and honor that name. That leads us to a third important truth.

A Solemn Warning

The commandment warns us not to shirk the responsibility it imposes upon us. "Thou shalt not take the name of the Lord thy God in vain." There are various ways of failing to sanctify the Lord's name and the third commandment warns against each of them.

Levity

From Psalm 96:4 we learn, "The Lord is great, and greatly to be praised; he is to be feared above all gods." We use the Lord's name properly only when we use it soberly and intelligently—that is, with reason and understanding, for a good purpose, for His glory, or for the good of ourselves or our fellowmen. To take the Lord's name in vain includes using it frivolously. God has created in us a sense of humor, but, as with every other faculty and gift, it must be sanctified and kept under the control of God and His Spirit. It is *never* permissible to use the name of God in a joke. Frequently preachers pollute the Christian pulpit with blasphemy by the levity with which they use the Lord's name. Any humor that includes the name of God, His person, His titles, or His works is of the devil. "Thou shalt not take the name of the Lord, thy God in vain" by levity.

Sorcery

Sorcery includes incantations using the Lord's name in occult practices. Interestingly, the Old Testament calls false prophecy a kind of sorcery. "When Balaam saw that it pleased the Lord to bless Israel, he went not, as at other times, to seek for enchantments" (Numbers 24:1). To the false prophet, the name of Jehovah was merely a magical charm. All magical incantations of the divine name belong to sorcery, not to Christianity. There is something chillingly evil about the constant repetition of the name *Jesus, Jesus, Jesus* in many Charismatic services, as if it were some kind of charm. Far from being godly, such a use of the Lord's name breaks the third commandment. It is dangerous, delusive, and devilish.

Perjury

Perjury is the act of confirming falsehood with an oath. It is lying with the added guilt of involving the name of the God of truth in the lie.

God's command is, "Ye shall not swear by my name falsely, neither shalt thou profane the name of thy God: I am the Lord" (Leviticus 19:12). Perjury is a serious and widespread evil in everyday life. It always has been. Jeremiah lamented, "Though they say, the Lord liveth; surely they swear falsely" (Jeremiah 5:2). We have as much cause as the prophet to lament. It is commonplace for people to invoke the name of God as a witness to their truthfulness, while all the time they are swearing lies.

Perjury is an evil not only in private life, but in public life also. Magistrates often profane God's name by including it in their oath of office and then blaspheming it by their insolent neglect of their oath. Ministers and elders often commit the same breach of the third commandment by unfaithfulness to the solemn vows they took before God at their ordination.

Blasphemy

Blasphemy is reproaching or reviling God. It is contempt for His person, worship, or word. In Leviticus 24:10–16 we read of the son of an Israelitish woman who cursed by the name of Jehovah, and of the punishment meted out to him: "And the son of an Israelitish woman, whose father was an Egyptian, went out among the children of Israel: and this son of the Israelitish woman and a man of Israel strove together in the camp; and the Israelitish woman's son blasphemed the name of the Lord, and cursed. And they brought him unto Moses: (and his mother's name was Shelomith, the daughter of Dibri, of the tribe of Dan:) and they put him in ward, that the mind of the Lord might be shewed them. And the Lord spake unto Moses, saying, Bring forth him that hath cursed without the camp; and let all that heard him lay their hands upon his head, and let all the congregation stone him. And thou shalt speak unto the children of Israel, saying, Whosoever curseth his God shall bear his sin. And he that blasphemeth the name of the Lord, he shall surely be put to death, and all the congregation shall certainly stone him: as well the stranger, as he that is born in the land, when he blasphemeth the name of the Lord, shall be put to death."

The Lord looks on blasphemy as an attack upon His person, His providence, or His promise. It has the malignity of Satan within it. According to Revelation 13:5, "There was given unto him [the beast, Satan's emissary on the earth in the end times] a mouth speaking great things and blasphemies."

Blasphemy particularly involves *speaking against God*. The Lord Jesus Christ made this abundantly clear: "All manner of sin and blasphemy shall be forgiven unto men: but the blasphemy against the Holy Ghost shall not be forgiven unto men. And whosoever speaketh a word against the Son of man, it shall be forgiven him: but whosoever speaketh against the Holy Ghost, it shall not be forgiven him, neither in this world, neither in the world to come" (Matthew 12:31–32). Blasphemy is speaking against the Lord, and the worst form of it is blasphemy against the Holy Ghost—which may be defined from the context in Matthew 12 as the deliberate attribution of the works of the Holy Spirit to the devil.

But there is a much more common form of blasphemy. As we have seen, one meaning of the Hebrew word translated "vain," is *emptiness, vanity, a nonentity, a worthless thing*. To blaspheme therefore is to hold God to be despicable or worthless, or negligible, or to treat Him as a nonentity. Thus, most sinners live in perpetual blasphemy. Anyone who lives as if God does not exist or has not spoken, blasphemes Him. To treat Almighty God as unimportant is the ultimate blasphemy.

Apostasy

Apostasy is the use of the Lord's name to depart from His truth or to deny His revelation. Jeremiah denounced the prophets who prophesied lies in the Lord's name saying, "I have dreamed, I have dreamed." Peter warns us that this apostasy will afflict the church: "There were false prophets also among the people, even as there shall be false teachers among you, who privily shall bring in damnable heresies, even denying the Lord that bought them, and bring upon themselves swift destruction" (2 Peter 2:1). Later in the same chapter he calls such apostates "natural brute beasts, made to be taken and destroyed" who "shall utterly perish in their own corruption" (2 Peter 2:12). To them "the mist of darkness is reserved for ever" (v. 17), or "the blackness of darkness for ever," as Jude puts it (Jude 13). What deepens the crime of such apostates is their use of the Lord's name to support their lying inventions. That is why divine retribution upon them is so severe. The Lord Jesus said, "Many will say to me in that day, Lord, Lord, have we not prophesied in thy name? and in thy name have cast out devils? and in thy name done many wonderful works? And then will I profess unto them, I never knew you: depart from me, ye that work iniquity" (Matthew 7:22–23). They cursed God by their apostasy; He cursed them with His judgment.

Hypocrisy

Hypocrisy lifts up the name of the Lord as a cover for sin. Jude 4 warns us of "certain men crept in unawares, . . . ungodly men, turning the grace of God into lasciviousness, and denying the only Lord God, and our Lord Jesus Christ." Peter warns us against our own inclination toward hypocrisy: "As free, and not using your liberty for a cloke of maliciousness, but as the servants of God" (1 Peter 2:16). Paul adds, "Brethren, ye have been called unto liberty; only use not liberty for an occasion to the flesh, but by love serve one another" (Galatians 5:13). What is hypocrisy? In the words of Jeremiah, hypocrisy is stealing, murdering, committing adultery, swearing falsely and then coming and standing before God in His house and saying, "We are delivered to do all these abominations" (Jeremiah 7:9–10).

Religious hypocrisy stands condemned on many counts: It is lying, it is the cover for many other sins, but primarily it is a blasphemy against God. We must abhor blasphemy in all its forms and live sincerely in the fear of God: "Servants, be obedient to them that are your masters according to the flesh, with fear and trembling, in singleness of your heart, as unto Christ; not with eyeservice, as menpleasers; but as the servants of Christ, doing the will of God from the heart" (Ephesians 6:5–6).

Profanity

Profanity is the most frequent and the most accepted form of taking the Lord's name in vain. It is an irreverent use of God's name or interests, using God's name without any fear of His person. It may be a light or thoughtless use of the divine name. Sometimes it takes the form of a passionate invective made more terrible by the invocation of the Lord's name. Often profanity is the use the Lord's name to curse. There is nothing new in this. Jeremiah says, "Because of swearing the land mourneth"

(Jeremiah 23:10). Hosea laments, "By swearing [cursing], and lying, and killing, and stealing, and committing adultery, they break out [in wanton fury—Calvin], and blood toucheth blood [violent crimes pile one upon another]" (Hosea 4:2). Here is a solemn truth: Breaking the third commandment never stands alone. When a nation loses the fear of God, it loses the mainspring of societal purity. Using God's name as an expletive is so common that people dismiss it as harmless. But God's word says that it is just the first link in a chain of lawlessness that produces the violent crime that is overwhelming our nation.

To make matters worse, profanity is almost exclusively practised against the Lord Jehovah. Heathens do not profane the names of their idols. Some secular Muslims have been known to use the name of Allah lightly, but even in Western countries there would probably be an uproar if television and radio programmes started using the name of Allah or of Muhammed as a swear word. But while such an insult may not be offered to the false gods of the heathen, it is freely directed against the name of the triune Jehovah.

Even professing Christians are guilty of profanity. We should pay careful attention to the things we say and never use the Lord's name lightly. We must never forget whose name it is. Angels cry, "Holy, holy, holy," and thus should we sanctify the name of the Lord. That is our solemn responsibility.

A Terrible Judgment

The Lord threatens certain judgment on the wicked misuse of His name. "The Lord will not hold him guiltless that taketh his name in vain." The Psalmist speaks of the wrath of God against those who break the third commandment: "Surely thou wilt slay the wicked, O God: depart from me therefore, ye bloody men. For they speak against thee wickedly, and thine enemies take thy name in vain" (Psalm 139:19–20). There is a day of reckoning coming for every abuser of God's name. Jesus said, "I say unto you, That every idle word that men shall speak, they shall give account thereof in the day of judgment. For by thy words thou shalt be justified, and by thy words thou shalt be condemned" (Matthew 12:36–37). God will use men's own words against them. His judgment against the despisers of His name will be swift and terrible. *GUILTY!* is the verdict that will ring out from the great white throne. The sentence that will follow will be the eternal punishment of hell, for that is the place of retribution for those who blaspheme God.

What makes the blasphemer's punishment all the more terrible is that the very name he has cursed is the name given to save him. Speaking to Joseph of the birth of Christ, the angel of the Lord said, "Thou shalt call his name JESUS: for he shall save his people from their sins" (Matthew 1:21). *Jesus* means "Jehovah our Saviour," and it is the name by which God has revealed His full plan of salvation. Peter said, "Neither is there salvation in any other: for there is none other name under heaven given among men, whereby we must be saved" (Acts 4:12). Again, "To him give all the prophets witness, that through his name whosoever believeth in him shall receive remission of sins" (Acts 10:43). That precious name brings salvation to all who sincerely call upon it "for whosoever shall call upon the name of the Lord shall be saved" (Romans 10:13). It is the ultimate folly for men to abuse the name God has revealed for their salvation and so make it the seal of their eternal destruction.

In a sense, the Lord's name will be the seal of our place in heaven or in hell. *It seals the saints for glory.* From His throne the Lord Jesus Christ describes the glory awaiting His overcoming people: "Him that overcometh will I make a pillar in the temple of my God, and he shall go no more out: and I will write upon him the name of my God, and the name of the city of my God, which is new Jerusalem, which cometh down out of heaven from my God: and I will write upon him my new name" (Revelation 3:12). *The Lord's name seals the profane in hell,* for God is jealous for His holy name and solemnly warns us, "Thou shalt not take the name of the Lord thy God in vain, for the Lord will not hold him guiltless that taketh his name in vain."

We should give earnest heed to this commandment. If it convicts us as lawbreakers, let it also drive us to Christ to "call upon the name of the Lord" for mercy and pardon. Then we may live a new life in Christ, joyfully observing the unspeakable sanctity of the eternal name.

CHAPTER SEVENTEEN

CALLING THE SABBATH A DELIGHT

THE FOURTH COMMANDMENT

"Remember the sabbath day, to keep it holy. Six days shalt thou labour, and do all thy work: But the seventh day is the sabbath of the Lord thy God: in it thou shalt not do any work, thou, nor thy son, nor thy daughter, thy manservant, nor thy maidservant, nor thy cattle, nor thy stranger that is within thy gates: For in six days the Lord made heaven and earth, the sea, and all that in them is, and rested the seventh day: wherefore the Lord blessed the sabbath day, and hallowed it."
Exodus 20:8–11

The Lord has invested each one of the Ten Commandments with an enduring and majestic authority. Each of them is a law, a commandment, first spoken by God and then written by His own finger on tables of stone. That goes for the fourth commandment as truly as for the other nine. "Remember the sabbath day, to keep it holy," or as we read in Deuteronomy 5:12, "Keep the sabbath day to sanctify it, as the Lord thy God hath commanded thee."

This commandment stands at the end of the first table of the law. The Lord first commanded our exclusive worship. Second, He laid down how we are to worship Him. Next, He commanded that we should reverence His name. Now in the fourth commandment He stipulates the observance of one day each week as His peculiar day to be sanctified for the Lord's glory and as His gift to men for their physical and spiritual good.

The Lord claims one day in seven. That alone should alert us to the importance of the fourth commandment. W. S. Plumer noted: "[This] is a law claiming to regulate a seventh portion of human life. If a man lives twenty-one years, this law claims control of three of them. It is therefore important. But it also devotes this portion of time to religious purposes; and these are the highest ends of all life. All other time is secular. This is holy. That *may* be occupied with things which perish in the using. This *must* be given to things which take hold on eternity."

Despite the clear importance of the law, no commandment has aroused more controversy and engendered more questions. Many Christians view the sabbath commandment as a ceremonial law, one that therefore passed away with the rest of the Jewish ceremonies after the resurrection of Christ. Martin Luther discarded sabbath observance as Jewish, and even John Calvin believed it was largely, though not entirely, ceremonial (maintaining on other grounds, however, the need for a Christian sabbath). Such views persist to this day.

In opposition to all such views, this chapter will seek to establish that *the fourth commandment is still in force* and that *it finds its proper observance in our sanctifying the first day of the week as the Lord's Day.* In seeking to establish this position we will face the objections that have been raised against it, in the hope that the result of this study will be that every reader will be able to "call the sabbath a delight" (Isaiah 58:13).

The Divine Institution of the Sabbath

The sabbath is divine in its institution. The Lord specifically claims this day as His own peculiar day. Nehemiah says, "[Thou] madest known unto them thy holy sabbath" (Nehemiah 9:14). While all of time belongs to God (Psalm 31:15), the sabbath is a day He calls His own in an exclusive way: "Verily my sabbaths ye shall keep: for it is a sign between me and you throughout your generations; that ye may know that I am the Lord that doth sanctify you. Ye shall keep the sabbath therefore; for it is holy unto you: every one that defileth it shall surely be put to death: for whosoever doeth any work therein, that soul shall be cut off from among his people" (Exodus 31:13–14).

The division of time into seven-day weeks is not of man, but of God. He set the pattern in creation and that is when He instituted the sabbath: "And on the seventh day God ended his work which he had made; and he rested on the seventh day from all his work which he had made. And God blessed the seventh day, and sanctified it: because that in it he had rested from all his work which God created and made" (Genesis 2:2–3). Some object that this text does not actually mention the sabbath and that God alone is said to have rested, not man. Further, the objectors argue, there is no mention of sabbath-keeping before Moses gave the law to Israel. If this argument is valid, its significance is far-reaching, for it forms the basis of the claim that sabbath observance is not a universal law. If, on the other hand, the Lord instituted sabbath observance at creation, then it cannot be dismissed as a merely temporary part of Jewish ceremonial law.

Despite its impressive sound, the argument against dating the sabbath to the creation is surely erroneous, for the following reasons:

First, it is beyond doubt that Genesis 2:2–3 speaks of the sabbath. The wording of the fourth commandment puts the matter beyond dispute: The basis of sabbath observance in the law of Moses was God's rest from His creation activity. According to God's own statement, "[The sabbath] is a sign between me and the children of Israel for ever: for in six days the Lord made heaven and earth, and on the seventh day he rested, and was refreshed" (Exodus 31:17).

Second, the Lord "sanctified" and "blessed" the sabbath. For whose use did He set the sabbath apart? To whom did He bless it? Man is the great beneficiary of the sabbath institution. Jesus said, "The sabbath was made for man" (Mark 2:27), not merely or exclusively for Jews.

Third, the silence of Scripture on the subject of the sabbath between Genesis 2 and the time of Moses does not prove that it was unknown during that period. Scripture is equally silent on the subject during the period between Moses and the time of the monarchy, but we know that the sabbath was certainly included in the Jewish legal code during all that time. So the silence of the biblical record does not prove that the sabbath was unknown

But is the Bible completely silent about the sabbath between the creation and the time of Moses? We have mentioned that the seven-day week was a divine institution. The patriarchs learned of it by revelation; they did not invent it for themselves or evolve it by a process of trial and error. Could they possibly have learned about the seven-day week from God without any reference to the sabbath? It seems unlikely, but the evidence of Exodus 16:23–30 puts the matter beyond speculation. These verses describe God's regulations governing the gathering of manna by the Israelites during a time before the giving of the law. "And [Moses] said unto them, This is that which the Lord hath said, To morrow is the rest of the holy sabbath unto the Lord: bake that which ye will bake to day, and seethe that ye will seethe; and that which remaineth over lay up for you to be kept until the morning. . . . See, for that the Lord hath given you the sabbath, therefore he giveth you on the sixth day the bread of two days; abide ye every man in his place, let no man go out of his place on the seventh day. So the people rested on the seventh day" (Exodus 16:23, 29–30). Here we see that before the giving of the law Moses speaks of the sabbath as already well known. It was obviously something with which the Israelites were expected to be familiar. How could this be if the sabbath was not revealed before the giving of the law at Mount Sinai? It is obvious that even at this time men understood the principle of the sabbath and that is why the fourth commandment is to "*remember* the sabbath day."

The fact that the Lord later made the sabbath a sign between Him and the people of Israel does not alter the fact that He instituted it before the Fall for all men. In his treatment of the fourth commandment, Timothy Dwight argues that it is incredible that God's resting after the creation of *man* was intended as a pattern only to the *Jews,* a miniscule fraction of mankind. All the evidence points to the conclusion the sabbath is a divine institution for all men, from Adam onwards.

The Moral Constitution of the Sabbath

The sabbath is moral in its constitution. John Calvin saw the sabbath as partly ceremonial. No doubt, Hebrews 4 teaches that what natural Israel enjoyed in earthly terms through sabbath observance was a figure of the salvation rest spiritual Israel (God's redeemed people in every age) enjoys in Christ. But that does not make the sabbath part of the ceremonial law. The law of the sabbath is one of the Ten Commandments, and it is moral, not ceremonial. There is nothing in the biblical statement of the Decalogue to set this commandment apart from the others. Dwight makes the following points to establish the case for recognizing the sabbath as a continuing part of the moral law:

- By divine design it was placed in the middle of the Decalogue.
- It was spoken with the awful and audible voice of God Himself from the midst of the thunders and lightnings which enveloped Mount Sinai.
- It was twice written by the finger of God on tables of stone.
- It was delivered in the same absolute manner as the other nine commandments.
- It has the same universal application as the other nine; that is, it provides the benefits of sabbath observance, needed by all men of all nations.

In the light of these facts, how can anyone have the temerity to excise the fourth commandment from the moral law of God, especially since the moral nature of the sabbath command has such important implications?

The Permanent Duration of the Sabbath

The sabbath is permanent in its duration. The permanence of the sabbath is hotly denied by many Christians. However, the word of God speaks of sabbath observance until the end of time. Isaiah 66:23 describes the worship of the millennial kingdom: "It shall come to pass, that from one new moon to another, and from one sabbath to another, shall all flesh come to worship before me, saith the Lord." The Lord instituted the observance of the sabbath at the creation. From this passage we learn that He will continue it through the millennium. We would therefore be greatly surprised if we were told that He had suspended it for the present—that He had made this the only period in the history of the world without His sabbath law. Certainly, man needs the sabbath as much today as ever.

It could be argued that the hectic pace of modern life renders the sabbath more precious and necessary than ever before. Despite this, many complain that sabbath observance is impractical in the modern world. The truth is that it has never been "practical" for self-seeking, self-indulging sinners to observe the Lord's sabbath (see, for example, Nehemiah 13:15–22, where even the Jews who had returned from Babylonian captivity had a "business as usual" attitude to the sabbath). The real reason for the rejection or desecration of God's day is the rejection or despising of God Himself. This may appear a rash or harsh judgment, especially since many evangelical Christians repudiate the entire idea of sabbath observance. But the judgment is neither rash nor harsh. Many Christians who *theoretically* reject sabbath observance, *practically* hallow the Lord's Day out of love for Him. Those who do not sanctify God's day can hardly claim to obey the injunction of 1 Peter 3:15 to "sanctify the Lord God," the One who gave the sabbath day.

God has never repealed any of the Ten Commandments. Antinomians disagree and argue that He has abrogated the law entirely for His redeemed people. In chapter 2 we stated the case for the permanence of the law, and we dealt with antinomian arguments in chapter 6. However, many Christians who are not generally antinomian deny the permanence of the fourth commandment. They cite the following Scriptures in favour of their position: "One man esteemeth one day above another: another esteemeth every day alike. Let every man be fully persuaded in his own mind. He that regardeth the day, regardeth it unto the Lord; and he that regardeth not the day, to the Lord he doth not regard it. He that eateth, eateth to the Lord, for he giveth God thanks; and he that eateth not, to the Lord he eateth not, and giveth God thanks" (Romans 14:5–6); "Let no man therefore judge you in meat, or in drink, or in respect of an holyday, or of the new moon, or of the sabbath days: which are a shadow of things to come; but the body is of Christ" (Colossians 2:16–17); "Ye observe days, and months, and times, and years. I am afraid of you, lest I have bestowed upon you labour in vain" (Galatians 4:10–11).

Usually, the bare recitation of these texts is considered sufficiently persuasive to dismiss all argument for the permanence of sabbath observance. It is confidently held that at the very least, sabbath observance is not mandatory for Christians, while at its worst sabbath-keeping may become legalism. Never was confidence more misplaced. The texts cited do not teach that sabbath observance has been discontinued or made optional. One vital fact must be noted: *None of the texts cited makes any reference to the weekly sabbath.* In Judaism there were *many ceremonial sabbaths.* Being purely ceremonial, they passed away with the coming of the gospel substance of which they were foreshadowings. But the Lord has never spoken a single word about abrogating the *weekly* sabbath.

Indeed, *He has retained it and has made it the memorial of the resurrection of Christ by changing its observance from the seventh to the first day of the week.* Saturday observance is not the essence of the sabbath. The word itself means *rest,* not *seventh.* The fourth commandment does not specify the seventh day of the week as the sabbath. It commands the seventh day—one following six days of labour—to be observed as the sabbath, *not necessarily the seventh day of the week.* It stipulates that one-seventh part of each week is the Lord's sabbath. The fact that the Jewish sabbath fell on the seventh day of the week does not invest observing Saturday as the sabbath with permanence for all time. The Old Testament sabbath was observed on the seventh day of the week because it celebrated the Lord's creation rest. The New Testament sabbath calls for a new day, the first day of the week, to celebrate Christ's resurrection on that day. So the Lord changed the sabbath for Christians from the seventh to the first day of the week.

Seventh Day Adventists and others dispute the claim that God changed the sabbath to the first day of the week. They often allege that it was the Roman Emperor Constantine who did so. They are wrong. After he professed Christianity, *Constantine made the observance of the first day of the week mandatory throughout society; he did not institute it in the Christian church.* It was the Lord of the church, not a Roman emperor, who authorized the observance of the first day of the week as the Christian sabbath. Consider the evidence:

1. The Lord Jesus Christ rose from the dead on the first day of the week. Attention to the time references in His post-resurrection appearances will show that He met His disciples in succeeding weeks on the first day. Pentecost came on the first day of the week (Leviticus 23:10–16—seven sabbaths from the sabbath at the end of the Passover week plus one day places the day of Pentecost on a Sunday). The New Testament churches met on the first day (1 Corinthians 16:1–2), a fact that is of vital importance, because meeting on that day must have caused a great practical difficulty, as no other religions sanctified it. All this sets a precedent for all Christians. Apostolic precedent has the same value as a command: What the apostles *did* was just as normative as what they *said.*

2. The Bible claims the first day of the week as "the Lord's Day" (Revelation 1:10). In the Greek text, *the Lord's Day* is not equivalent to "the day of the Lord," but is parallel to *the Lord's Supper* (1 Corinthians 11:20). Just as the Lord's Supper replaced the Passover, the Lord's Day replaced the seventh day for the observation of the sabbath. As the Old Testament sabbath was "the sabbath of the Lord thy God" (Exodus 20:10) in commemoration of God's creative work, the day of Christ's resurrection is "the Lord's Day" in commemoration of His redemptive work.

3. The Old Testament prepares us for this change of day. In Psalm 118:22–24 we read, "The stone which the builders refused is become the head stone of the corner. This is the Lord's doing; it is marvellous in our eyes. This is the day which the Lord hath made; we will rejoice and be glad in it." As Acts 4:10–11 makes plain, Christ became the head stone of the corner by His resurrection from the dead: "Be it known unto you all, and to all the people of Israel, that by the name of Jesus Christ of Nazareth, whom ye crucified, whom God raised from the dead, even by him doth this man stand here before you whole. This is the stone which was set at nought of you builders, which is become the head of the corner." So it was by resurrection that the Lord Jesus became the head stone. Well might the Psalmist say, "This is the Lord's doing; it is marvellous in our eyes." Notice carefully: As soon as he makes reference to Christ's resurrection,

the Psalmist says, "This is the day which the Lord hath made." The verb *made* means formed, fashioned, or appointed. Is it mere coincidence that David follows his reference to Christ's resurrection with the declaration that God has appointed a day in which we are to rejoice and be glad? While the full significance of David's words may transcend the observance of the first day of the week as our special day of rejoicing (2 Corinthians 6:2), it certainly includes it.

4. The New Testament plainly intimates the change to the first day of the week for Christians to observe the sabbath. That is the significance of Hebrew 4:9–10: "There remaineth therefore a rest to the people of God. For he that is entered into his rest, he also hath ceased from his own works, as God did from his." This is a crucial text, and one that is not well understood by most Christians. Let us follow carefully the argument of the passage:

- Canaan rest was typical of the spiritual rest of salvation.
- That salvation rest is in the Lord Jesus Christ, through His finished work (verse 10). He completed the work of redemption just as God completed the work of creation. This is the real meaning of the verse. It does *not* say that we who have entered Christ's rest have ceased from our works. It is true that we have given up all trust in our works, but there is no parallel between a sinner ceasing his self-righteous works and God's rest at the end of the creation week. The only one in all history who commenced a work and finished it to rest from his works as God did from His, is the Lord Jesus Christ. Having finished His work, Christ entered into His rest.
- On that basis "there remaineth therefore a rest to the people of God." Two words here demand our attention, *remaineth* and *rest.* The word *remaineth* carries the idea of something left over from what has gone before. The book of Hebrews speaks a lot about the state of things during Old Testament times, things that have now been taken away. The sacrifices, holy days, Levitical rituals, tabernacle, and temple of the old dispensation have all been removed. But according to Hebrews 4:9 there is a *rest* that has not been taken away. The Greek

word translated "rest" in verse 9 is *sabbatismos*, "a keeping of sabbath." Amidst all that God removed at the resurrection of Christ, *a keeping of sabbath remains.* That is the unavoidable message of this text. And according to verse 10, this sabbath-keeping celebrates the finished work of Christ, His resurrection from the dead. He arose on the first day of the week and His people therefore worship on that day.

The Simple Precept of the Sabbath

The sabbath is simple in its precept. First, *it requires us to rest, to refresh ourselves, and to worship*. It is a day to devote to the Lord, who calls on us to "hallow" or "sanctify" it and to celebrate our Saviour's resurrection. The sabbath precept is binding on us. Remembering that in apostolic times Christian assemblies met on the first day of the week, we can appreciate the significance of the injunction of Hebrews 10:25 that we should not forsake "the assembling of ourselves together, as the manner of some is." We are commanded to guard the privilege of meeting together with God's people each Lord's Day. This is the best way to recover from the pressures of the week just ended and to prepare for the challenges of the week to come. So the sabbath precept enjoins rest, refreshment, and worship. This is how we should observe the Christian sabbath.

Second, *the sabbath precept forbids work on this special day and the wilful neglect of sabbath duties:* "In it thou shalt not do any work" (Exodus 20:10). In Isaiah 58:13–14, the Lord commands us to turn aside from our own pleasure, purposes, and activities, and to delight in attending to His work and worship: "If thou turn away thy foot from the sabbath, from doing thy pleasure on my holy day; and call the sabbath a delight, the holy of the Lord, honourable; and shalt honour him, not doing thine own ways, nor finding thine own pleasure, nor speaking thine own words [literally, *speaking a word*]: then shalt thou delight thyself in the Lord; and I will cause thee to ride upon the high places of the earth, and feed thee with the heritage of Jacob thy father: for the mouth of the Lord hath spoken it." What is the significance of *not speaking a word*? It does not mean that the sabbath is a day of silence. There is no biblical evidence that such a standard was ever taught or observed among God's people. So what are we to conclude from this part of the commandment? The Old Testament sabbath celebrated God's finished creation. For six days He created by His word (Genesis 1; Psalm 33:9), but on the sabbath He did not put forth His creative word; He had finished His work. The force of the command not to speak our own words would simply be that on other days of the week we legitimately attend to our words, purposes, or business, but not on the sabbath. Christians should not treat the sabbath as just another day to work, or to pursue their own pleasure, recreation, or pursuits.

Third, *the sabbath precept permits works of necessity, mercy, and piety.* It is not a harsh, cruel imposition, surrounded by endless legalistic hair-splitting. The Lord Jesus Christ made that plain by word and deed. Much to the chagrin of the Pharisees, He did certain works on the sabbath. He allowed His disciples to pluck corn on the sabbath to satisfy their hunger. He said, "The sabbath was made for man, and not man for the sabbath: therefore the Son of man is Lord also of the sabbath" (Mark 2:27–28). According to the Lord of the sabbath, man was not made to be the slave of a burdensome list of man-made do's and don'ts.

As Lord of the sabbath, Christ allows works of necessity. "Which of you shall have an ass or an ox fallen into a pit, and will not straightway pull him out on the sabbath day?" (Luke 14:5). The ox in the ditch represents that class of duties that calls for immediate action, even on the sabbath. Jesus Himself observed this rule by healing on the sabbath (for example, John 9:14). He pronounced His disciples guiltless of any sin in plucking ears of corn to alleviate their hunger (Matthew 12:7). They needed food and could not obtain it otherwise than by plucking some ears as they followed the Lord through a field of corn. Whatever activities legitimately come under the heading of "works of necessity" will change from generation to generation, and Christians need to have their consciences instructed by the word of God. What we must avoid is the tendency to label whatever we wish to do as "necessary." As a rule of thumb, if a work can be as well done before or after the sabbath, or if its urgency arises from our wilful negligence, we should not consider it a work of necessity.

The Lord of the sabbath allows works of mercy. He posed some penetrating questions that emphasized this permission: "Is it lawful to do good on the sabbath days, or to do evil? to save life, or to kill?" (Mark 3:4). These remarkable questions were based on the case of the man He had just healed. "Was it better to heal this poor sufferer before Him with the withered hand, or leave him alone? Was it more sinful to restore a person to health on the Sabbath, than to plot murder, and nourish hatred against an innocent person, as they were doing at that moment against Himself? Was He to be blamed for saving a life on the Sabbath? Were they blameless who were desirous to kill. No wonder that before such a question as this, our Lord's enemies 'held their peace'" (J. C. Ryle, *Expository Thoughts on the Gospels*). There is no blame attached to works of mercy performed on the sabbath. Doctors, nurses, hospital workers, suppliers of emergency services are all called upon to perform works of mercy every day of the week, including the sabbath. Such sabbath work does not break the fourth commandment.

The Lord of the sabbath allows works of piety on the sabbath. "Have ye not read in the law, how that on the sabbath days the priests in the temple profane the sabbath, and are blameless?" (Matthew 12:5). Preachers, evangelists, prison and hospital visitors, and sabbath school teachers all know from experience that they must work hard on the Lord's Day to accomplish the spiritual service of their master.

In the light of Christ's allowance for the works of necessity, mercy, and piety, we can see how empty is the common complaint that sabbath observance is a harsh, restrictive requirement. In truth, it is a spirit of rebellion against the Lord that counts the honouring of His day as an intolerable burden. Like the people of Nehemiah's day, some reject sabbath observance out of greed (Nehemiah 13:15–22). Others reject it because of pleasure, insisting on doing what they please (Isaiah 58:13). And some compromise by using only a brief portion of the sabbath for church services and then spending the rest of the day in pursuit of business or pleasure. Every week, many Christians rush out of church to restaurants, stores, golf courses, business meetings, or home to watch a sports event on television. When Christians treat the fourth commandment in such a carnal manner, why do they express surprise when the ungodly treat the rest of the law of God with equal indifference? Such desecration of the sabbath, the *Lord's* Day, is both scandalous and costly, not only in terms of weakened testimony but also of personal enjoyment of the benefits its observance confers.

The Gracious Purpose of the Sabbath

The sabbath is gracious in its purpose. All too many people, including many Christians, resent what they see as the restrictions the sabbath imposes. To them sabbath observance makes the Lord's Day a day of grinding boredom and dullness. Admittedly, the kinds of human additions to, or misinterpretations of, the divine law of the sabbath that the Pharisees imposed, were (and still are) a cruel bondage. But the sabbath itself, as a divine institution, was and is a gift of freedom, not a chain of bondage. The Lord *gave* the sabbath and He intended it to be a boon to man.

First, *He gave it as a day of rest and refreshment.* This is clear from the Bible's description of the Lord's sabbath rest after the creation and of His people's weekly rest after six days of labour: "In six days the Lord made heaven and earth, and on the seventh day he rested, and was refreshed" (Exodus 31:17); "Six days thou shalt do thy work, and on the seventh day thou shalt rest: that thine ox and thine ass may rest, and the son of thy handmaid, and the stranger, may be refreshed" (Exodus 23:12). The expression *may be refreshed* is from the Hebrew word for breath and could be translated "may catch your breath." That is what the sabbath is for. It gives us time to catch our breath after the activity of our work-week and to be refreshed through rest for the labours that await us in a new week.

The Lord insists that this rest be extended to all men, servants as well as masters. That was probably one reason for the strict legislation in Israel forbidding even the lighting of a fire on the sabbath (Exodus 35:3). Thus the institution of the weekly sabbath was a powerful piece of social legislation to guarantee even the poorest of men a day of rest and refreshment. Even animals had to be permitted to rest, and so did the land, which was kept fresh and fertile by means of a sabbath *year.* Generations of men have found the sabbath a wise and beneficial gift from God.

Second, *the Lord gave the sabbath as a day of worship.* He did not intend us to consume sabbath rest on worldly business or pursuits. The sabbath is meant to be a day free from such considerations so that we may worship the Lord our God without distraction. Thus Moses called for a holy convocation—a public assembly of worshippers—on the sabbath: "Six days shall work be done: but the seventh day is the sabbath of rest, an holy convocation; ye shall do no work therein: it is the sabbath of the Lord in all your dwellings" (Leviticus 23:3). Again, in Leviticus 19:30 he said, "Ye shall keep my sabbaths, *and reverence my sanctuary:* I am the Lord." From the response of the husband of the Shulamite woman to her decision to go to the prophet Elisha, we conclude that the sabbath was a day for hearing God's word: "Wherefore wilt thou go to him to day? it is neither new moon, nor sabbath" (2 Kings 4:23).

The Lord Jesus practised sabbath worship: "He came to Nazareth, where he had been brought up: and, *as his custom was, he went into the synagogue on the sabbath day,* and stood up for to read" (Luke 4:16). In the light of such evidence, there can be no reasonable doubt that the Lord intended the sabbath to be a day of public worship.

Third, *in the sabbath the Lord testifies to His people of their special relationship to Him.* At first it was merely a memorial to His creation, but when He redeemed Israel he made it a sign of His saving grace: "Remember that thou wast a servant in the land of Egypt, and that the Lord thy God brought thee out thence through a mighty hand and by a stretched out arm: therefore the Lord thy God commanded thee to keep the sabbath day" (Deuteronomy 5:15). Here is the testimony of the sabbath to us today. To every *person* it is a reminder that he is God's creature. To every *Christian* it is a glorious statement of his redemption by grace. Thus we keep the sabbath, not out of legalistic bondage, but out of gratitude to God for the special relationship into which He has brought us in Christ.

Fourth, *in the sabbath the Lord points us to His perfect work for us, in which we are to rest for eternal life and salvation.* The sabbath speaks of His finished work, first in creation, and then in redemption. It therefore points us to the cross and to the empty tomb and impresses upon us the merits of Christ's mediation. It assures us of the all-conquering grace of Christ who *finished* the work of procuring our salvation and entered into His rest. By that work we have entered into the rest of pardon and acceptance in Christ. All this the sabbath testifies. It is a constant sermon on the love of God. It speaks mightily of His purpose of grace.

The Blessed Observance of the Sabbath

The sabbath is blessed in its observance. God's word assures us of many rich, spiritual, temporal, and eternal benefits that flow from a humble, holy observance of the sabbath. "Blessed is the man that doeth this, and the son of man that layeth hold on it; that keepeth the sabbath from polluting it, and keepeth his hand from doing any evil" (Isaiah 56:2). Having spoken of making the sabbath a delight, Isaiah describes the blessing that follows: "I will cause thee to ride upon the high places of the earth, and feed thee with the heritage of Jacob thy father: for the mouth of the Lord hath spoken it" (Isaiah 58:14). The Lord will make the observance of His special day a festival for us, a time when He will refresh our bodies and feed our souls as we guard the honour of the sabbath at *our* house and *His* house. This festival expresses three spiritual blessings that are precious to every believer:

First, it expresses the blessing of *our likeness to our God.* The reason the fourth commandment gives for sabbath observance is that the Lord rested on the sabbath and hallowed it. We are to be conformed to His image in this as well as in every other aspect of holiness. "Be ye therefore followers [imitators] of God, as dear children" (Ephesians 5:1). Faithful, spiritual sabbath observance obeys this injunction.

Second, this weekly festival expresses the blessing of *our liberty in Christ.* Far from being a leftover from legalistic bondage, the observance of the sabbath is an eloquent testimony of gospel liberty: "Remember that thou wast a servant in the land of Egypt, and that the Lord thy God brought thee out thence through a mighty hand and by a stretched out arm: therefore the Lord thy God commanded thee to keep the sabbath day" (Deuteronomy 5:15). The logic of this verse is notable: The Lord has delivered you from the shackles of sin; therefore He commands you to keep the sabbath. In the light of such a statement it is amazing that any redeemed soul should accept the perverted idea that sabbath observance is a chain of bondage!

Third, the festival expresses the blessing of *our love for Christ.* In Isaiah 58:13 the Lord equates calling the sabbath a delight with honouring *Him.* Protestations of love for God ring hollow when accompanied by the wilful desecration of His day. We certainly cannot claim to love someone whom we dishonour. A scriptural observance of the sabbath declares our love and loyalty to the Lord and witnesses to heaven, earth, and hell that we put His commands and interests before any other.

A weekly festival that does us good in body and soul and that expresses our likeness to, liberty in, and love for Christ is the precious gift of our kind heavenly Father. According to the word of God, it is big with blessings on all who observe it.

The Evangelical Message of the Sabbath

The sabbath is evangelical in its message. First, *it points us constantly to Christ,* for as we have seen from Hebrews 4:9–10 it celebrates His finished work of redemption. This is a fact that too many Christians ignore. The Christian sabbath is a beautiful message of the fulfilment of the law by Christ and of the redemption rest He has merited for His believing people.

Second, *the sabbath challenges us to look beyond the things of the world to those of eternity.* In an age of crass materialism it tells us that there is something more important than business, or money, or any other earthly pursuit. These will all soon perish forever. We will leave them all behind when the Lord calls us into eternity. When we step aside from the ceaseless round of worldly activity to observe the Lord's Day as our sabbath rest, we confess that we have an eternal dimension to our purposes and pursuits. Thus the sabbath challenges us to show by our actions that we really believe what we profess about the supreme importance of eternal things.[1]

Third, *the sabbath calls for the exercise of faith and dependence upon the Lord.* To give up one-seventh of the earning power of every week makes no sense to the carnal mind. At times, shortage of money may tempt us to

[1] Imagine the consternation of a friend who agreed to attend a church with Christians who assured him that the worship of God and the preaching of His gospel were of paramount importance, only to hear the preacher announce that there would be no evening service the next Lord's Day so that everyone would be free to stay at home to watch the Super Bowl on television! Those people forfeited all credibility and authority to witness to him of the preeminence of the gospel and its claims.

rationalize departing from biblical standards of sabbath observance. In such times, the sabbath becomes a trial of our faith. But it is also an opportunity to prove God by placing our dependence upon Him to meet our needs and to bless our labours during the remainder of the week. *Faith is always an obedient response to a divine revelation.* An obedient response to the fourth commandment will accept whatever hardship comes to us because of our faithfulness to God. Such faith will receive a rich reward. As we trust God we will prove not only that He is able to supply our needs according to His riches in glory by Christ Jesus (Philippians 4:19), but that He has solemnly pledged to do so. Those who seek first the kingdom of God and His righteousness will not lack the necessities of life (Matthew 6:33). "The Lord God is a sun and shield: the Lord will give grace and glory: no good thing will he withhold from them that walk uprightly" (Psalm 84:11). This is the faith we express by a scriptural observance of the sabbath.

Fourth, *the sabbath builds up individuals, families, and churches* in the faith of the gospel and teaches them to obey God rather than men.

This is the Christian sabbath. We should call it a delight. We should guard it as a gift more precious than gold. Most of all, we should ensure that we use it to hear and receive the gospel it so clearly declares. Only then can we be ready to enter the eternal rest it foreshadows.

CHAPTER EIGHTEEN

HONOUR IN THE HOME
THE FIFTH COMMANDMENT

"Honour thy father and thy mother."
Exodus 20:12

Thomas Watson appropriately likened the Ten Commandments to Jacob's ladder. The first table of the law—that is, the first four commandments—like the top of Jacob's ladder, reaches to heaven and deals with our moral and spiritual attitude to God. The second table—commandments five through ten—is like the bottom of the ladder and deals with our moral and spiritual attitude toward men. As Watson said, a man cannot be good in regard to the first who is bad in regard to the second.

That makes the second table of the law a matter of great importance. At first sight it may appear that compared to the weighty matters of the first table, things like "Honour thy father and thy mother" are matters of small moment. But that is far from the truth. No man can be right in relation to God if he is wrong in his relation to his fellow men.

It is interesting that the second table of the law starts as it does. The question is, why? If we were to ask most people which commandment they felt should head the second table of the law few would choose "Honour thy father and thy mother." Human wisdom would probably opt for "Thou shalt not kill." So why did the Lord place "Honour thy father and thy mother" first in this table? On reflection we will see that there are very good reasons for His doing so.

First, *the fifth commandment raises the matter of legitimate authority and its source and enjoins godly submission to it.* The remaining commandments deal with our moral and social responsibilities, but before we can discharge these we must learn to respect legitimate authority. It is essential to recognize that our moral and social responsibilities are not mere human conventions to be changed at will. They have the weight of God's law behind them and the human authority that enforces them has the strength of divine ordination behind it.

Second, *if we get our home life right we will get every other part of society right*. The fifth is the only commandment that explicitly mentions any human authority, and it firmly sets that authority in the family. It is there that all moral and social good must begin. So there is good reason for the fifth commandment to appear where it does.

In the light of all this it is obvious that this commandment does more than regulate the relationship of children to their parents. It does that. But it does much more: It regulates our attitude and relations to legitimate authority in general, in society, in the church, and in the state. That is why the *Shorter Catechism* (Question 64) says:

> *The fifth commandment requireth the preserving the honour, and performing the duties, belonging to every one in their several places and relations, as superiors, inferiors, or equals.*

To many that will appear to be stretching the simple words of the commandment. On first hearing, the Israelites probably understood it to refer exclusively to their domestic arrangements. However, it is obvious that the Lord soon disabused them of any such notion. He set up the institutions of the church and the state as extensions of their domestic arrangements, employing the terms *father* and *mother* to denote much more than biological parenthood. Therefore He extended the duty of honour far beyond parents to include many others. For us, this means that God uses *father* and *mother* in a variety of ways and commands us to honour those to whom He has given such a title.

Rulers: "Kings shall be thy nursing fathers, and their queens thy nursing mothers" (Isaiah 49:23). "The inhabitants of the villages ceased, they ceased in Israel, until that I Deborah arose, that I arose a mother in [or, *to*] Israel" (Judges 5:7).

Prophets: "Elisha . . . cried [to Elijah], My father, my father" (2 Kings 2:12). King Joram addressed Elisha as "My father" (2 Kings 6:21).

Soulwinners: "Though ye have ten thousand instructors in Christ, yet have ye not many fathers: for in Christ Jesus I have begotten you through the gospel" (1 Corinthians 4:15). The apostle John wrote, "I have no greater joy than to hear that my children walk in truth" (3 John 4).

To these, add the texts that speak of honouring those who bear the titles of father or mother. Moses commanded, "Thou shalt rise up before the hoary head [or, *stand up before grey hairs*), and honour the face of the old man" (Leviticus 19:32). Paul says, "Rebuke not an elder, but entreat him as a *father* . . . the elder women as *mothers*. . . . Honour widows that are widows indeed" (1 Timothy 5:1–3). Later, in verse 17, he says, "Let the elders that rule well be counted worthy of double honour." Peter adds, "Honour the king" (1 Peter 2:17).

Thus, *father* and *mother* and the duty of giving honour to them apply much more widely than to the single relationship of children to their parents. As the Westminster Divines (the compilers of the *Shorter Catechism*) saw so clearly, the fifth commandment regulates our attitude and behaviour towards *all earthly authority.*

This includes the authority of the state. The Lord commands us to respect and obey our rulers and the laws they enact in so far as they do not call on us to disobey the Lord. "Let every soul be subject unto the higher powers. For there is no power but of God: the powers that be are ordained of God" (Romans 13:1).

It also includes the authority of the church. Paul refers to "Jerusalem which is above is . . . the mother of us all" (Galatians 4:26). The "true spiritual church," as John Brown calls it, the gospel church proclaiming the covenant of grace is our mother and we are duty-bound to honour her as such. Her authority is not to be despised: "Obey them that have the rule over you, and submit yourselves: for they watch for your souls, as they that must give account, that they may do it with joy, and not with grief: for that is unprofitable for you" (Hebrews 13:17).

But even this is not the whole story: The fifth commandment directs us how we must react to God's authority over our entire earthly existence. "Ye are the children of the Lord your God" (Deuteronomy 14:1).

The Lord Jesus Christ instructed His people to pray to God as "our Father" (Matthew 6:9). The apostle Paul reminded us of this special relationship in Romans 8:15–16: "For ye have not received the spirit of bondage again to fear; but ye have received the Spirit of adoption, whereby we cry, Abba, Father. The Spirit itself beareth witness with our spirit, that we are the children of God." John says, "Behold, what manner of love the Father hath bestowed upon us, that we should be called the sons of God. . . . Beloved, now are we the sons of God" (1 John 3:1, 2). In all these references *Father* speaks of God as our Saviour in Christ. But Malachi 2:10 uses the term to describe Him as Creator of all men: "Have we not all one father? hath not one God created us?" So the fifth commandment means that all men should honour the Lord because He created them, and Christians especially should honour Him because He saved them.

Here then is the full extent of the commandment, "Honour thy father and thy mother": God has ordered all human society on the basis of legitimate authority which every one of us should acknowledge and respect because we acknowledge and respect the authority of God Himself. That is a huge subject, one that is much too vast for us to cover in the course of a study such as this.[1] To do justice to it we would have to consider the biblical teaching on the following subjects:

- What constitutes legitimate authority and its proper exercise in church and state;
- The duties of citizens toward the state;
- The limits of state authority, the difference between *power* and *authority,* the right of protest against the tyrannical abuse of power, and when and by whom a revolution against a government may be pursued;
- The proper use of church power by elders, and the nature and necessity of joyful Christian submission to it—the proud or selfish despising of the legitimate rule of the elders of the church being a flagrant breach of the law of God, as despising God Himself.

[1] For a more complete discussion see "Fomenting Rebellion" in chapter 21, p. 277.

These are undeniably important matters. The Bible has clear teaching about all of them. The main thing for us to recognize is that the law of God forbids unbridled individualism and commands true respect for legitimate authority.

We must, however, confine ourselves to the primary reference of the fifth commandment: the proper attitude and actions of parents and children toward each other.

Duties of Parents

Again, some will see this as stretching the meaning of the commandment. After all, the fifth commandment is addressed to children, not to parents. So why commence with the duties of parents? Indeed, why include this subject in the treatment of the commandment at all? Simply because this is what the inspired commentary on this commandment does. In Ephesians 6:1–4 we read, "Children, obey your parents in the Lord: for this is right. Honour thy father and mother; (which is the first commandment with promise;) that it may be well with thee, and thou mayest live long on the earth. And, ye fathers, provoke not your children to wrath: but bring them up in the nurture and admonition of the Lord."

Parents are to be more than merely the biological producers of their children. They are to be all that the Scriptures include in the terms *father* and *mother.*

Fathers should reflect the Fatherhood of God for it is after that Fatherhood that "the whole family in heaven and earth is named" (Ephesians 3:15). To fail to do so is destructive to our children and will often warp their response to the message of the gospel. Most pastors have had to confront the tragedy of hardened and embittered young people who find it difficult to listen to a gospel that proclaims the Fatherhood of God because all they ever met with in their earthly father was cruelty or incestuous abuse. Our fatherhood is meant to be a representation of God to our children. Woe be to the man whose representation is such a vicious caricature of God as to make his children loathe the very thought of another "father."

Mothers should reflect the role and rule of the church as they rear their children, for the church is, as we have seen, "the mother of us all." If mothers fulfil this role they not only bear their children but care for them. They teach them and are careful to point them to Christ, not only by their words but by their own evident love for and submission to their Saviour.

These are high standards. They are also necessary standards. We must not derive our ideas of parenting from the latest fad in psychology. We must not model our family relationships after the fashion of the ungodly example or philosophy of those who are living in rebellion against God and His word. Nowhere is it more imperative that we know and obey God's word than in the area of rearing our children. We have no excuse for not knowing what we should do, for the Scriptures are clear in setting forth the duties of parents to their children.

First, *parents are to instruct their children.* Teaching children is the primary duty, not of the state nor even of the church, but of parents. Moses makes this clear in Deuteronomy 6:6–7: "These words, which I command thee this day, shall be in thine heart: and thou shalt teach them diligently unto thy children, and shalt talk of them when thou sittest in thine house, and when thou walkest by the way, and when thou liest down, and when thou risest up." *Teach them diligently unto thy children.* That is the fundamental duty of every parent. As our heavenly Father is careful to instruct His children (Deuteronomy 32:10; Nehemiah 9:20; Isaiah 28:26), so we should follow His example with our children. We must make sure they are reared under the influence of the word of God, that they learn its truth and memorize its very words. And we must make sure we demonstrate to them by our lives what it is to know, love, and obey God's word.

The Lord praised Abraham because "I know him, that he will command his children and his household after him, and they shall keep the way of the Lord, to do justice and judgment; that the Lord may bring upon Abraham that which he hath spoken of him" (Genesis 18:19). God means parents to spend time with their children teaching them His word. This is not solely the mother's work. It belongs in a very special way to the father also. In too many homes the fathers never pray with their children, never teach them the divine word. They leave such things to their wives. That is a mistake that will usually be very costly.

We should repeat that the Lord means us to have time to spend with our children. Moses speaks of sitting down with them, walking with them, talking with them. How many parents, especially fathers, actually do such things nowadays? Parents cannot really teach their children without spending time with them. This may mean major rearrangements of work and leisure schedules. So be it. We naturally wish to prepare our children educationally and culturally to hold an honourable place in society. To this end we will work to earn the money necessary to make these things possible. All of that is good. However, in pursuing these goals we must not overlook the primary goal: to see our children come to the greatest knowledge anyone can attain on this earth, the knowledge of Christ as Saviour, for this is eternal life (John 17:3).

No Christian parent can be content to see his children grow up as strangers to the gospel of grace. Nor can he console himself that he is working hard for their good while he neglects their highest good. What the apostle John said of his spiritual children every parent who knows Christ can say of his natural children: "I have no greater joy than to hear that my children walk in truth" (3 John 4).

All this is obviously addressed to Christian parents. Without doubt there are unsaved parents who are "good" parents, doing their best for their children according to their lights. But to be the best parents we must be Christian parents. The teaching our children most need is *biblical* teaching. Those who would teach their children biblically must themselves have submitted to the message of Scripture—that is, to have repented and received Christ.

Parents must take the task of educating their children very seriously. This is not to say that the education of children is the exclusive task of parents. Some people have interpreted Moses' command to mean that no one but a child's parents should educate him. However, the Lord has specifically mentioned other teachers whose responsibility, at least in part, included the teaching of children. In the Old Testament, the Levites had a particular role in teaching. There was a school for young prophets, a kind of college or seminary they attended. In the New Testament, the ascended Christ gave the gift of pastor-teachers to His church. There is a place for school and Sunday school. Teaching children is not necessarily the exclusive task of parents. But it is primarily their task.

Parents must not be mere onlookers in the education of their children. Nowadays the state claims the role of the primary educator and usually excludes the Bible from its curriculum. The results have been predictable. It used to be that the church was the centre of even secular education. The church established the school, set the curriculum and the rules, and administered the discipline according to the word of God. Family and church worked together. But as parents have abdicated responsibility to be fully involved in the development of their children and have deputed their God-given task to the state, families have disintegrated and the state itself has suffered the consequences. For the benefit of children, families, church, and state, parents must reassume the primary role in teaching their children. In doing so they must be sure to make the word of God foundational in their teaching.

Second, *parents should provide for their children.* "The children ought not to lay up for the parents, but the parents for the children" (2 Corinthians 12:14). Parents have the responsibility to provide materially for their children. This is not the state's role. That is not to say that the state should be indifferent to the needs of the poor or that it should not make ready a safety net for children in need. When God instructed Moses about the establishment of Israelite society He made particular provision for the poor (Exodus 23:11; Leviticus 19:10; 23:22; Deuteronomy 15:7; 24:14). But children must never become the property of the state—and that is the inevitable result of giving the state instead of the parents the primary job of providing for them. Communism makes children the possession of the state; Christianity makes them the treasure of their parents and gives those parents the task of providing for them.

As we have seen in Ephesians 6, rearing children means nurturing them. That is, feeding them, caring for them. This nurture extends far beyond mere material provision. It includes emotional, moral, and spiritual provision. Parents must provide the best possible homes for their children. This has little to do with wealth and luxury. Some of the worst homes children have to live in are opulent palaces. Some of the best are humble abodes with little of this world's wealth. Nowadays there is such an emphasis on material possessions that parents feel they have to work night and day to give their children plenty of "things." In doing so, they often give up the opportunity to provide the spiritual and emotional environment their children need. We must never forget that the calling of parents is to nurture their children in the fullest sense of the word.

It follows then that no parent has the right to abuse a child. The term *abuse* is carelessly thrown around by social engineers who think they know better than God. They would include all forms of corporal punishment. As we shall see, there is a need for biblical discipline and the neglect of it is detrimental to the development of a child (Proverbs 13:24). But it must always be measured, controlled, consistent, loving, and set in the context of carefully explaining the teachings of Scripture. It is not revenge but a means of recalling children from the paths of wickedness (Proverbs 22:15; 23:13–14). Biblical discipline is not a form of abuse.

But we all know that there is widespread abuse of children by parents. Some parents look on their children as chattels and treat them as slaves. Many more practise mental and physical cruelty on them as foul-tempered fathers and mothers try to hide their sin behind the Bible's teaching on discipline. In all too many cases homes are dens of incest and gross perversion. Preachers—we dare not call them Christians—are far from guiltless in this regard. I have known of preachers who raped their own daughters and had the hypocrisy to command their silence by quoting the fifth commandment, "Honour thy father and thy mother." It is not obedience to the law of God that covers such a monster's sin. It is sheer intimidation. Whatever the profession of Christianity such a pervert makes, however he seeks to justify his actions, he should be turned over to the law. No punishment is too severe for him. He has betrayed the most sacred trust a parent can receive from God: He has robbed those whom he should have nurtured.

Third, *parents should discipline their children.* They should establish biblical standards for their families along with appropriate sanctions for the breach of those standards. Then they must impose those standards, visiting appropriate punishment on violations of them. This is vital. God has ordained parents to be parents, not big brothers or sisters to their children. While they must seek the closest and most vital and intimate relationship possible with their children, parents must never forget that they represent God and His law in their family. They must have the spiritual wisdom, courage, and faith to establish the standards demanded by the word of God. They must avoid the sin of Eli. Eli was a godly man who did nothing to restrain the wickedness of his sons (1 Samuel 2:27–34; 3:12–14). He failed to observe the standards of godliness and discipline that the Scriptures demanded for his family. True, he did plead with them to desist from the worst of their vices, but it was too little too late. When his sons ignored his pleadings and continued to mock the Lord and His sacrifice, Eli should have visited the full rigour of the law on them. He was both their father and their judge. But he did nothing. Having failed to establish godly standards for his family he also failed to carry out godly discipline. The results were disastrous and his failure damned his sons. That was a terrible price to pay for neglecting godly standards in the home.

Many Christians adopt Eli's method of child rearing. Often they are swayed by human opinion or current conventions. What they need to do is to stand by faith on the word of God, rule their homes by that word, and teach their children the truth of both the law and the gospel. In other words parents must teach their children what it is to respect both divine and human authority. By teaching them to respect God's word, God's name, God's day, and God's worship they teach them to acknowledge divine authority. By teaching them filial obedience they teach them to respect legitimate human authority, not only in the home but in the church and in the state.

All this must be according to the word of God, patterned after the love and kindness of our heavenly Father. This holds good even, rather, especially when punishment is necessary. Our heavenly Father chastises in love and afflicts in faithfulness (Hebrews 12:5; Psalm 119:75; Proverbs 3:11–12). As God has treated us we should treat our children (Proverbs 13:24). Parents have neither the calling nor the right to squelch self-expression and development in a child. They must be careful not to injure his personality or to inflict emotional scars that he must carry for the rest of his life. They are forbidden to provoke a child to wrath (Ephesians 6:4), which includes all abusive attitudes, words, and behaviour that produce long-term anger and bitterness. What parents must seek to do is to regulate the development of their child's personality by the word of God.

The fifth commandment includes teaching a child how to behave in relation to others, that he cannot always have his own way, and that he cannot always indulge his own pleasures. In Bible times children called their father "lord," bowed to their parents, and stood in the presence of their elders. Customs have changed, but the principle behind them remains the same. Good manners should not be corrupted. Someone has said that manners are the brakes conscience puts on the expression of the lusts of the flesh. They teach children to take time to consider the effect their actions may have on others.

That raises a very important point: By their discipline parents must teach their children to take the long view of things. Children have a very narrow time reference for all their decisions. They live for the moment. For parents to exercise godly discipline is to refuse to be manipulated into accepting the child's demand for instantaneous gratification of every whim. They must teach him that while he needs some things at once, he needs to wait for some other things—or even to forgo them entirely. Part of the purpose of this kind of discipline is to teach children what it is to wait, labour, or even suffer for the moment in order to achieve long-term benefit. Every wise parent should want his children to learn the lesson Dr. Bob Jones, Sr., taught the students of Bob Jones University: Don't sacrifice the permanent on the altar of the immediate.

Children find self-control difficult, and lazy or self-indulgent parents make it even more difficult for them. Parents who live under a crushing burden of debt because they refused to wait until they could afford the luxuries they see others enjoy will have a hard time teaching children to control their craving for instant gratification. Parents who play fast and loose with their marriage vows will sound like the basest hypocrites if they try to teach their children moral restraint. People who are ruled by immediate passions are ill-equipped to train children in the necessary discipline of godly self-control. We should particularly remark that parents who sacrifice the eternal welfare of their own souls for the sake of the momentary gratification sin brings, inculcate the grossest form of indiscipline into their children. They certainly communicate a disdain of Christ and of the glory of heaven to their children. "What shall it profit a man, if he shall gain the whole world, and lose his own soul?" (Mark

8:36). Anyone who sells his soul for a little piece of the world is playing the fool. A fool is in a poor position to teach his children wisdom. Children will most naturally follow in the footsteps of their parents.

These are the duties of parents—they must instruct, provide for, and discipline their children. These duties are part of the domestic arrangement God has ordained for happy and prosperous homes. Children are our most precious possessions on earth because they are immortal souls. That thought should weigh very heavily on every parent's heart. It is enough to make even the best of parents cry out, "Who is sufficient for these things?" Parental responsibilities are so heavy that most parents feel a deep sense of failure. So how can parents meet the standards set for them in the fifth commandment?

The first thing is for them to make sure they personally know Christ as Saviour. To be the best parent, a person needs to be a Christian. The second thing is to maintain a close walk with the Lord by faith in the gospel. Christian parents should take care to understand the gospel of grace and live in the full enjoyment of it. This is the best equipment for doing right in the home. Living by the faith of the gospel—that is, letting what we believe about the Lord Jesus Christ govern how we act—keeps parents from laziness on the one hand and from excessive worry about their parental duties (so often the cause of harshness) on the other. It means obeying and believing the Lord even when their children don't obey them or respond to the word of God. And it means calling on the Lord to fulfil His word in every family situation, however apparently hopeless. We can express God's grace most beautifully and effectively when we are enjoying it. In other words, though the law tells us what to do, the gospel gives us the power to do it.

The Duties of Children

"Honour thy father and thy mother" is the commandment. Paul expresses its meaning in Ephesians 6:1, 2: "Children, obey your parents in the Lord: for this is right. Honour thy father and mother; (which is the first commandment with promise)." In order that we may understand clearly the duties of children to their parents, God's word sets before us three ideas: a plain precept, a perfect pattern, and a gracious promise.

First, *the Lord gives us a plain precept.* He says, "Honour thy father and thy mother." Some have wondered why the Bible does not say, "*Love* your parents." In all of Scripture there is no actual command for children to love their parents. Now we must be careful that we do not jump to the conclusion that the Bible does not teach children to love their fathers and mothers. When God tells us to love our neighbour that obviously includes our parents, and as we shall see, honour encompasses the idea of real love. We are apt to confine our idea of love to having tender feelings of affection. But God tells us to honour our parents not because of how we feel toward them but because He commands it.

Paul's statement in Hebrews 12:9 will enable us to understand the force of the word *honour:* "We have had fathers of our flesh which corrected us, and we gave them reverence: shall we not much rather be in subjection unto the Father of spirits, and live?" Clearly honour includes love, respect, godly fear, obedience, submission, and the discharge of our filial duties.

The Hebrew word for honour simply means "heavy." Thus to honour our parents is to give due weight to their person, position, reputation, instruction, and judgments. It is the opposite of treating them lightly. Exodus 21:17 pronounces a severe sentence on all who treat their parents lightly: "He that curseth his father, or his mother, shall surely be put to death." Here the Hebrew word translated *curse* means "to esteem lightly," or as Jochem Douma suggests, "to treat as indecent or despicable." It is a strong word that clearly means more than common acts of disobedience. Yet disobedience is a perilous step on the way toward it.

The Bible notes that the wickedness of setting light by parents is one of the marks of a society given over to judgment for its sin. In Romans 1 we read of God's "giving up" men (vv. 24, 26, 28). The marks of societies under this judgment are listed, including the flagrant breach of the fifth commandment: "Backbiters, haters of God, despiteful, proud, boasters, inventors of evil things, disobedient to parents" (v. 30). Paul told Timothy that this sin would be especially prevalent in the last days: "Men shall be lovers of their own selves, covetous, boasters, proud, blasphemers, disobedient to parents, unthankful, unholy" (2 Timothy 3:2). This is what disrespect for parents really is. It is inherently pagan. It is part of a mindset that is anti-God. It calls for and will receive the judgment of the Lord: "They which commit such things are worthy of death" (Romans 1:32).

In contrast to this pagan breach of the biblical model for the family, God commands us, "Honour thy father and thy mother." We are gratefully to love, respect, and obey them while we are young. This idea of gratitude must not be omitted from the honour due to parents. Our parents brought us into the world, nurtured us, fed, clothed, and sheltered us. Whatever their deficiencies, real or imagined, they have done a work for us without which we would not be alive. It is sad many parents have done nothing more for their offspring than to bring them into the world. Their little ones need to be rescued from them. Of such parents it is true that "the tender mercies of the wicked are cruel" (Proverbs 12:10). This evil tribe is increasing all the time—which should remind children and young people who enjoy a much better situation, especially those who have Christian parents, that they have much for which to be thankful. They should respond with gratitude, not with surly, thankless disrespect.

Any child or young person who has the blessing of Christian parents should make sure to learn well from them the wisdom of the word of God. Proverbs 4:1–4 says, "Hear, ye children, the instruction of a father, and attend to know understanding. For I give you good doctrine, forsake ye not my law. For I was my father's son, tender and only beloved in the sight of my mother. He taught me also, and said unto me, Let thine heart retain my words: keep my commandments, and live." Again in Proverbs 7:1–3 we read, "My son, keep my words, and lay up my commandments with thee. Keep my commandments, and live; and my law as the apple of thine eye. Bind them upon thy fingers, write them upon the table of thine heart."

It is an inestimable privilege for children to have fathers and mothers who teach them God's word. There is only one proper and godly response to such a privilege: Honour those parents by paying respectful, obedient, submissive attention to their ministry of love. Do not despise them to align yourself with the wicked principles and practices of those who advise you to "liberate" yourself from parental control. As children, honour your parents with grateful love and respect.

Even when we become adults we are to continue to give due weight to our parents' position and advice. Wise parents rear their children to be able to live their own lives and to make wise decisions for their own families. In this sense a man must "leave his father and his mother" to be joined to his wife (Mark 10:7). The maturity to assume full responsibility for running a home does not come all at once. Parents should train their children to make decisions in the light of the word of God. When those children become adults the parents cannot continue to run their lives. Parents who attempt to do so are usually manipulative and domineering. If they have done their parenting work well they will not need to intrude into the lives of their adult children's homes and families. That does not mean they will not have good advice to give. Normally they should wait until they are asked for it. The asking is part of the honour their children should accord them. Giving due weight to their opinion is another part of the same honour.

In cases where adult sons or daughters still live under the parental roof they should realize that they especially should continue to show respect for the standards of that home. They do not shed the duty of obeying the fifth commandment simply because they have reached their twenties or thirties. Again, if their parents have done their work well, these young adults will be equipped to make wise decisions and will live with their parents in an atmosphere of mutual respect. If they refuse to do so, the parents must remember that they still have the authority to set the standards for their own home and to impose necessary sanctions on the breach of those standards. Parents often feel trapped into putting up with drunkenness, drug abuse, immorality, and even physical, mental, and verbal abuse—and a host of lesser evils such as laziness, slovenliness, and general insensitivity—because their adult children "need" them or may become worse if they depart the family home. Such parents would be better to use what has been called "tough love"—love that expresses itself in establishing and observing the biblical standards and sanctions of the home. The alternative is to become prisoners in their own home and accessories to the very sins they see ruining their son or daughter.

The duty of honouring parents particularly includes the care, support, and relief of those parents in their old age. Even when parents are still in the work force, wage-earning children who remain in the family home should contribute to the family budget (even when they are wealthy enough not need such contributions, wise parents will usually seek to inculcate financial responsibility in their adult children). Jesus said, "God commanded, saying, Honour thy father and mother: and, He that curseth father or mother, let him die the death. But ye say, Whosoever shall say to his father or his mother, It is a gift, by whatsoever thou mightest be profited by me and honour not his father or his mother, he shall be free" (Matthew 15:4–5). This duty increases as parents become old. In old age they will need more than money. They will need care, affection, assurance, and attention. Their children should honour them by meeting these needs. Paul gave clear instructions: "If any widow have children or nephews, let them learn first to shew piety at home, and to *requite their parents:* for that is good and acceptable before God. . . . But if any provide not for his own, and specially for those of his own house, he hath denied the faith, and is worse than an infidel" (1 Timothy 5:4, 8).

Probably no part of the duty of honouring parents causes more questioning than this. Nowadays, most families feel they cannot afford to look after aged parents, or don't have room for them, or cannot be at home to meet their needs, especially where husbands and wives both need to hold down jobs. There isn't always a simple answer to these problems and many godly families have agonized over how to solve them. What must be grasped is that adult children have the God-given duty to take the care and support of their parents seriously. They do not meet that responsibility simply by paying a third-party care giver (usually a nursing home) to house, wash, and feed their parents. Nursing home care may be necessary, but we also owe our aged parents our time, respect, love, and company. We should do what we can so that there can be no doubt that to the best of our abilities and resources we have obeyed God in honouring our parents in their old age.

It is easy to state the duties of children; it is another thing to put the precept into action. Some parents show little sense or biblical wisdom. Sometimes they are dishonourable and difficult to respect. Nevertheless, the fifth commandment still stands. Given the difficulty many face in obeying it, we may be grateful that the word of God not only gives us the precept but also an example of the perfect observance of it.

Thus the second thing we must note is that *the Lord gives us a perfect pattern, the Lord Jesus Christ.* Take the subject we have just been considering, the care adult children should have for their parents. Here the Saviour supplies us the perfect example of filial concern. As He hung on the cross, amid all the agonies of death, He remembered His mother Mary and her special needs (John 19:26–27). By that time she must have been widowed and now she was losing her eldest son. So the Lord Jesus committed her to the care of John the beloved disciple, probably a close relative. The point is that Jesus took the welfare of His mother seriously and even in His personal suffering was careful to maintain His duty toward her.

In doing so He was continuing the pattern He had established from the very beginning of His relationship with His earthly parents. We read of Him as a twelve-year-old boy: "He went down with them, and came to Nazareth, and was subject unto them" (Luke 2:51). The Greek verb translated "was subject" denotes "a voluntary attitude of giving in, co-operating, assuming responsibility, and carrying a burden." Thus the Lord placed Himself under the control of Mary and Joseph. He obeyed them and subordinated Himself to them. He honoured them. We should consider this relationship very carefully for it will give us invaluable insights into how we should meet the difficulties of honouring our parents.

The Lord Jesus was truly the son of Mary, but He was also the Son of God. At times that led to conflicting viewpoints. For example, we read in Luke 2:41–51 of Mary and Joseph going up to the temple when Jesus was about twelve years old. When it was time to return to Nazareth they set off, thinking, but obviously not making sure, that Jesus was in the company. In fact, He was still in Jerusalem doing "my Father's business" (v. 49). Clearly, His Father had led Him to remain in Jerusalem to converse with the doctors of the law. But Mary was grieved at Him and rebuked Him. She faulted Him when she, not He, had been remiss. Parents all too often do that. However, Jesus remained subject to His earthly parents and as far as it was consonant with obedience to His heavenly Father, obeyed them.

That is a good rule for us all to live by. Obedience to our heavenly Father is the overarching duty of every man. It dictates our response to every other situation. Children should obey their parents "in the Lord: for this is right" (Ephesians 6:1). When parents command what is contrary to God's word, children have the duty to disobey their command. This refers to cases of open defiance of the plain command of God, not to some personal or whimsical interpretation of a Scripture text. Here is a rather startling example: One of our missionaries recently reported that some young girls had been converted under the preaching of the gospel and had gone on to establish good testimonies. However, when these girls entered their teenage years their mothers commanded them to sell themselves as prostitutes. When they refused, the mothers brutally beat them into submission. Did the young girls do right in disobeying their mothers? Undoubtedly. No parent has the right to command a child to break the law of God.

Thankfully, for most of us that kind of situation does not arise. Therefore the duty of children to disobey ungodly commands must not be used as an excuse to disobey their parents' perfectly legitimate directions simply because they run counter to the children's desires. The example of the Lord Jesus Christ is clear: We must obey to the full extent that such obedience is consonant with obedience to God.

The Lord Jesus evidently did not always please His parents but He always honoured them. We know that at least in the case of the Jerusalem journey, Mary was displeased with Him. She was also probably among the family members who were displeased with Him and who sought to stop Him when He launched into His public ministry (Mark 3:21, 31–33). It certainly was due to no fault in the Lord Jesus that His parents were ever displeased with Him. It was due solely to their inadequacies and their sin. But instead of making their unjust displeasure a cause for casting off His filial duty, the Saviour maintained a perfect honour and respect for Mary and Joseph.

This example is of immediate value to many whose parents become angry with them for no good reason or who heap guilt on them to cover their own failures. How should children deal with such a situation? As Jesus did—by respectfully refusing to disobey God; by rejecting the false imputation of guilt Mary sought to lay upon Him; and by continuing to give cheerful, wholehearted submission to His parents' will in all matters that involved no disobedience to God.

Of course, Mary and Joseph were basically honourable people, worthy of respect. Wise parents seek to be worthy of their children's respect. They remember that they derive their authority from God and therefore will try never to use it to drive their children from Him. They will not be petty tyrants. They will endeavour not to provoke their children to anger (Ephesians 6:4) or to be so critical as to break their spirits and leave them discouraged. As they see their children approach and enter adulthood they will seek to transfer more and more personal responsibility to them. Wise parents will distinguish between moral absolutes and passing preferences. They will be careful not to make every little failure in their children into a momentous spiritual problem. They will recognize that part of their teaching role is to be ready to talk to their children and explain their position. In all they do they will seek to be good representatives of their Lord.

Wise parents will act together. If children are to honour father and mother, then father and mother should never put them in the position of having to disobey one to obey the other, of having to despise one to honour the other.

It would be wonderful if all children had wise parents. Sadly, they don't. The example of the Lord Jesus establishes the duty of every child to his parents, especially those children and young people who profess to be saved. It would be wonderful if wise parents never had rebellious children. Again, this is sadly not the case. Sometimes their very wisdom arouses their children to violent anger and rejection. But they must remain faithful to their calling.

Every young person should gladly respect such parents, even in the most challenging situations. Children should subordinate their desires and plans to the directions of their parents. Parents set the rules of the house—the times their children may go out and when they should come in; where they may go and with whom. Even in the matter of dating and choosing a marriage partner parents have great authority. For years parents invest themselves in their children. Should they not have a major say in the most important relationship decisions of those children's lives? Where they show from Scripture that a particular relationship is wrong, their children should instantly submit to their call to abandon it. Where they forbid a relationship because they consider it harmful, their children should accept their ruling with good grace until such time as they change their opinion or the children in question are old enough and self-sufficient enough to become independent. Wise parents will be willing to pray these matters through with their children and will not equate their personal preferences with the will of God—and will not use God's word as a tool to manipulate their children into submitting to their whims as if they were Scripture principles. Wise parents will give time for mature reflection and will seek agreement in the light of Scripture. They will avoid conflict arising out of personal prejudice.

Basically, then, the duty of children to their parents is to be in godly submission to them, just as the Lord Jesus Christ was subject to His earthly parents. Obedience does not come easily or naturally to most of us. Even young children betray a rebellious nature. Teenagers very often imagine that they have outgrown the need for parental control. As a result many a home—the place God ordained to be earth's nearest expression of heaven (Deuteronomy 11:20-21)—has become a battlefield. Many teenaged children have become sullen, arrogant, and stubborn. To all such the message of God is clear and plain: "Remember the fifth commandment. You will be able to go your own way soon enough. If the Lord Jesus Christ submitted Himself to His parents, how much more should you!"

The Lord Jesus Christ is a pattern to us also in dealing with authority that is not honourable. For many believers this is a big problem. How are we to honour and respect dishonourable people? Particularly, how is a son or daughter to honour a drunken, deceiving, lecherous, or otherwise criminally irresponsible parent? There is no easy answer, but we would do well to ponder the manner in which Christ treated the rulers He confronted. Those rulers were for the most part far from honourable. Yet despite their personal moral decrepitude He acknowledged their position. He obeyed all He could. He spoke honestly but temperately in denouncing their sin. He sought their good—as we see in His interview with Pilate. He "witnessed a good confession" (1 Timothy 6:13).

Paul followed His master's example in his appearances before Felix, Festus, and Agrippa. Every child of parents who have not earned much honour should do the same. This is especially true for Christians. Christians above all people glory in grace, unearned favour. We know from experience the power of grace to change us. It can do the same for our unsaved parents. So, while repudiating their wickedness, we respect them in the God-given role of parent. Where we must dissent from them we will be careful to set our behaviour in the light of the higher claim God has upon us. Even as we dissent we will seek to honour our parents in the belief that the grace that saved us can do the same for even the worst of parents.

Third, *the Lord gives us a gracious promise:* "Honour thy father and thy mother: that thy days may be long upon the land which the Lord thy God giveth thee" (Exodus 20:12). In his commentary on Exodus 20, C. J. Ellicott remarks, "The promise may be understood in two quite different senses. (1) It may be taken as guaranteeing national permanence to the people among whom filial respect and obedience is generally practised; or (2) it may be understood in the simpler and more literal sense of a pledge that obedient children shall, as a general rule, receive for their reward the blessing of long life."

Paul terms this fifth commandment "the first commandment with promise" (Ephesians 6:2). *First* here may be better understood as "foremost," that is, the outstanding example of God's attaching a specific promise to a commandment. The world may not set much stock upon honouring parents, but God does—so much so that He promises richly to bless those who do so. Honouring our parents is a major factor in a long and happy life. It produces much happiness in both the short term and the long term. Thus, even self-interest calls us to obey the fifth commandment.

We should have a greater concern than *long* life, however. Having *eternal* life is what really matters. No amount of respect for parents—or of obeying any other law for that matter—will ever merit this life. The honour that yields the fruit of eternal life is that which is directed toward our heavenly Father. And no man can honour Him who does not receive His Son as Saviour and Lord. Jesus said: "Whosoever shall receive me receiveth him that sent me" (Luke 9:48), and "He that despiseth me despiseth him that sent me" (Luke 10:16). Here is our ultimate responsibility to recognize and respect the most fundamental authority of all, God's authority. Honouring parents will ordinarily bring long life and happy results. Honouring the Lord by receiving His Son will invariably produce everlasting life and happiness.

CHAPTER NINETEEN

THE RIGHT TO LIFE
THE SIXTH COMMANDMENT

"Thou shalt not kill."
Exodus 20:13

The sixth commandment sounds absolute. At first sight it appears to be without conditions or exceptions. As it stands it seems to prohibit taking any life of any kind, animal as well as human. Timothy Dwight—born in 1752, the grandson of Jonathan Edwards and certainly no freak of the modern environmentalist lobby—said: "The command which is given us in this text is expressed in the most absolute manner: *Thou shalt not kill.* To *kill* is the thing forbidden; and by the words it is forbidden in all cases whatever. Whenever we kill any living creature, therefore, we are guilty of transgression of this command; unless we are permitted to take away the life in question *by an exception which God himself has made to this rule"* (*Dwight's Theology,* 4.159, emphasis his).

Many have taken Dwight's position. J. Douma, a modern Dutch Calvinist, uses the sixth commandment as a springboard for a strong plea for "environmental stewardship" to prohibit the continued forced extinction of various species of plants and animals. Douma uses the sixth commandment to attack deforestation and overplanting that have made vast tracts of the earth infertile. Similarly, he inveighs heavily against industrialization gone mad, industrialization that cares nothing about death-dealing pollutants as long as the profit line remains strong.

This manner of employing the sixth commandment deserves thoughtful and respectful attention. We would be foolish and unscriptural to advocate a careless disregard for animal life or for environmental sanity.

However, the commandment addresses such matters only in so far as they threaten human lives. It is the taking of human life that is in view in the sixth commandment. *Kill* is the Hebrew word *ratsach* and it is never used of killing animals or plants. Except where it refers to the judicial slaying of one who left the safety of a city of refuge, it always means *to take away a human life unlawfully.* Thus the commandment is, "Thou shalt not unlawfully kill a human being." This understanding of the commandment was endorsed by the Lord Jesus Christ who quoted it as, "Thou shalt do no murder" (Matthew 19:18).

By prohibiting the unlawful taking of human life, the sixth commandment presupposes that there are *lawful* ways of taking human life. The Scriptures mention some.

First, there is *self-defence.* God's law enacted that "If a thief be found breaking up, and be smitten that he die, there shall no blood be shed for him" (Exodus 22:2). However, if the thief gets away from the premises and is caught in daylight there is no ground for killing him: "If the sun be risen upon him, there shall be blood shed for him" (verse 3). Even the life of a criminal is precious.

Second, *capital punishment.* When Noah left the ark after the flood, the Lord enacted the fundamental law of social justice: "Whoso sheddeth man's blood, by man shall his blood be shed: for in the image of God made he man" (Genesis 9:6). There were exceptions. The Lord was careful to mark the difference between criminal murder and involuntary manslaughter. For manslaughter He instituted the cities of refuge. He also instituted the practice of vigorous legal investigation to establish the guilt or innocence of one charged with murder (Numbers 35).

Third, *just wars.* Most wars are unjust. In most cases throughout history nations have been committed to the horrors of war by the political intrigues of unscrupulous leaders. Even where war is just it is something horrible, not something to be glorified. While the exploits of brave men and women may justly be remembered and celebrated we should never forget the words of Robert Hall: "War is nothing but the temporary repeal of all the principles of virtue."

Still, at times war is unavoidable. Abraham (Genesis 14) had to fight the hosts of Chedorlaomer to rescue Lot. At the Lord's command Israel fought Amalek (Exodus 17) in Rephidim. Those were just wars. So is a war of self-defence or a war to defend our allies. Killing the enemy in these cases does not breach the sixth commandment. David was a man of war from his youth *and also* a man after God's own heart (1 Samuel 16:18; Acts 13:22). It was in a centurion that Jesus found the greatest faith in Israel (Matthew 8:10). Cornelius was a centurion, a commander in the Roman army, but God respected his prayers and almsgiving (Acts 10:4).

Obviously the sixth commandment does not refer to such taking of human life as is justified by the Scriptures. The *Shorter Catechism* grasps its proper force. In answering Questions 68 and 69 the *Catechism* says: "The sixth commandment requireth all lawful endeavours to preserve our own life, and the life of others. The sixth commandment forbiddeth the taking away of our own life, or the life of our neighbour unjustly, or whatsoever tendeth thereunto." We may state the full force of the commandment: We should so respect human life that we ensure its protection and preservation by all scriptural means.

Disregard for Human Life

The sixth commandment forbids us to disregard human life and condemns every murderous act or intention against it. There are various ways in which people disregard this divine prohibition.

Homicide

Homicide is the deliberate act of unlawfully slaying another—and here the emphasis must be on God's law, not on the brutal enactments of criminal rulers who cloak the killings they endorse under the cover of evil legislation or executive orders. The word of God absolutely condemns homicide whether by the state, by individuals, or by any other organized group—especially when that group claims to perpetrate its crime in God's name. Historically, the church of Rome has made herself "drunken with the blood of the saints, and with the blood of the martyrs of Jesus" (Revelation 17:6). Her Inquisition slew millions. Her prolonged persecutions slew millions more. The hypocritical incantations of her bishops and priests only served to make Rome's murderous deeds more heinous.

In the twentieth century state-inspired murders claimed more victims than ever before in human history, perhaps more than in all previous centuries combined. Some put the number of victims at 125 million. That is probably a conservative estimate. The Communist government of China approached that number all by itself. The old Soviet Union was not too far behind. Indeed the evil pattern of state killings stained Africa, South America, Europe, and Asia. By the end of the century genocide, ethnic cleansing, and other brands of politically inspired murder were commonplace.

Add to the awful tally of state murders the explosion of terrorist killings. Terrorists driven by political, social, or religious fanaticism sometimes attract the misplaced support of Western idealists, but God's word labels them murderers. No cloak of philosophical or theological apology can shield the vicious activities of gangs of anarchists, communists, Irish Republicans, or Ulster (so-called) Loyalists from the condemnation of the sixth commandment.

Feticide

Feticide means abortion for a reason other than the saving of a mother's life, and it is a national scandal. Since 1973, in the United States alone some thirty to forty million unborn infants have been massacred in their mothers' wombs. To cloak the fact that an abortion is the destruction of a baby, advocates prefer to use the word *fetus*. Thus abortionists depersonalize the child in the womb—it is merely an "unviable fetus." But according to God's word—and modern science agrees—a human fetus is a human baby in the early stages of development.

The Old Testament has no such word as *fetus*. It speaks plainly of the unborn baby as a child, using the very same terms to describe it before its birth as after. In Exodus 21:22–25 we have unequivocal proof that God considers the unborn child as much a person as any other person and accords him the same rights and protection as others: "If men strive, and hurt a woman with child, so that her fruit depart from her [so that she miscarry], and yet no mischief follow [the baby is born alive and well]: he shall be surely punished, according as the woman's husband will lay upon him; and he shall pay as the judges determine. And if any mischief follow [if the baby is delivered dead or injured], then thou shalt give life for life, eye for eye, tooth for tooth, hand for hand, foot for foot, burning for burning, wound for wound, stripe for stripe." From this Scripture we may state unequivocally that God looks on the child in the womb as a real person, to be protected from injury as any other person. The New Testament bears similar witness. At a time when the son of Zacharias and Elisabeth would be written off as a mere fetus by modern abortionists, God's word plainly calls him a baby (Luke 1:41).

The arguments advanced in favour of abortion are empty. "A woman has the right to do as she decides with her own body. She has the right to choose for herself whether she has a baby. She cannot be forced to have children she does not wish to have." These arguments miss the point: A woman has a right to decide not to conceive and it is at that stage she should exercise her control over her body. The argument is not that anyone has the right to force her to have children. It is that she has no right to murder a child she has already conceived. *Murder* is the proper word for abortion on demand. According to the law of God, feticide is the culpable killing of the unborn.

Suicide

Suicide is self-murder. Many who commit suicide do so when they are so mentally unbalanced or deeply depressed that they are incapable of rational or logical thought. Others do so because they are engulfed by a feeling of hopelessness. Acts 16 describes the Philippian jailer on the point of killing himself because he had reached the conclusion that his prisoners had all escaped. In his despair he could see no alternative to killing himself. It was a rash conclusion, as he learned when Paul cried out, "Do thyself no harm: for we are all here" (v. 28). However bleak and black the outlook, there is hope and there is help. But however depressed or despairing people may be, they must seek that hope and that help in obedience to the sixth commandment, "Thou shalt not kill." That includes killing oneself.

Homicide, feticide, and suicide are murder even when they are paraded as "mercy killings." Mercy-killing homicide is called *euthanasia*. Euthanasia is murder and defies the sixth commandment. Mercy-killing feticide may hide under the term *eugenics,* but it is still murder and a breach of the sixth commandment. David Fields, in his book *God's Good Life,* tells the story of a lecturer at a seminar on abortion who confronted some medical students with the following case study: "The father has syphilis; the mother tuberculosis. They have had four children—the first is blind, the second died, the third is deaf and dumb, and the fourth has tuberculosis. Now the mother is expecting her fifth child. She will have an abortion if you advise it. What would you advise?" Overwhelmingly the medical students said they would advise the mother to have an abortion. The lecturer responded, "Congratulations, you have just murdered Beethoven!" One wonders how many Beethovens have been destroyed over the years. But every child slaughtered in the womb is as precious and real a person as Beethoven. And murdering any of them—no matter how weak or deformed—is explicitly condemned by the law of God.

There are other forms of murder: plotting a person's death, as Saul did against David (1 Samuel 18:17); being an accessory to other men's murderous actions, as Saul of Tarsus was at the killing of Stephen (Acts 7); and putting someone in harm's way to prevent our sin from being exposed, as David did when he sent Uriah to the hottest part of the battle (2 Samuel 11–12). In addition we may mention three ways of breaking the sixth commandment that few people recognize.

Hatred

We may kill a person with hateful words and thoughts as well as with swords. This is not to say that a person is as extensively injured by our wicked words or by our desire to kill him as by our actually doing the deed. Human law properly recognizes the difference. But the law of God is far more penetrating and exacting than any human standard. According to the spirituality of the law, hatred is murder in the embryo, but murder nonetheless.

The Bible says, "Whosoever hateth his brother is a murderer: and ye know that no murderer hath eternal life abiding in him" (1 John 3:15). The Lord Jesus Christ warned, "Ye have heard that it was said by them of old time, Thou shalt not kill; and whosoever shall kill shall be in danger of the judgment: but I say unto you, That whosoever is angry with his brother without a cause shall be in danger of the judgment: and whosoever shall say to his brother, Raca, shall be in danger of the council: but whosoever shall say, Thou fool, shall be in danger of hell fire" (Matthew 5:21–22). God regards the hatred that treats a brother with utter contempt as a breach of the sixth commandment.

Reckless Negligence

There is a very far-reaching requirement in Deuteronomy 22:8: "When thou buildest a new house, then thou shalt make a battlement for thy roof, that thou bring not blood upon thine house, if any man fall from thence." The meaning is inescapable: The neglect of obvious safety measures amounts to reckless endangerment of life. Any death resulting from it is not to be dismissed as an unfortunate accident but as an unlawful killing.

Significantly, the Bible singles out the home for attention in this matter. The home should be a place of safety. Such things as dangerous wiring and open medicine cabinets to which inquisitive children may gain access may seem to be examples of mere carelessness. According to Scripture, they are rather examples of recklessness. So is the failure to erect moral barricades in the home to protect children from the constant bombardment of wickedness the world hurls at our homes. For example, parents who use Hollywood to baby-sit their little ones by allowing them almost unrestricted access to television, will answer to God for jeopardizing them just as much as if they had carelessly exposed them to physical harm. Recklessness that leads to death breaks the sixth commandment.

The same standard applies to industry. Companies have no right to disregard human health and life in their quest for ever larger profits. We may have a healthy suspicion of government regulation, but however unwelcome it is and however it eats into profit margins, we should insist that the law of the land reflect the law of God and demand the highest safety standards for both workers and the public.

The nuclear industry furnishes a good example. America had its "almost accident" at Three Mile Island. Russia had its actual disaster at Chernobyl. Given the potential for unimaginable destruction following a nuclear accident, it stands to reason that the safeguard principle of Deuteronomy 22:8 be strictly observed. In other words, not just the extreme left wing anti-nuclear radicals but all who love God's law should be demanding the highest possible standards of safety at nuclear plants and in the disposal of nuclear waste.

The tobacco industry gives us another clear example of industrial responsibility. In the United States individuals and entire states are suing tobacco companies because their products have killed so many smokers. While people who continued to smoke despite all the health warnings put out by the government are as guilty of suicide as the tobacco companies are of killing them, the fact is that the tobacco industry has deliberately continued to deal in death for no other reason than money. It is an industry of death for dollars.

The same is true of the liquor industry. Big business spends big money to present alcohol consumption as a pleasant, stimulating, and very civilized habit. Carefully hidden are the sordid facts that alcohol is a depressant, a poison, and one of the leading causes of death in modern society. Because it would hurt their profits, the beer barons do not want people to know that according to the United States National Highway Traffic Safety Administration, thirty-eight percent of all traffic fatalities are alcohol related; and according to the National Institute of Alcohol Abuse and Alcoholism, almost twenty-five percent of those admitted to general hospitals have alcohol problems. This figure does not appear to include accident victims or others whose admission to hospital is the result of another person's alcohol impairment. When *all* hospital admissions as the result of alcohol are considered, the figure of twenty-five percent rises dramatically. All this dealing in death for the sake of what the Bible calls "filthy lucre" is a reckless defiance of the sixth commandment.

There are many other examples of such reckless negligence. Perhaps the most obvious is the recklessness of many car and truck drivers. Accidents happen, even to the safest of drivers. People make mistakes, even the most careful of people. But the driver who drives under the influence of alcohol or drugs or in flagrant disregard of his own and others' safety cannot hide from the condemnation of the sixth commandment under the cloak of "It was an accident," or "I didn't mean this to happen." Reckless negligence is a crime for which God will hold men responsible.

Deicide

The killing of the Lord Jesus Christ was murder. It was homicide greatly aggravated for He was "God manifest in the flesh" (1 Timothy 3:16). Peter told the Jews, "Ye denied the Holy One and the Just, and desired a murderer to be granted unto you; and killed the Prince of life" (Acts 3:14–15). We can easily agree with that assessment of the crime of killing Christ—though as the gospel records show it may be as truly charged against the Gentile Romans as against the Jews. However, we are not so quick to recognize that the guilt of this crime extends to many more than those who actually condemned and crucified Jesus. In Hebrews 6:6 we learn that repudiaters of Christ "crucify to themselves the Son of God afresh, and put him to an open shame." And Paul warns us that those who eat and drink unworthily at the Lord's Table are "guilty of the body and blood of the Lord" (1 Corinthians 11:27).

The sixth commandment forbids us to disregard human life and condemns every way in which we do so.

Protection and Preservation of Human Life

The sixth commandment calls for the protection and preservation of human life by all lawful means. In most cases this is a plain command and its implementation presents no moral dilemma. However, there are cases of acute difficulty in which our duty to the law of God in this matter of protecting and preserving human life is hard to understand.

Abortion

Abortion advocates often put the case for abortion in the emotive terms that a woman should not be forced to bear a child conceived by rape. As a reason for abortion on demand the argument is a red herring. Very few abortions take place because of a rape. The percentage is minimal. There is an old saying that hard cases make bad laws and certainly it is very bad law to allow wholesale abortion because of the few hard cases of rape victims.

However, where a woman is pregnant because of rape, we must sympathize with her in her very real grief. Nothing in our stand against the abortion industry should give anyone any cause to doubt our honest, heart-felt, Christian love for a woman traumatized by rape. But though we try to understand the feelings of a woman who finds herself with child by a man who criminally assaulted her, we must kindly seek to show her that the advice of the abortionists is bad advice.[1]

Several important facts should be borne in mind. First, by whatever means, she has become a mother. The child is really and truly hers. Nothing any abortion doctor can do will change that. Second, is it by any stretch of the imagination right to kill an innocent child—as truly the victim in this case as the mother herself—because she abhors its father and his actions? Killing the innocent child in her womb for the sin of its father is unjust. Third, the hurt and pain of the rape victim will not be alleviated by the additional burden of knowing that she has killed her child. This is a case where the protection and preservation of human life comes at a high cost, but the law of God surely requires it.

Take another hard case. Should a woman be permitted to abort her baby to save her own life? The Roman Catholic church has always answered, "No," but Protestantism has taken the position that such an abortion is legal and ethical. If indeed doctors must choose between the life of the mother and the life of the baby, Protestant theology allows the woman the same protection every other person has when his life is threatened. It would appear to be simple and scriptural logic that if the mother has no right to kill her child, neither does the child have any inherent right to kill its mother. A surgery to save a pregnant woman's life—as, for example, the removal of a malignant tumor—in the knowledge that the surgery will kill her unborn baby, does not deserve to be described as an abor-

[1] The same understanding and kindness should, of course, be evident in our counselling of a woman who has already had an abortion. Any statement of God's law and its condemnation of the killing of the unborn should be accompanied by an equally clear exposition of the gospel of redeeming grace. Women with deep feelings of guilt as the result of wrong decisions in earlier life need to hear of the love of God in Christ and of the power and reality of justifying grace. The guilt of abortion is intrinsically the same as the guilt of all other sin and the gospel is the message of how God graciously removes guilt by Him "whom God hath set forth to be a propitiation through faith in his blood" (Romans 3:25).

tion. Nor does any other case where a doctor presents a family with the dilemma: "I can save only one life, the mother's or her baby's. You tell me which it is to be." To put the mother's life before the baby's is as much the legitimate protection and preservation of human life as putting the baby's before hers. To accuse grief-stricken women who have to lose their babies to save their own lives of unlawful killing would be not only insensitive but unscriptural.

Euthanasia

Euthanasia is wrong. It flies in the face of the plain and simple meaning of the command of God. But is there not a difference between taking a human life and allowing that life to succumb to natural processes without invasive procedures? Does the principle of protecting and preserving human life mean that we must always employ every possible medical and surgical procedure to stave off inevitable death? These are not easy questions. The more science progresses in its knowledge of the human genome the more delicate ethical questions we will have to face. However, we must never confuse these difficult decisions with the crime of euthanasia. And we must never allow them to obscure the central duty the sixth commandment imposes on us to protect and preserve human life. John Calvin stated that duty very well:

> *Since the Lord has bound the whole human race by a kind of unity, the safety of all ought to be considered as intrusted to each. In general, therefore, all violence and injustice, and every kind of harm from which our neighbour's body suffers, is prohibited. Accordingly, we are faithfully required to do what within us lies to defend the life of our neighbour, to promote whatever tends to his tranquility, to be vigilant in warding off harm, and when danger comes, to assist in removing it. . . . Man is both the image of God and our flesh. Wherefore, if we would not violate the image of God, we must hold the person of man sacred—if we would not divest ourselves of humanity, we must cherish our own flesh.*
>
> (Institutes, book 2, chap. 8, sec. 39)

Spiritual and Eternal Application

The sixth commandment not only forbids us to disregard human life but it also calls on us to protect and preserve human life. In addition, it requires us to acknowledge these truths as much in regard to the next world as to this. The words *life* and *soul* are translations of the same Hebrew and Greek terms. Every crime against the life is a crime against the soul. And every crime against the soul is equally a crime against the life. Life and soul cannot be separated. So if it is murder to take our own or another's life, it is murder to kill our own or another's soul. Indeed, according to the Lord Jesus Christ, the soul is more important: "I say unto you my friends, Be not afraid of them that kill the body, and after that have no more that they can do. But I will forewarn you whom ye shall fear: fear him, which after he hath killed hath power to cast into hell; yea, I say unto you, Fear him" (Luke 12:4–5). To commit ourselves or others to the "second death" (Revelation 20:14) is much more serious than committing them to the first death.

He who by false doctrine, or by evil influence, leads souls to hell is a murderer of the worst sort. Peter speaks of "false prophets" bringing in "damnable heresies," meaning *heresies of perdition* (2 Peter 2:1). False prophets, apostate preachers, perverters of the gospel—however we describe them—are wolves in sheep's clothing (Matthew 7:15). They are the false shepherds of whom the prophet Ezekiel spoke: "When I say unto the wicked, O wicked man, thou shalt surely die; if thou dost not speak to warn the wicked from his way, that wicked man shall die in his iniquity; but his blood will I require at thine hand" (Ezekiel 33:8).

He who lives for sin murders his own soul. "When lust hath conceived, it bringeth forth sin: and sin, when it is finished, bringeth forth death" (James 1:15).

He who rejects the Lord Jesus Christ commits spiritual suicide. This is clear from the words of Paul and Barnabas to the Jews of Antioch in Pisidia: "Paul and Barnabas waxed bold, and said, It was necessary that the word of God should first have been spoken to you: but seeing ye put it from you, and judge yourselves unworthy of everlasting life, lo, we turn to the Gentiles" (Acts 13:46).

God has made a way for dying sinners to obtain eternal life in Christ. Jesus said, "I am the way, the truth, and the life: no man cometh unto the Father, but by me" (John 14:6). Eternal life is to know Him (John 17:3). It is the gift of God through Him (Rom. 6:23). His invitation to sinners to receive this life is clear and sincere: "The Spirit and the bride say, Come. And let him that heareth say, Come. And let him that is athirst come. And whosoever will, let him take the water of life freely" (Revelation 22:17). This *whosoever* includes those who have broken the sixth commandment. David contrived to have Uriah slain, yet he found forgiveness. Saul of Tarsus was an accessory to the murder of Stephen, but God saved and transformed him. What He did for David and Saul He can do for others. That is why Christian workers visit criminals on death row. God can save even them. He can do the same for those guilty of breaking the sixth commandment who have escaped any censure from the state. Abortion doctors may find salvation at the foot of the cross. Women who have destroyed their children in the womb may find complete forgiveness in Christ. His love and power are real and available. His promise is true. He will not cast out any sinner who comes to Him (John 6:37).

The sixth commandment obligates each of us to receive God's gift of life in Christ. Moses said, "I call heaven and earth to record this day against you, that I have set before you life and death, blessing and cursing: therefore choose life, that both thou and thy seed may live" (Deuteronomy 30:19).

Thou shalt not kill. Thus the Lord commands us to do everything scripturally possible to protect and preserve our own and our neighbour's life on earth, and to "lay hold on eternal life" (1 Timothy 6:12, 19) purchased by the Lord Jesus Christ and freely offered in the gospel.

CHAPTER TWENTY

MARRIAGE AND MORALITY
THE SEVENTH COMMANDMENT

"Thou shalt not commit adultery."
Exodus 20:14

Preaching or writing on the seventh commandment presents a problem. It is one that preachers have often expressed. W. S. Plumer described the difficulty as follows:

> *It is both man's crime and misery that he often acquires a habit of thinking lightly of the most weighty and serious things. Such levity is not reconcilable with wisdom towards ourselves, or of duty towards God. . . . It is still worse when we learn so to think and speak of matters of great moment as that the introduction of them is a temptation to impurity of thought. . . . These remarks apply with great force to almost all topics belonging to the seventh commandment. Such is the state of the public mind that it is exceedingly difficult to write or speak on any of them without giving offence to some, or occasion of evil thoughts to others.*
>
> (Law of God, p. 452)

Many Christians feel uncomfortable when preachers address the subject matter of the seventh commandment. Timothy Dwight, the grandson of Jonathan Edwards and president of Yale University, said that in his day (and he was referring to the late eighteenth and early nineteenth centuries) there was a prejudice of long standing against any pulpit treatment of the sins of immorality (Dwight, *Works,* vol. 4, p. 235). The difficulty these preachers felt is all the more acute today. The commandment forces us to deal honestly with the issue of sexual morality. The English language furnishes us with a vocabulary that is both specific and chaste, and that should allow us to deal with the subject honestly yet modestly. Such is the general ignorance of the language, however, that the terms we should be able to use are well nigh meaningless, even to educated people nowadays. To make matters worse, the terms that remain for our use are used so thoughtlessly and immodestly that it is difficult to convey the urgently needed message of the seventh commandment with the delicacy the word of God demands.

Yet the commandment is there. It demands to be considered. It is God's law for all of us and will be profitable to us, despite the difficulties we face in conveying its message forthrightly but without debasement.

Thou shalt not commit adultery. Possibly none of the ten commandments is less intelligible to the people of our generation than this—not only unintelligible but totally unwelcome. It is so unacceptable that living in flagrant defiance of it is a way of life for millions. Even in churches and among professing Christians chastity is becoming a rare jewel indeed. One would think that the printer's error in the 1631 edition of the Authorised Version of the Bible—which made Exodus 20:14 read, "Thou shalt commit adultery"—was what the Bible really taught. The printer who committed the error was fined £300, a huge sum in those days. Nowadays he would be heralded as a friend and champion of our moral anarchists!

Despite the revolution in morals that has debased our society, the seventh commandment is still the word of God. Any breach of it is sin. It is no small matter to break it, for under Israel's theocratic government this commandment, along with the six commandments that precede it, carried the death penalty (Leviticus 19:20). That shows just how seriously the Lord views personal chastity. Perhaps the simplest and most comprehensive summary of *thou shalt not commit adultery* is in Paul's words to Timothy, "Keep thyself pure" (1 Timothy 5:22). That is the meaning and message of the seventh commandment.

The Basis of the Seventh Commandment

The terms of the seventh commandment show us that *it is based on the uniqueness and sanctity of the marriage relationship.* Adultery is the sin of marital infidelity, the physical union of a married person with someone other than his spouse. That is the essence and grossness of the sin: It is a fundamental breach of the marriage relationship. Thus, underlying the seventh commandment is the biblical doctrine of marriage.

There is a clear development in the Ten Commandments. They first deal with our duty to God, to His name, and to His day. They proceed to the subject of the family, dealing with the mutual relations and duties of parents and children. It is often said that the family is the fundamental building block of society. Certainly, the word of God recognizes its importance. But if the home is to be the power for good that God intended it to be there must be some absolute hedge of protection raised around the marriage union. That God has indeed raised such a hedge is the message of the seventh commandment.

Marriage is a divine institution. Tennyson said, "Marriages are made in heaven." While we may well doubt that many marriages are entered upon with any knowledge of divine guidance, we must be clear that the institution is of divine, not human, origin. The Lord Jesus Christ said that it was God who made the first man and the first woman and brought them together in the bonds of the marriage union (Matthew 19:3–6). So close is the marriage bond that by divine decree it takes precedence even over that between parent and child: "For this cause shall a man leave father and mother, and shall cleave to his wife: and they twain shall be one flesh"(Matthew 19:5).

Marriage is not the product of societal evolution. It is not something dreamed up by the wit of man. It is the institution of our Creator and the terms of its enjoyment are established by Him.

Marriage is a solemn covenant witnessed by God Himself. Jurists may argue that marriage is neither more nor less than a civil contract. That is the basis on which the powers that be allow the easy dissolution of the marriage bond, the result being that the parties who enter into the contract may just as easily decide to terminate it. Such reasoning may suit the immoral aims of our self-centred society but it is wrong nonetheless. Marriage is a civil contract, but only in a secondary manner. It is first and foremost a solemn contract witnessed by the Almighty. In Malachi 2:14 we read, "The Lord hath been witness between thee and the wife of thy youth, against whom thou hast dealt treacherously: yet is she thy companion, and the wife of thy covenant." Proverbs 2:16–17 condemns the sin of the "strange woman" because she "forsaketh the guide of her youth, and forgetteth the covenant of her God." This is clearly a reference to a wicked woman, not an errant saint. Indeed the Hebrew word *zur* carries the idea that it is an apostate who is referred to. That establishes a clear truth: Even those who deny God cannot escape the responsibility of treating marriage as a divinely witnessed covenant. When they enter into the rights and privileges of the married state they enter a realm that God has bounded by His solemn laws. He will hold them to His standards for their marriage, not theirs.

Marriage is the union of one man and one woman. Nowadays, under the constant clamour of the homosexual lobby, governments are under pressure to recognize same-sex marriage. The very idea is as lewd as it is ludicrous. Remember that marriage is a *divine* institution. God inaugurated it and He alone may define it. Marriage is what He says it is, not what some society of sexual deviants says it is, or even what a state government says it is. At the beginning, God created one man and one woman and joined them in marriage. That is His definition of marriage. Two men living in a perverted sexual liaison can never be a marriage. Two women changing "the natural use into that which is against nature" (Romans 1:26) are not a marriage. Marriage is the union of a man and a woman.

It is the union of *one* man and *one* woman. That is how it was at the institution of marriage in the garden of Eden: "Therefore shall a man leave his father and his mother, and shall cleave unto his wife: and they shall be one flesh" (Genesis 2:24). Christ quoted this passage in His discussion of marriage in Matthew 19:3–9, indicating that the law of marriage that God established in Eden is perpetual.

We must note the full force of the statement, "they twain shall be one flesh." From this we gather that polygamy is no part of the institution of marriage. Polygamy has scarred the earth for millennia. At times God "winked" at it because a strict visitation of judgment on it would have obliterated man from the earth. But His standard for marriage is one man and one woman. There is a passage in Malachi 2:15 that has caused interpreters great difficulty: "Did not he make [two] one [pair, or flesh]? Yet had he the residue of the spirit [and therefore could have made many wives for Adam]. And wherefore one [pair]? That he might seek a godly seed. Therefore take heed to your spirit, and let none deal treacherously against the wife of his youth."

Marriage is a life-long union. According to the Lord Jesus Christ, a man should *cleave* to his wife. He should cling to her. The meaning is that he should remain faithful to her and tenaciously resist any force that would weaken his marriage bond. God allows for no easy dissolution of marriage. He hates "putting away" (Malachi 2:16). Jesus said, "Whosoever shall put away his wife, except it be for fornication, and shall marry another, committeth adultery: and whoso marrieth her which is put away doth commit adultery" (Matthew 19:9; see also 5:32).

Marriage is a union of personal commitment and enduring love, in which God has made the only lawful provision for the sexual needs and pleasure of men and women, and for the procreation and nurture of children. The Bible says, "Husbands, love your wives, even as Christ also loved the church, and gave himself for it" (Ephesians 5:25). Could there be any higher commitment? Any higher description of marital love and fidelity? The special, selfless, sacrificial, sanctifying love with which Christ loved His church should be the pattern for the love of a husband to his wife.

Likewise, wives should reverence their husbands as the church does Christ (Ephesians 5:33). And they should love them: "Young women [should be taught] to love their husbands [and] to love their children" (Titus 2:4).

It is in this union and commitment of enduring love that God has ordained the enjoyment of physical intimacy between a man and a woman. Proverbs 5:18–19 admonishes, "Let thy fountain [wife] be blessed: and rejoice with the wife of thy youth. Let her be as the loving hind and pleasant roe; let her breasts satisfy thee at all times; and be thou ravished always with her love" (see also Genesis 1:28 and Psalm 127:3–5). The idea that the Bible frowns on physical intimacy and the pleasure of sexual satisfaction is a prudery that is foreign to the word of God. The Scriptures celebrate the pleasures of wedded bliss but insist that marriage is the only place for the lawful satisfaction of sexual desire. Outside of marriage, sexual union is mere lust. "Marriage is honourable in all, and the bed undefiled: but whoremongers and adulterers God will judge" (Hebrews 13:4)

Marriage is the basis of the seventh commandment. "Thou shalt not commit adultery" is a commandment to husbands and wives to maintain marital purity. But it is more.

The Breadth of the Seventh Commandment

The scope of the seventh commandment is aptly set out in the *Shorter Catechism* (Questions 71, 72). The *Catechism* summarizes the implications of the commandment and says that it *requires* the preservation of our own and our neighbour's chastity in heart, speech, and behaviour; and *forbids* all unchaste thoughts, words, and actions.

At first sight this seems to go beyond the seventh commandment. How do we get from a law governing marriage morality to a law of universal chastity? The answers are easy to discover. First, it should be obvious that God does not intend to restrict chastity to married people—that would be to overthrow the very institution He had established and sanctified. Again, it should be obvious that pre-marital unchastity is a threat to the uniqueness and holiness of marriage. Thus the principle of the seventh commandment addresses the subject of *universal* sexual morality. John Calvin shows the full intent of the commandment: "As the law under which man was created was not to lead a life of solitude, but enjoy a help meet for him . . . the Lord made the requisite provision for us in the institution of marriage, which, entered into under his authority, he has sanctioned with his blessing. Hence, it is evident, that any mode of cohabitation different from marriage is cursed in his sight" (*Institutes*, vol. 1, book 2, sec. 41).

Paul makes the same point in 1 Corinthians 7:2, where he shows that marriage allows a physical union, a union that is utterly sinful outside of marriage: "Nevertheless, to avoid fornication [sexual impurity], let every man have his own wife, and let every woman have her own husband." Thus the seventh commandment demands chastity in both the married and the unmarried and utterly disallows all cohabitation outside of marriage. All such sexual activity is sin.

Thus the seventh commandment calls for purity of thought. Unchastity captures the mind before it expresses itself in action. The Lord Jesus said, "Ye have heard that it was said by them of old time, Thou shalt not commit adultery: but I say unto you, That whosoever looketh on a woman to lust after her hath committed adultery with her already in his heart" (Matthew 5:27–28). It is of prime importance, therefore, for us to guard our minds.

Peter commands us, "Wherefore gird up the loins of your mind, be sober, and hope to the end for the grace that is to be brought unto you at the revelation of Jesus Christ; as obedient children, not fashioning yourselves according to the former lusts in your ignorance: but as he which hath called you is holy, so be ye holy in all manner of conversation; because it is written, Be ye holy; for I am holy" (1 Peter 1:13–16). This language describes someone preparing to run an errand or do a service. Peter refers to the long, flowing garments people wore in those days. To make sure they could run freely they would hitch up the skirts under their belt or girdle. The spiritual equivalent to hitching up the skirts is to tie up our thoughts to the gospel. This is how we are to guard and control our minds and how we are then to live in holiness in a wicked world.

Paul made the same point in Philippians 4:8. He said, "Finally, brethren, whatsoever things are true, whatsoever things are honest, whatsoever things are just, whatsoever things are pure, whatsoever things are lovely, whatsoever things are of good report; if there be any virtue, and if there be any praise, think on these things."

The seventh commandment also calls for purity in all that produces thought in ourselves and in others. The world is constantly bombarding our minds. It assaults our eyes and ears in order to captivate our minds. It produces every sort of perverted philosophy to pollute our thinking. Therefore we must be careful what we look at, listen to, and read. The Psalmist said, "I will set no wicked thing before mine eyes" (Psalm 101:3). In Psalm 119:37 there is this prayer: "Turn away mine eyes from beholding vanity; and quicken thou me in thy way." Job said, "I made a covenant with mine eyes; why then should I think upon a maid?" (Job 31:1).

Not only must we be careful what we allow into our minds, we must be equally careful what we cause to enter into the minds of others. In other words, we must take care how we present ourselves to others. The law of God commands purity of thought and thereby prohibits us from saying or doing anything that is calculated to cause others to indulge impure thoughts. It is for good reason that the Scriptures call for modesty of dress. Proverbs 7:10 speaks of the "attire of an harlot." This is a form of dress that brazenly and immodestly proclaims the harlot's desire to excite lustful attention to herself. It is sensual and provocative dress—and it breaks the clear commandment of God.

Sometimes even professing Christians dress immodestly. "Because the daughters of Zion are haughty, and walk with stretched forth necks and wanton eyes, walking and mincing as they go, and making a tinkling with their feet: therefore the Lord will smite with a scab the crown of the head of the daughters of Zion, and the Lord will discover their secret parts" (Isaiah 3:16–17). What a shame it is when the Lord has to speak like this to the daughters of the church and chide them for parading themselves, not as becomes chaste women walking in the sight of God, but as unclean worldlings. Paul's concern for the spiritual chastity of the Corinthians has a very literal application to the moral standards Christians should follow: "I am jealous over you with godly jealousy: for I have espoused you to one husband, that I may present you as a chaste virgin to Christ. But I fear, lest by any means, as the serpent beguiled Eve through his subtilty, so your minds should be corrupted from the simplicity that is in Christ" (2 Corinthians 11:2–3).

Not only should we be careful about our appearance, we should also pay particular attention to our speech. There should be a reserve and a modesty of speech among Christians that seeks to promote moral purity. There is no room among God's people for the blue joke, *double entendre,* and the suggestive smut that all too often masquerade as humour.

This is particularly true of the language of the pulpit. There are times when the subjects of marriage and morality must be dealt with. The word of God deals with them. It does not indulge in Victorian prudery, but neither does it allow the vulgar, immodest explicitness that stirs up passion and lust. Nowhere is the Bible's command to let our speech be seasoned with the salt of grace more relevant than in dealing with matters that by their very nature may produce evil thoughts in those who hear us.

The seventh commandment calls for purity of action. The area of moral purity is one where the principle "touch not, taste not, handle not" must be followed absolutely. Only within marriage does God sanction and bless sexual union. Outside of marriage it is a moral defilement and a curse. Christians' bodies are the temples of the Holy Spirit. They are united to Christ. Thus when Paul wrote to the Corinthians to upbraid them for immorality he argued that they must act as members of Christ: "Know ye not that your bodies are the members of Christ? shall I then take the members of Christ, and make them the members of an harlot? God forbid. What? know ye not that he which is joined to an harlot is one body? for two, saith he, shall be one flesh. But he that is joined unto the Lord is one spirit. Flee fornication. Every sin that a man doeth is without the body; but he that committeth fornication sinneth against his own body. What? know ye not that your body is the temple of the Holy Ghost which is in you, which ye have of God, and ye are not your own? For ye are bought with a price: therefore glorify God in your body, and in your spirit, which are God's" (1 Corinthians 6:15–20).

The Evils Condemned by the Seventh Commandment

The seventh commandment identifies and denounces every threat to the uniqueness, sanctity, and permanence of the marriage bond. The word *marriage* signifies a union of a man and a woman. It comes from the Latin word for husband. Marriage is really the act of becoming or taking a husband. The verb *to marry* was one used by horticulturalists to describe the grafting of a branch into a tree. That is a very clear statement of what marriage is: It is the grafting of one life into another so as to produce a perfect union.

We usually define the union effected by marriage with three terms that reveal its three fundamental aspects.

Marriage is a connubial state. Connubial is from two Latin words, *cum,* "with," and *nubere,* "to veil," or "to marry." It is from this word *nubere* that we get our description of a wedding as *nuptials.* It is an important key to understanding what the marriage union really is. Remember the reference to veiling and consider Abimilech's words to Sarah: "Behold, he [your husband] is to thee a covering of the eyes, unto all that are with thee, and with all other" (Genesis 20:16). Marriage is meant to veil a husband and wife from the eyes, desire, and touch of all others. For a married person to seek the attention, the desire, or the touch of anyone other than his spouse—or to confer them on anyone other than his spouse—falls under the condemnation of the seventh commandment. The marriage service very properly includes the vow of both bride and groom to "keep thee only unto him/her as long as you both shall live."

This prohibits more than adultery and fornication. It also outlaws sodomy, transvestism, bestiality, and erotic fantasy. Nowadays these gross impurities are widely practised and even promoted. Erotic fantasy is encouraged and indeed is the driving force behind multi-billion dollar industries. But it is destructive and wrong. No husband—even if he never touches another woman—is faithful to his wife and to God if he gives himself over to such uncleanness.

Marriage is a conjugal state. Conjugal comes from the Latin words *cum,* "with," and *jungere,* "to unite." As a conjugal state, marriage is the union of a man and a woman as one flesh. This "one flesh" clearly emphasizes the physical union husbands and wives enjoy, but it must not be limited to the physical level. Husbands and wives belong to each other and each is incomplete without the other. They should think of themselves as one in every area of their lives. Even those who maintain a physical intimacy will find that their marriage will weaken if the husband is happy to go his own way apart from his wife or if the wife is happy to live most of her life apart from her husband. Paul addressed this point in 1 Corinthians 7:3–5: "Let the husband render unto the wife due benevolence: and likewise also the wife unto the husband. The wife hath not power of her own body, but the husband: and likewise also the husband hath not power of his own body, but the wife. Defraud ye not one the other, except it be with consent for a time, that ye may give yourselves to fasting and prayer; and come together again, that Satan tempt you not for your incontinency."

Here the apostle denounces uncleanness, not only outside of marriage, but within it. Husbands and wives are to live as one, with a proper regard to the needs and dignity of each other. "Due benevolence" means goodwill or kindness, and covers the entire area of mutual regard and respect. "Neither is the man without the woman, neither the woman without the man, in the Lord" (1 Corinthians 11:11). They are not to use their marriage selfishly. They must not indulge in practices that estrange them from their spouses. The modern mania for erotic materials and the widespread distribution of pornography are constant challenges to the sanctity of marriage. The paid pimps and strumpets of Hollywood and Madison Avenue along with the gutter press outdo each other in their attempts to seduce people from being satisfied with their marriages and spouses. No one should allow himself to be manipulated by such evil people, either into open infidelity or into any form of autoeroticism. It is vicious for anyone to substitute autoeroticism, excited by the moral scum of the world, for a faithful husband or wife. This is a form of selfish indulgence in sin that will tear the heart out of a marriage.

Marriage is a matrimonial state. Matrimonial comes from the Latin word *mater,* "mother" and it points to one of the chief ends of the marriage union, which is the procreation of children. "Did not he make [husband and wife] one? . . . And wherefore one? That he might seek a godly seed" (Malachi 2:15). There may be a true marriage without children. Abraham and Sarai were a legitimately married couple during the long years of their childlessness, as were Elkanah and Hannah, and Zacharias and Elisabeth. Nevertheless, childlessness is an affliction to be borne. Unless there are reasons that can endure the scrutiny of God our judge, it is wrong to enter upon the marriage union with the express intention of refusing to have children. The worldly selfishness that looks on children as an intrusion into the freedom of adults places a marriage under great stress. It often stretches marital fidelity to the breaking point and denies one of the basic purposes for which God instituted marriage.

Since producing a godly seed is a major divine purpose in marriage, many adopt the Roman Catholic position that the procreation of children is the sole justification for conjugal relations. In their view it is sinful for married couples to take any steps to limit the number of children they may have, except by abstention from conjugal relationships. Some make a further exception to allow the rhythm method of birth control that utilizes the "safe period" in the wife's menstrual cycle when it is probable that she will not conceive. This position appears to lack candour, since the intention to avoid conception contravenes the theological assumption that procreation is the sole reason and justification for conjugal relations. This assumption has no basis in Scripture.[1] The quotation of texts that describe the blessings of a large family, or of God's command to Adam to be "fruitful and multiply" (Genesis 1:28) does not address the issue. There is nothing in Scripture that can justify the position that sexual relations between husbands and wives are illicit unless they are with a view to procreation. This is not to say that all steps to limit the size of families are legitimate. Some forms of birth control are clear violations of the law of God. Abortion is the outstanding example, but *the same fundamental objection is valid against all forms of birth control that are not forms of contraception but methods of destroying the products of conception*. The Scriptures say nothing about contraception—the oft-quoted case of Onan in Genesis 38:8–10 addresses the issue of what was later known as Levirate marriage, not of contraception—but it does forbid the unlawful taking of human life. Thus any method of birth control that kills a life already conceived, however early in a pregnancy, is illegal before God.

The matrimonial aspect of marriage raises a problem of a very different kind for childless couples. The progress of medical technology now offers many such people the hope of having children. The Roman Catholic Church frowns on all such efforts, but not on any biblical basis. *Fertility drugs* raise ethical questions for Christians. The risk of multiple births usually means that doctors will "cull" most of the fetuses. Does this amount to abortion? Even some anti-abortion Christian doctors argue that allowing a mother to carry seven or eight babies to term would most likely cause all of them to die and that taking away some of them at a very early stage is a legitimate medical procedure to save the lives of the rest. But is that a decision Christians feel qualified to make?

[1] We are not here discussing the use of the rhythm method of birth control by Christians who exercise their own judgment as to the desirability of procreating but wish to leave room for the Lord to overrule their judgment by giving conception.

In some instances where a husband or wife is infertile, couples have turned to *artificial insemination.* In those cases where her own ovum fertilized by her husband's sperm is employed to overcome a wife's inability to conceive normally—due for example to blocked or diseased fallopian tubes—there is no violation of the sanctity of the marriage union. There may, however, be other ethical considerations similar to those we discussed above. Will the doctors fertilize a number of the wife's ova? What will become of those not used in the insemination? Is destroying them tantamount to abortion, or is abortion possible only where a fetus has been within the mother's womb?

Artificial insemination by donor is an entirely different matter. The use of another man's sperm to impregnate a wife is surely a violation of the sacredness of the marriage union. The fact that the impregnation is the result of a medical procedure rather than by sexual intercourse does not change the fundamental ethic of marriage relations: It is adulterous for a woman to become pregnant by a man other than her husband.

The use of a *surrogate mother* who allows herself to be impregnated with the sperm of the husband of an infertile wife, whether by sexual intercourse or by medical procedure, falls into the same category. A more difficult case is the one where husband and wife are both fertile but where a pregnancy would be fatal to the wife. In such a case, may a couple employ medical technology to fertilize an ovum from the wife with her husband's sperm and allow a surrogate to carry the baby to term? Here the issue of violating the union of husband and wife is not the same as in the case of artificial insemination by *donor*, but there are still ethical concerns. Since she is certainly pregnant with a child not begotten by her husband, is *she* guilty of adultery? The issue of unused fertilized ova again arises, along with other difficult questions: Is a surrogate mother really a mother? Who would really be the mother of the child of such a procedure, the wife whose ovum was fertilized or the surrogate who actually bore the child? There are other practical, social, and legal difficulties that must be faced, but the major consideration for Christian couples must be whether such a procedure is consistent with the word of God. His law is unchanging and every use of modern technology must be according to its moral imperatives. That includes every aspect of the issues raised by the *matrimonial* aspect of marriage.

Divorce

Understanding the three aspects of marriage—as a connubial, conjugal, and matrimonial state—enables us to appreciate why the Lord Jesus condemned any breach of the marriage union as serious sin. "Wherefore they are no more twain, but one flesh. What therefore God hath joined together, let not man put asunder" (Matthew 19:6). Marriage is intended to be the life-long union of a man and a woman: "The woman which hath an husband is bound by the law to her husband so long as he liveth; but if the husband be dead, she is loosed from the law of her husband. So then if, while her husband liveth, she be married to another man, she shall be called an adulteress: but if her husband be dead, she is free from that law; so that she is no adulteress, though she be married to another man" (Romans 7:2–3). In the light of this, one of the most glaring sins that the seventh commandment condemns is the practice of easy divorce. Even though human law allows divorce at the request of one or both marriage partners, God's law condemns it. No individual or church has the right to substitute man's law for God's law. Short of death, the Bible allows only one ground for divorce: *porneia,* translated "fornication" in our Authorised Version. The word signifies gross immoral impurity—which may be adultery, fornication, sodomy, bestiality, trans-sexualism, or other intolerable sexual perversion or activity.

This was the standard that Moses laid down: "When a man hath taken a wife, and married her, and it come to pass that she find no favour in his eyes, *because he hath found some uncleanness in her:* then let him write her a bill of divorcement, and give it in her hand, and send her out of his house. And when she is departed out of his house, she may go and be another man's wife" (Deuteronomy 24:1–2). The Lord Jesus Christ endorsed this standard: "Whosoever shall put away his wife, *saving for the cause of fornication,* causeth her to commit adultery: and whosoever shall marry her that is divorced committeth adultery" (Matthew 5:32). Similarly, in Matthew 19:9 He said, "Whosoever shall put away his wife, *except it be for fornication,* and shall marry another, committeth adultery: and whoso marrieth her which is put away doth commit adultery."

The exceptive clause means exactly what it says: Remarriage after a divorce is adulterous except when the divorce has been caused by fornication. In such a case remarriage is allowable. Paul expounds this standard in 1 Corinthians 7. Christians should not divorce or separate (v. 10), but if they do, they should remain unmarried or be reconciled (v. 11). Paul's main objective is to address the problems of a Christian married to an unbeliever. In those cases where the unbeliever is willing to maintain the marriage, he teaches, "The woman which hath an husband that believeth not, and if he be pleased to dwell with her, let her not leave him" (v. 13). This is an important rule of Christian behaviour. *It is never allowable for a Christian to forsake an unbelieving spouse because he is not a Christian.* Often Christians feel a great loneliness and lack of fellowship because their partners are unsaved. In church they may meet Christians of the opposite sex to whom they feel attracted, and they may be tempted to rationalize that they would be happier and better Christians if they were free to marry them. Paul's inspired command is absolute: She must not leave her husband. No amount of rationalization can change the fact that to do so would be to pursue adultery.

If an unbelieving spouse forsakes a Christian the situation is different: "If the unbelieving depart, let him depart. A brother or a sister is not under bondage in such cases: but God hath called us to peace" (v. 15). *Not under bondage* simply means "free." Free from what? Obviously, from the marriage bond and the restriction imposed by the general rule stated in Romans 7. Desertion as Paul envisaged it was a form of *porneia,* probably because it was with a view to cohabitation with another. The remarriage of the deserted party in such a case is not prohibited as a breach of the seventh commandment.

Desertion of a spouse with a view to cohabitation with another is obviously a gross sin. It is just as great a sin, possibly even greater, in a Christian than in an unbeliever, for a Christian should live to a higher moral standard than the ungodly. The excuses for divorce and remarriage that are so easily accepted among Christians today cannot stand the scrutiny of God's word.

Incompatibility, for example, is a frequently cited reason for divorce. Where people are willing humbly to seek a scriptural solution to such problems, they will find that God can make them compatible. *Unhappiness* is another reason given for divorce. There are usually effective spiritual remedies for unhappy marriages, especially where both spouses are believers. An unhappy marriage is a tragedy, but it is better to be unhappy in a legitimate marriage than happy in an adulterous relationship. When it becomes impossible for a Christian to live any longer with a spouse—for example, because of drunkenness, violence, or insanity—the word of God is clear as to what should be done: "Let not the wife depart from her husband: *but and if she depart, let her remain unmarried, or be reconciled to her husband*: and let not the husband put away his wife" (1 Corinthians 7:10–11). In other words, though there are certainly hard cases in which Christians are deprived of the comforts of marriage through no fault of their own, nothing but gross moral impurity in their spouses provides biblical grounds for divorce and remarriage.

An important truth arises from Moses' legislation in Deuteronomy 24. A woman guilty of uncleanness may be divorced—that is, *the guilty party* in the divorce—and once she is legitimately divorced she is free to marry another without the stigma of adultery. Today there is a lot of well-meant but unscriptural reference to "the innocent party" in a divorce having the sole right to remarry. The fact is that when that innocent party pursues a divorce—or acts upon a divorce obtained by his partner by contracting another marriage—he thereby frees the guilty party to remarry as well.

Another important truth is that a divorced person who marries another cannot ever remarry a former spouse: "If the latter husband hate her [who has been divorced and remarried], and write her a bill of divorcement, and giveth it in her hand, and sendeth her out of his house; or if the latter husband die, which took her to be his wife; her former husband, which sent her away, may not take her again to be his wife, after that she is defiled; for that is abomination before the Lord" (Deuteronomy 24:3–4).

While gross impurity is a breach of the seventh commandment and provides a ground for legitimate divorce, it does not always follow that divorce is either necessary or wise. Repentance, forgiveness, and restoration are possible and usually infinitely preferable and God-honouring than a divorce, however legitimate. But it must be conceded that the moral evils that the seventh commandment condemns are peculiarly vicious and destructive.

The Power to Obey the Seventh Commandment

Immorality is no modern phenomenon. In Old Testament times, Reuben and Bilhah (Genesis 35:22), Judah and Tamar (Genesis 38:13–26), Abraham and Sarai (Genesis 12:11–20; 20:2–7), and David and Bathsheba (2 Samuel 11:1–5) all defiled the sacred beauty of their marriage bonds. In New Testament times, the Corinthian church suffered gross moral lapses, and the urgent calls to purity from the apostles indicate that they were aware of the constant danger that faced their converts (see, for example, Galatians 5:19–21; Ephesians 5:1–5; Colossians 3:5; 1 Thessalonians 4:1–5; Revelation 21:8). Church history attests the widespread plague of impurity that constantly challenged the church's testimony.

In modern society, it is even more difficult for Christians to remain pure. Pornography meets us at almost every turn—whether at work, or at home, in public or in private, in the press, on television, and now on the Internet. Ours is a society obsessed with sexual "freedom," that is, the freedom to flout every biblical standard of decency and morality, and to glory in openly lecherous or provocative behaviour.

Natural heterosexual desires in human beings are God's gifts by creation. They are strong but not wrong, unless they are nurtured and indulged outside of marriage. If they are so indulged, they cause a deep sense of guilt and hurt and leave lasting scars. But there is pardon from impurity. After reciting a list of the most wicked of moral vices, Paul says, "And such were some of you: but ye are washed, but ye are sanctified, but ye are justified in the name of the Lord Jesus, and by the Spirit of our God" (1 Corinthians 6:11). The gospel has not changed: "Come now, and let us reason together, saith the Lord: though your sins be as scarlet, they shall be as white as snow; though they be red like crimson, they shall be as wool" (Isaiah 1:18).

To those thus pardoned God gives the promise of victory over the sins that once dominated: "Sin shall not have dominion over you: for ye are not under the law, but under grace" (Romans 6:14). Paul's confidence was well grounded: "If any man be in Christ, he is a new creature: old things are passed away; behold, all things are become new" (2 Corinthians 5:17). Thus he could lay down the simple rule of victorious Christian living: "Walk in the Spirit, and ye shall not fulfil the lust of the flesh" (Galatians 5:16). In Colossians 3 he makes the same point by commanding God's people to "put on" Christ, or the new man, and to "put off" the old man. This is where Christians obtain the power to be pure. "If the Spirit of him that raised up Jesus from the dead dwell in you, he that raised up Christ from the dead shall also quicken your mortal bodies by his Spirit that dwelleth in you. Therefore, brethren, we are debtors, not to the flesh, to live after the flesh. For if ye live after the flesh, ye shall die: but if ye through the Spirit do mortify the deeds of the body, ye shall live" (Romans 8:11–13).

Victory over impurity comes by setting our thoughts and affections on Christ. In Romans 13:14 Paul says, "Put ye on the Lord Jesus Christ, and make not provision for the flesh, to fulfil the lusts thereof." *Make not provision for the flesh.* When a man claims to desire victory over impurity of thought and action he must be careful about what he watches on television and what he reads or listens to. For a man who has a struggle to remain pure in thought and deed to fill his mind with the impure output of most of the entertainment media is sinful folly. If he makes provision for the flesh he will fulfil its lusts. If he makes no provision for it but feasts his mind on Christ and His gospel he will live in moral purity. "Finally, brethren, whatsoever things are true, whatsoever things are honest, whatsoever things are just, whatsoever things are pure, whatsoever things are lovely, whatsoever things are of good report; if there be any virtue, and if there be any praise, think on these things" (Philippians 4:8).

The seventh commandment is a powerful indictment of the purest of people. It exposes the hidden wickedness of the heart as well as the open wickedness of the life. It crucifies easy self-righteousness and leaves us no place of refuge in ourselves. In doing so, it drives us to the gospel, the gospel leads us to Christ, and Christ enables us to delight in the law of

God after the inward man and to live in obedience to it. Our obedience is not perfect, but our Saviour is. He is able to keep us from falling (Jude 24) as we walk with Him. "If we walk in the light as He is in the light, we have fellowship one with another and the blood of Jesus Christ his Son cleanseth us from all sin" (1 John 1:7). That is the best way to fulfill the command of 1 Timothy 5:22, "Keep thyself pure."

CHAPTER TWENTY-ONE

HONEST WORKS
THE EIGHTH COMMANDMENT

"Thou shalt not steal."
Exodus 20:15

Despite its simplicity and brevity, the eighth commandment opens up an entire volume of biblical ethics. As with the other commandments, what is stated negatively contains a positive law that binds all men's consciences and constitutes the standard of God's judgment of them. This commandment lays down what to many is a revolutionary requirement: All business and all financial matters—as well as all personal attitudes to all earthly possessions—must be regulated by the law of God. Too many people have the idea that religion is for church, that it does not reach the business world because it is altogether *otherworldly,* not *this* worldly. But this is a grave mistake. If a man's religion is not good enough to live by, it is not good enough to die by. So the eighth commandment gets right down to where we live in the trenches of this world's occupations. It speaks to us about property and money and about our attitude toward their acquisition and use and asserts the Lord's sovereign right to regulate both.

No one can doubt that the eighth commandment has to do with the sanctity and safety of our neighbour's property. It has a lot to say about the rights of property and about the just and unjust acquisition of property in this world. But he who sees only a law governing property and commercial matters is blind to the far-reaching applications that the Bible makes of this commandment. The *Larger Catechism* addresses these matters, dealing first with the duties required and then with the sins forbidden by the commandment, "Thou shalt not steal."

> *The duties required in the eighth commandment are, truth, faithfulness, and justice in contracts and commerce between man and man; rendering to every one his due; restitution of goods unlawfully detained, from the right owners thereof; giving and lending freely, according to our abilities, and the necessities of others; moderation of our judgments, wills, and affections concerning our worldly goods; a provident study to get, keep, use, and dispose these things which are necessary and convenient for the sustentation of our nature, and suitable to our condition; a lawful calling, and diligence in it; frugality; avoiding unnecessary lawsuits, and suretyship, or other like engagements; and an endeavour, by all just and lawful means, to procure, preserve, and further the wealth and outward estate of others, as well as our own.*
>
> *The sins forbidden in the eighth commandment, besides the neglect of the duties required, are theft, robbery, manstealing, and receiving anything that is stolen, fraudulent dealing, false weights and measures, removing landmarks, injustice and unfaithfulness in contracts between man and man, or in matters of trust; oppression, extortion, usury, bribery, vexatious lawsuits, unjust inclosures [seizing or appropriating lands unjustly] and depopulations [dispossessing people of their homes for self-aggrandizement]; ingrossing commodities [artificially creating shortages] to enhance price; unlawful callings [illicit occupations], and all other unjust ways of taking or withholding from our neighbour what belongs to him, or enriching ourselves; covetousness, inordinate prizing and affecting [loving] worldly goods; distrustful and distracting cares and studies in getting, keeping, and using them; envying at the prosperity of others; as likewise idleness, prodigality [reckless wastefulness], wasteful gaming; and all other ways whereby we do unduly prejudice our own outward estate, and defrauding ourselves of the due use and comfort of that estate which God hath given us.*
>
> (Questions 141, 142)

These are intimidating lists of duties and sins—all the more so when we consider that on the judgment day the Lord will judge by a stricter standard than even the far-seeing Westminster Divines could imagine! From what we have seen of the scope of the eighth commandment, we recognize that its central theme is one of maintaining honour and honesty in safeguarding our own and others' rights.

The Principles Expounded

This commandment is based on certain clear, scriptural principles. Many texts shed light upon it. For example, "Let no man seek his own, but every man another's wealth" (1 Corinthians 10:24); "Render therefore to all their dues: tribute to whom tribute is due; custom to whom custom; fear to whom fear; honour to whom honour. Owe no man any thing, but to love one another: for he that loveth another hath fulfilled the law" (Romans 13:7–8; This is not a proof text, as some think it is, of the position that a Christian should never borrow. Rather it teaches that we should give to every man what is due to him); "Recompense to no man evil for evil. Provide things honest in the sight of all men" (Romans 12:17). These Scriptures help us to establish the principles that underlie the eighth commandment.

Property Rights

The command, "Thou shalt not steal," rests on a recognition of property rights. It presupposes that what a man justly possesses is his by divine right. The Bible does not teach a universal community of resources, goods, and property. Though liberal churches have espoused this philosophy, it is a communist, not a Christian doctrine, which lacks any biblical support. Scripture records that Abraham purchased property as a burial ground and it remained his by right from that point onward. When Israel entered the Promised Land, the Lord allotted to each tribe its own particular property, insisting that the inheritance of the tribe could never be alienated from it. Within the tribe, He gave each family its allotment and hedged its right of ownership with strong protections (see, for example, Leviticus 25:13, 23–28; Numbers 36:7, 9). When the early Christians in Jerusalem entered into a community of goods, they did so *volun-*

tarily, not under coercion, and they recognized that their brethren had the right to maintain ownership of their own properties. Peter made this clear in announcing God's judgment on Ananias's duplicity: "Whiles it remained, was it not thine own? and after it was sold, was it not in thine own power? why hast thou conceived this thing in thine heart? thou hast not lied unto men, but unto God" (Acts 5:4). Clearly, a man has the God-given right to acquire, use, and dispose of personal property, so long as he does so justly. All the Marxist denials of this not only run contrary to Scripture, but also are destructive of human progress and happiness.

But if anyone thinks that the word of God endorses untrammelled capitalism, he should think again. It does not. The Bible forbade the permanent transfer of land in Israel from one tribe to another. In this way, God ensured that the straitened circumstances of the poor would not open the door for the rich to amass great holdings at their expense. For example, in the event that a poor man had to raise money on his property, the rich could purchase only a temporary lease of it and had to release it to its original owner or to his estate in the year of jubilee (Leviticus 25:26–28). In addition, God commanded employers to pay just wages to their employees and to pay them on time (Deuteronomy 24:14–15; Leviticus 19:13). He also required the rich to provide generously for their poor brethren, lending to them without charging interest and without exacting a pledge of their goods as security (Deuteronomy 15:7–11; Exodus 22:25–26; Leviticus 25:36–37; Deuteronomy 24:10–13). The Lord further enacted that on releasing an indentured servant, an employer must send him away with fitting rewards for his years of service (Deuteronomy 15:12–14). So the Lord gives no support for unrestrained capitalism.

From these passages we can see that the Bible does acknowledge the property rights of men. But it also reminds them that they hold their portion of this earth as God's stewards, and that therefore they are responsible to Him for how they employ the goods and resources He has entrusted to them, "for the earth is the Lord's, and the fulness thereof" (1 Corinthians 10:26, 28).

Personal Rights

The second principle upon which the eighth commandment rests is the recognition of personal rights. "Thou shalt not steal" outlaws all oppression and extortion: "Thou shalt neither vex a stranger, nor oppress him: for ye were strangers in the land of Egypt" (Exodus 22:21); "If thou sell ought unto thy neighbour, or buyest ought of thy neighbour's hand, ye shall not oppress one another" (Leviticus 25:14); "Thou shalt not oppress an hired servant that is poor and needy, whether he be of thy brethren, or of thy strangers that are in thy land within thy gates" (Deuteronomy 24:14). Here the Scriptures address the area of what we call human rights. Human rights are not the gift of human governments or the United Nations. They are not the recent discovery of liberal politicians. They are the endowment of our Creator. He has given all men certain inalienable rights, and no government has the right to curtail or abrogate them. The prohibition of stealing and oppression applies to governments as much as to individuals.

Personal Responsibility

The third great principle upon which the eighth commandment rests is the recognition of personal responsibility. *We have the responsibility to be honest*. *Honesty* comes from a Latin word that has in it the twin ideas of justice and honour. This is what God's law requires of us: to live justly and honourably, according to the standards that it has established. *We have also the responsibility to work*. The *Larger Catechism* rightly emphasized the diligent pursuit of a lawful occupation as part of the duty of fulfilling this commandment. In other words, freeloading is sin. Those who refuse to do honest work and expect to live off the product of other people's labour are thieves. When God says, "Thou shalt not steal," He places upon us the responsibility to do honest work for honest wages. Paul combines the ideas of honesty and work in 1 Thessalonians 4:11–12: "Study to be quiet, and to do your own business, and to work with your own hands, as we commanded you; that ye may walk honestly toward them that are without, and that ye may have lack of nothing." In 2 Thessalonians 3:10 he added, "For even when we were with you, this we commanded you, that if any would not work, neither should he eat." The word of God is eloquent in its demand for the compassionate treatment of the poor, but it gives no comfort to poor people who assume little or no responsibility for their own welfare by refusing honest employment and who make their poverty a right to other people's property. It strikes a balance here between rights and responsibility, and it demands that we do the same.

Spiritual Priorities

A fourth principle underlies the eighth commandment: the recognition of spiritual priorities. Behind every action lies an attitude. When the Bible commands, "Thou shalt not steal," it inculcates a spiritual attitude towards material possessions. In 1 Timothy 6:6–9, Paul clearly defines the proper attitude we should have toward all earthly goods: "Godliness with contentment is great gain. For we brought nothing into this world, and it is certain we can carry nothing out. And having food and raiment let us be therewith content. But they that will be [desire to be] rich fall into temptation and a snare, and into many foolish and hurtful lusts, which drown men in destruction and perdition" (see Proverbs 28:20).

The Prohibition Enacted

The eighth commandment is stated in the form of a prohibition. We must understand the definition of stealing and then proceed to see how extensive is the Bible's prohibition of it. *Stealing is the illegal or unjust appropriation of another's rightful property, or its appropriation without his consent, whether by violence, deceit, or fraud*—always remembering that ultimately it is God's law, not man's, that determines what is legal and what is illegal. That is the standard by which God will judge us. It is possible to remain within human laws on fraud and theft and yet stand condemned by the eighth commandment. Human law tends to come down hard on certain types of stealing, while turning a blind eye to others. Martin Luther denounced the practice—as prevalent today as it was in his lifetime—of the legal system pursuing petty thieves with vigour and rigour, while ignoring the great thieves, the princes and the barons of industry. In Luther's day, the princes, the Pope, and their business partners, raped and pillaged entire countries and kept the populace in grinding poverty, often leaving the common people without food, clothing, or means of providing them. And they did so with the full support of the law. A poor man met with swift retribution for stealing a chicken to feed his family, while his oppressors went unpunished. But according to *God's* law, those rich oppressors, though supported by the legal systems of both church and state, stood condemned as thieves and robbers. We must never forget this important proviso in establishing our definition of stealing as an unjust or illegal appropriation of another's property: It is God's law that establishes what is just or unjust, legal or illegal.

The prohibition, "Thou shalt not steal," extends to every conceivable kind of theft. The Scriptures are careful to lay bare the details of this crime, demonstrating that not only is it a social injustice against our fellow men, but also it is a defiance of the law of the Lord God.

Stealing People

At the head of the list of the ways in which men may break the eighth commandment, the word of God places the crime of stealing people. This is the vilest form of robbery. God regards it as a capital offence: "He that stealeth a man, and selleth him, or if he be found in his hand, he shall surely be put to death" (Exodus 21:16). He labelled it an evil that must be put away from Israel: "If a man be found stealing any of his brethren of the children of Israel, and maketh merchandise of him, or selleth him; then that thief shall die; and thou shalt put evil away from among you" (Deuteronomy 24:7). Theft of property in Israel did not carry the death penalty, but theft of people did. That states God's abhorrence of slave dealing in the plainest terms. The New Testament establishes the same standard. Writing to Timothy, Paul listed representative breaches of many of the commandments and chose this crime as the most remarkable breach of the eighth: "The law [is made] for the lawless and disobedient, for the ungodly and for sinners, for unholy and profane, for murderers of fathers and murderers of mothers, for manslayers, for whoremongers, for them that defile themselves with mankind, for *menstealers*, for liars, for perjured persons, and if there be any other thing that is contrary to sound doctrine" (1 Timothy 1:9–10).

A man's most precious possessions are his own body and soul. If it is illegal to steal his property, how much worse it is to steal his person! The Bible condemns the evil practice of kidnapping men and making them slaves. We sometimes hear about the biblical basis of slavery. It does not exist! Throughout much of history, men have bought and sold their fellow men. Those stolen and sold were treated as the "property" of their "owners." Until fairly modern times this practice enjoyed the support of the laws of "Christian" nations, but it never enjoyed the sanction of God's law. The slave trade was—and where it still exists, is—illegal, immoral, and unchristian. No amount of money could ever make it legitimate.

Attempts to justify slave trading by comparing it to Israel's practice of indentured servitude or to her treatment of the remnants of the Amorite nations God had commanded her to extirpate, are inadmissible. An indentured servant was not a slave. He received wages for his labour (Leviticus 25:40), and his period of service was limited to six years (Deuteronomy 15:12). When he had fulfilled his contract, he went free with a liberal gift from his employer (Deuteronomy 15:13–14). The protections were even stronger for an indentured maidservant, for her entrance into service was on the basis of betrothal, which guaranteed her matrimonial and familial privileges and protections (Exodus 21:7–11). Even the case of the servant who wished to make his indenture permanent offers no support to the defenders of slavery. The decision to remain in service was voluntary and the servant retained substantial legal protections (Exodus 21:5–6). The permanence of his bond to his master did not make him a slave. To argue from this case that God sanctioned the violent removal of human beings from their homeland to be sold as forced labourers to enrich those who stole them and those who bought them is to treat God's word with recklessness.

It is true that God permitted the Israelites to use people from the surrounding nations as slaves (Leviticus 25:44–46). The first instance of such bond service resulted from the Gibeonites' deceiving Joshua into entering a peace pact with them (Joshua 9:3–27). The Gibeonites realized that they were doomed to die along with the other Canaanite nations who occupied the area that the Lord had promised to Israel. Understandably they chose servitude as a better option. Servitude actually spared their lives, for God had sent Israel into Canaan with a commission to slay the nations of the Promised Land for their sin (Deuteronomy 7:1–3, 23–24). None of this furnishes a basis for the evil trade in men that is the hallmark of slavery.

The apostles of Christ confronted the institutionalized slavery of the Roman Empire with the great equalizing message of the gospel. They did not attack it as if they were leading a political pressure group, but by their doctrine and practice—especially their insistence on the central truth of the equality of all believers before God (Galatians 3:26–28)—they laid the groundwork for its ultimate overthrow.[1] Their stand certainly lends no sanction to the practice of stealing and selling people. The sooner all Christians admit that there is no justification for slave trading and that the good men we admire for their contributions to the progress of church and state but who endorsed the evil trade in human beings were utterly misled, the better.

Slavery is Babylonish, that is, antichristian, not Christian. The Bible describes Babylon, the system of antichrist, as the great proponent of slave dealing. Prominent in her trade are "slaves, and souls of men" (Revelation 18:13). The Greek text simply reads "the bodies and souls of men," but our translators quite correctly discerned that any trade in men's bodies and souls is slave trading. Christianity's task is to "make disciples of all men" (Matthew 28:19, Greek), not to make merchandise of them. What the law condemns—in this case, stealing men—the gospel cannot endorse.

Theft of Every Kind

1. *Violent robbery, petty theft, grand larceny.* The Bible condemns theft in every guise. It denounces violent robbery: "They know not to do right, saith the Lord, who store up violence and robbery in their palaces" (Amos 3:10). It condemns everything from petty theft to grand larceny. Business fraud, dishonest pricing, deliberate lateness in settling accounts, and wasting an employer's time but claiming payment for the time wasted, are all forms of theft. Even stealing to eat is sin (though it should be remembered that in Israel, the laws governing harvesting guaranteed that

[1] For a fuller explanation of the apostles' attitude toward slavery see my treatment of Paul's epistle to Philemon in *A Sure Foundation* (Belfast: Ambassador, 1996), 220.

there would be sufficient gleanings for the poor and hungry to take [Leviticus 19:9] and that the hungry had the right to pick and eat [Deuteronomy 23:25]). The wise man says (Proverbs 30:8-9), "Remove far from me vanity and lies: give me neither poverty nor riches; feed me with food convenient for me: lest I be full, and deny thee, and say, Who is the Lord? or lest I be poor, and steal, and take the name of my God in vain."

2. *Benefitting from another's theft.* The Bible also labels benefitting from another's theft as stealing. Receiving stolen goods while knowing them to be stolen, is morally equivalent to performing the robbery. "Whoso is partner with a thief hateth his own soul" (Proverbs 29:24).

3. *Defrauding workers of a just wage.* For employers to defraud workers of a just wage is theft (Leviticus 19:13). Operators of modern sweatshops, and those who employ illegal immigrant workers, not only rob legitimate citizens of gainful employment, but they break God's law. Jeremiah pronounces a woe on all who do so: "Woe unto him that buildeth his house by unrighteousness, and his chambers by wrong; that useth his neighbour's service without wages, and giveth him not for his work" (Jeremiah 22:13). Employees should give a just day's work for their wages, but God's word reserves its strongest denunciation for those who defraud the labourer of his hire. "Behold, the hire of the labourers who have reaped down your fields, which is of you kept back by fraud, crieth: and the cries of them which have reaped are entered into the ears of the Lord of sabaoth [hosts]" (James 5:4).

4. *Social injustice.* The eighth commandment also condemns social injustice. The clearest voice against oppression should be that of the Christian church because the word of God is powerful in its denunciation of it. Regrettably, Bible-believing Christians too often equate the call for social justice with liberal theology and left-wing politics. It is not, or at least it ought not to be, as the following statements of the word of God will make clear:

"I returned, and considered all the oppressions that are done under the sun: and behold the tears of such as were oppressed, and they had no comforter; and on the side of their oppressors there was power; but they had no comforter" (Ecclesiastes 4:1).

"Woe unto them that join house to house, that lay field to field, till there be no place, that they may be placed alone in the midst of the earth!" (Isaiah 5:8).

"Thus saith the Lord . . . I will not turn away the punishment [of Israel]; because they sold the righteous for silver, and the poor for a pair of shoes. . . . Hear this word, ye kine of Bashan, that are in the mountain of Samaria, which oppress the poor, which crush the needy, which say to their masters, Bring, and let us drink. . . . Hear this, O ye that swallow up the needy, even to make the poor of the land to fail" (Amos 2:6; 4:1; 8:4).

"For the oppression of the poor, for the sighing of the needy, now will I arise, saith the Lord; I will set him in safety from him that puffeth at him" (Psalm 12:5).

"I will come near to you to judgment; and I will be a swift witness against the sorcerers, and against the adulterers, and against false swearers, and against those that oppress the hireling in his wages, the widow, and the fatherless, and that turn aside the stranger from his right, and fear not me, saith the Lord of hosts" (Malachi 3:5).

God has a word for all who are guilty of imposing social deprivation on others to enrich themselves: "Is not this the fast that I have chosen? to loose the bands of wickedness, to undo the heavy burdens, and to let the oppressed go free, and that ye break every yoke? (Isaiah 58:6).

5. *Swindling.* Another form of stealing censured by the law is swindling, especially the betrayal of public or private trust. All too often this passes as cleverness, but not with the Lord. "If a man shall deliver unto his neighbour money or stuff to keep, and it be stolen out of the man's house; if the thief be found, let him pay double. If the thief be not found, then the master of the house shall be brought unto the judges, to see whether he have put his hand unto his neighbour's goods" (Exodus 22:7–8).

6. *Usury.* Usury, in the sense of exorbitant interest rates, is another form of stealing that is roundly condemned by the word of God. The Hebrew word for usury carries the idea of *biting.* "Thou shalt not lend upon usury to thy brother; usury of money, usury of victuals, usury of any thing that is lent upon usury" (Deuteronomy 23:19); "He that by usury and unjust gain increaseth his substance, he shall gather it for him that will pity the poor" (Proverbs 28:8); "He that putteth not out his money to

usury, nor taketh reward against the innocent. He that doeth these things shall never be moved" (Psalm 15:5). A surface reading of such texts has led some to the belief that God's law disallows *all* lending or borrowing with interest. However, as John Calvin was careful to point out, these texts speak of lending to the *poor*, not to *investors*. God's law prohibits His people from exacting usury from a poor brother who borrows to sustain life or to supply the necessities of life. It does not prohibit lending at a fair rate of interest to those who borrow to invest to make more money. The Lord Jesus evidently did not repudiate all borrowing and lending with interest (Matthew 25:27); so there is a clear distinction between lawful and unlawful usury. The burden of God's law on the matter is to protect the poor, the weak, and the vulnerable. To this day, these are the people who are most exploited, often having to borrow for the essentials of life at interest rates many times greater than rates available to those better off. Many a "respectable" businessman has climbed to wealth on the backs of the poor. But there is a day of reckoning coming when such moneymongers will be judged by the standard of divine—not human—law, and when their business dealings will stand exposed as naked greed, and they will be condemned as thieves in the sight of God.

7. *Deceptive trade practices.* The word of God pays particular attention to what men often look upon as a "soft crime," namely, deceptive trade practices. Business carried on by lying, deceit, leading people to believe they are buying one thing, or a certain amount of that thing, when in reality they are receiving something else—all these are common examples of such practices. The Bible sets a clear standard for business integrity: "A false balance is abomination to the Lord: but a just weight is his delight" (Proverbs 11:1); "Ye shall do no unrighteousness in judgment, in meteyard, in weight, or in measure" (Leviticus 19:35); "Thou shalt not have in thy bag divers weights, a great and a small [pretending that they weigh the same, using the heavy when you are buying and the light when you are selling]" (Deuteronomy 25:13); "The getting of treasures by a lying tongue is a vanity tossed to and fro of them that seek death" (Proverbs 21:6). The business of deception is theft.

8. *Bribery.* Bribery is another form of theft condemned by the eighth commandment. Bribery perverts justice and honour—and therefore is

inherently dishonest. It robs both the briber and the bribed of integrity, and all interested parties of their dues. Though unjustly directed against Job, the words of Eliphaz strike a note of truth: "Fire shall consume the tabernacles of bribery" (Job 15:34). As with every other form of theft, the gain of bribery is illusory, for God will certainly visit it with burning retribution.

9. *Stealing from God.* Stealing from God is a particularly evil form of theft. Avariciously *turning God's house from a house of prayer into a place of merchandise* is one way of stealing from God (Matthew 21:13). Peter tells us that this is what apostates do when they lead people away from the gospel (2 Peter 2:1–3), and we can see how true is his description of their activities. On every hand we have evidence of it: Once-great churches, built by and for the preaching of the gospel of redeeming grace, have been commandeered by deniers of every fundamental truth of that gospel, and subverted to become instruments of antichrist.

Another form of stealing from God is the *withholding of the tithe* from His work. "Will a man rob God? Yet ye have robbed me. But ye say, Wherein have we robbed thee? In tithes and offerings. Ye are cursed with a curse: for ye have robbed me, even this whole nation" (Malachi 3:8–9). In support of God's work, we should give out of love, cheerfulness, and faith, grateful for all the Lord has given to us and assured that He will meet our needs both now and in the future (Philippians 4:19). But also, we should remember that God has a right to our tithe. That is the basic standard of giving He has established, and to fail to give it is stealing from God. Once again we must remember that we are but stewards, not absolute owners, of all with which He has entrusted us. As with everything else in life, what we do with our money must be for His glory (1 Corinthians 10:31). We can never glorify God by robbing Him.

10. *Fomenting rebellion.* Stealing men's hearts away from lawful authority is the final form of theft we will mention as coming under the censure of the eighth commandment. This was Absalom's crime: "Absalom stole the hearts of the men of Israel" (2 Samuel 15:6), fomenting a spirit first of discontent and then of open rebellion. The same tactics are still in frequent use. Unscrupulous men rise up to steal hearts and install themselves in places of illegitimate power. Such usurpation is sin,

a breach of the fifth and eighth—and usually the sixth and tenth—commandments. Christians can offer no support or comfort to such revolutionaries, even when they do not find much to admire in the government under which they are called to live. Paul, who lived as a Jew and a Christian under the iron rule of imperial Rome, was emphatic about what God requires of a Christian in his relation to the state: "Let every soul be subject unto the higher powers. For there is no power but of God: the powers that be are ordained of God. Whosoever therefore resisteth the power, resisteth the ordinance of God: and they that resist shall receive to themselves damnation. For rulers are not a terror to good works, but to the evil. Wilt thou then not be afraid of the power? do that which is good, and thou shalt have praise of the same" (Romans 13:1–3).

This recognition of the legitimacy of the magistracy is not a blanket endorsement of every self-appointed rebel who succeeds in grasping power. Absalom was not legitimate merely because he was able to drum up enough short-term popular support to exploit a time of weakness in his father's reign and grasp power. As Samuel Rutherford and the leaders of the seventeenth-century Puritan revolution in Britain maintained, legitimate power is derived from God through the people, for their good, and for the establishment and implementation of just laws. In the words of the title of Rutherford's famous book, *Lex Rex,* "Law is King," or "Law Reigns." This principle may be deduced from Paul's words in Romans 13:3, "Rulers are not a terror to good works, but to the evil"—the idea being that *legitimate* rulers use their position against the evil and in support of the good. Defining *good* is, of course, difficult, for governments tend to define goodness as whatever furthers their agenda. Nevertheless, the implementation of just laws, and the mediation of power through the people, are principles of legitimacy that provide substantial protection from governmental abuse of power.

Additionally, some Reformed theologians have been careful to maintain that not only the supreme magistracy in a nation is ordained of God, but each level of the magistracy. Each level of government is subject to the law it is sworn to uphold, and should act as a monitor, or as a part of a system of checks and balances, of the total operation of government. When in the exercise of their legitimate activities, lesser magistrates overthrow repressive rulers, they are not guilty of Absalom's sin, or of breaking God's law. Cromwell and his Roundheads had a just cause to maintain against Charles I's perfidious betrayal of his own people to a foreign power. Whether or not they were justified in executing the king as a traitor divided opinion then and continues to do so today, even among their keenest supporters. But there is no question as to the legitimacy of the government they established. Similarly, when just over a century later the leaders of the American Revolution overthrew George III's tyrannical rule, they were exercising their legitimate authority, and the government they established had every right to be regarded as legitimate.

Obviously this is all very different from the sin of Absalom. His rebellion was *theft,* an unlawful alienation of the affection and loyalty of a people from their lawful rulers. This is not a small sin. Christians should not be political revolutionaries. They should respect legitimate authority and, as much as in them lies, obey it. True, they "ought to obey God rather than men" (Acts 5:29), but they must not become fanatics who steal men's hearts, or who allow fanatics to steal their hearts.

This principle holds good for all areas of legitimate authority. Satan has often destroyed not only nations, but also churches and homes, by the alienation of affection and the undermining of submission to the authorities God has ordained in these spheres. "Thou shalt not steal" the hearts of men by fomenting bitterness or discontent in the church or in the family. If there are legitimate matters of concern, address them in the manner God has ordained in His word, but do not sink to the level of thieves by weakening the love and loyalty Christians should have for their rulers, elders, and parents. That is the standard of the eighth commandment.

To summarize: We are not to steal from the poor (and that is as true of nations as it is of individuals); neither are we to steal from the rich. A poor man stealing from a rich man must not escape the rigour of the law because his victim can afford the loss: "Neither shalt thou countenance a poor man in his cause" (Exodus 23:3). Again, this principle of not stealing from the rich applies to nations as well as to individuals. Communist and socialist state-sponsored schemes to redistribute wealth by confiscation or taxation—as distinct from lawful taxes equitably applied to the entire populace—are forms of theft.

We are not to steal from the state. "Jesus . . . said unto them, Render to Caesar the things that are Caesar's, and to God the things that are God's" (Mark 12:17). Cheating on tax returns, avoiding our legal liability for our portion of the tax burden, and enjoying the benefits of orderly government while failing to pay what we should towards its maintenance, are not merely criminal in the eyes of the law of the land, but in the sight of God. On the other hand, the state is not to steal from its citizens. State lotteries, exorbitant or unjust taxation, and pandering to special interests, are some of the most obvious ways in which it frequently does so. Employees are not to steal from their employers, or employers from their employees. Nor are we to rob God. Finally, we must not steal men's hearts from God-ordained authority. That is the prohibition of the eighth commandment.

The Pattern Exemplified

The eighth commandment exemplifies a pattern of life that puts material possessions in a proper perspective. It calls for a commitment to hard work, honesty, and spiritual priorities. It teaches us that we must obtain our possessions by lawful means, not by theft: "Trust not in oppression, and become not vain in robbery: if riches increase, set not your heart upon them" (Psalm 62:10). It also directs us to set our hearts on something higher and better than possessions: "Wilt thou set thine eyes upon that which is not? for riches certainly make themselves wings; they fly away as an eagle toward heaven" (Proverbs 23:5); "Set your affection on things above, not on things on the earth" (Colossians 3:2).

These are plain commands, but the biblical pattern of the eighth commandment goes even further. The opposite of stealing is not mere honesty, but Christlike generosity. It is a life of *giving*, rather than a fixation on *getting*. Paul shows that this is the true antithesis of stealing: "Let him that stole steal no more: but rather let him labour, working with his hands the thing which is good, that he may have to give to him that needeth" (Ephesians 4:28). Our greatest example of such selfless giving is the Lord Himself (John 3:16; 2 Corinthians 8:9). Having experienced His love and the fulness of His giving, we must be generous in giving to meet the needs of others: "Whoso hath this world's good, and seeth his brother have need, and shutteth up his bowels of compassion from him, how dwelleth the love of God in him?" (1 John 3:17). Giving is the positive grace implied by the prohibition against stealing.

Most of all, the antithesis of stealing is the giving of ourselves to the Lord. "What? know ye not that your body is the temple of the Holy Ghost which is in you, which ye have of God, and ye are not your own? For ye are bought with a price: therefore glorify God in your body, and in your spirit, which are God's" (1 Corinthians 6:19–20). Let us not steal from our Creator, or give either our substance or ourselves grudgingly to Him. Rather, as we look at Him who gave His Son for us, let us give ourselves and our substance cheerfully to Him, as Paul exhorted us, "He which soweth sparingly shall reap also sparingly; and he which soweth bountifully shall reap also bountifully. Every man according as he purposeth in his heart, so let him give; not grudgingly, or of necessity: for God loveth a cheerful giver. And God is able to make all grace abound toward you; that ye, always having all sufficiency in all things, may abound to every good work" (2 Corinthians 9:6–8). This is how to live in joyful, spiritual obedience to the commandment, "Thou shalt not steal."

CHAPTER TWENTY-TWO

HONEST WORDS

THE NINTH COMMANDMENT

"Thou shalt not bear false witness against thy neighbour."
Exodus 20:16

The tongue has incalculable power for both good and for evil. Its potential for good is immense. James said, "Therewith bless we God" (James 3:9). To what nobler use could the tongue of man ever be put than the praise of our God, our Creator, and our Redeemer? Scripture records no more exhilarating scene than that described in the book of the Revelation when the myriads of the redeemed surround the throne of God and of the Lamb, singing praises unto Him who redeemed them with His blood and brought them to glory (Revelation 5:9–14). What an immense potential for good is in the human tongue! On the other hand, its potential for evil is enormous. James went on to say in the very same sentence, "Therewith curse we men, which are made after the similitude of God."

It is significant that God directs two of the Ten Commandments to the use of the tongue: the third governing how we speak of God, and the ninth governing how we speak of men. What is true of the commandments generally, is true of the ninth particularly: He who is careful to attend to his duty toward God will not neglect his duty toward man. The person who shuns taking the Lord's name in vain will be a man of honour and truth; he will also shun bearing false witness against his neighbour.

As with the other commandments, the simple prohibition extends to a great number of sins. The *Larger Catechism* takes almost thirty lines, with Bible proof texts at each step of its statement, to list the duties required, and the sins forbidden, by the simple commandment, "Thou shalt not bear false witness against thy neighbour." Among the required duties, the *Catechism* calls attention to the following: preserving and promoting truth and our neighbor's reputation; standing for the truth; speaking only the truth from the heart; having charitable esteem for our neighbours; discouraging talebearers and slanderers; keeping lawful promises; and studying what is true, honest, and of good report. Among the sins denounced by the ninth commandment, the *Catechism* mentions these: giving false evidence, suborning false witnesses, pleading an evil cause, and handing down unjust sentences; calling evil good and good evil; speaking the truth with evil intention; lying, slandering, backbiting, and detracting; talebearing, whispering, scoffing, and reviling; misconstruing meanings, acts, or intentions; flattering and vain boasting; denying the gifts of God; wilfully overstating small faults and unnecessarily exposing faults; raising or receiving false rumours and reports; refusing to hear a just defence; harbouring evil suspicion; looking on others with scornful contempt; and failing to keep a promise. These and other sins like them fall under the general commandment, "Thou shalt not bear false witness against thy neighbour." We may summarize its message: *The ninth commandment obliges us to be faithful and true witnesses and to use our tongue for the good and not for the hurt of our neighbour.*

A Widespread Sin Condemned

The ninth commandment condemns every aspect of a widespread sin. "Thou shalt not bear false witness." Note the words very carefully. They are couched in legal terms. This commandment is a divine safeguard of the integrity of the legal system. In matters before the courts, every witness must tell the truth. In the juridical process of the Old Testament, witnesses played a vital role. It lay with witnesses to establish guilt or innocence; quite literally, the power of life and death was in their hands: "At the mouth of two witnesses, or three witnesses, shall he that is worthy of death be put to death; but at the mouth of one witness he shall not be put to death" (Deuteronomy 17:6); "One witness shall not rise up against a man for any iniquity, or for any sin, in any sin that he sinneth: at the mouth of two witnesses, or at the mouth of three witnesses, shall the matter be established" (Deuteronomy 19:15). Witnesses were important under Jewish law because much depended on their truthfulness: "Keep thee far from a false matter; and the innocent and righteous slay thou not: for I will not justify the wicked" (Exodus 23:7). Such a command was urgently needed because the potential for abuse in the witness system was substantial.

The word of God recognizes the devastating effects of a *false* witness: "A man that beareth false witness against his neighbour is a maul [war club], and a sword, and a sharp arrow" (Proverbs 25:18). Clubs, swords, and arrows are instruments of war, apt descriptions of those weapons employed by false witnesses against their victims. Jezebel used them against Naboth when, in Ahab's name, she ordered the elders and the judges of Naboth's home town to suborn witnesses who would swear that Naboth had blasphemed God and the king (1 Kings 21:8–12). On the strength of their false witness Naboth was put to death, and Ahab and Jezebel took possession of his property—the reason for the plot in the first place. The lies of the false witnesses were certainly weapons of death. The priests of Israel used these weapons against the Lord Jesus Christ. Failing to find any ground on which they might accuse Him, they stooped to hearing liars—false witnesses—in order to convict him (Matthew 26:59–60). The same scenario was repeated in the accusation of Stephen (Acts 6:13).

False witness was a grave danger. That is why under the law, God commanded Israel to do everything possible to ensure the integrity and the honesty of witnesses. For example, *witnesses in a capital case had to be first in executing judgment* (Deuteronomy 17:7). Many who would lie to secure the destruction of another might baulk at being the one to perform the execution. That was the first safeguard built into the system. The second was even stronger: If shown to be lying, *witnesses exposed themselves to the same punishment they sought to bring on those they accused*. "If a false witness rise up against any man to testify against him that which is wrong; then both the men, between whom the controversy is, shall stand before the Lord, before the priests and the judges, which shall be in those days; and the judges shall make diligent inquisition: and, behold, if the witness be a false witness, and hath testified falsely against his brother;

then shall ye do unto him, as he had thought to have done unto his brother: so shalt thou put the evil away from among you" (Deuteronomy 19:18–19).

Not only did God call for honest witnesses, He also warned *judges* to judge righteously. Jehoshaphat commanded his judges, "Take heed what ye do: for ye judge not for man, but for the Lord, who is with you in the judgment" (2 Chronicles 19:6). Moses expressed the duty of judges even more plainly: "Thou shalt not wrest judgment; thou shalt not respect persons, neither take a gift: for a gift doth blind the eyes of the wise, and pervert the words of the righteous" (Deuteronomy 16:19).

This is the basic meaning of the ninth commandment. It is a divine directive to establish a pure and just judicial system that will be equally accessible to all under its authority. When a nation fails to maintain such a system, it becomes an easy prey to tyranny and to anarchy. This places a great burden on the legal profession. Lawyers are people we love to hate, and lawyers' jokes always abound. But it was God who established lawyers in Israel. Theirs was, and is, a noble task. Tragically, lawyers have all too often prostituted their office for financial or political gain. The prosecutor, or the witness, who presents only those aspects of the facts as he deems will suit his cause—which is no longer the cause of truth and justice, but the cause of obtaining a conviction, rather than the establishment of truth—is a liar, according to the ninth commandment. The defence counsel whose only concern is to have his client acquitted, whatever the cost in the malignant slurs on honest witnesses, or who distorts the truth to free a criminal to prey again on society, will not find the judgment bar of God a place where his specious arguments obtain a hearing. He will be damned as a liar (Revelation 21:8). Not long ago a man with a fifteen-year history of flouting the law against driving while drunk, stood trial for wiping out an innocent family. He was represented by an able lawyer who told the press that his only aim was to get his client off. The facts of the case were indisputable and the best defence would have been to plead guilty. But no, the lawyer assailed every witness, twisted every fact, and did everything possible to have his criminal client set free to kill again. In this case he failed, but he boasted that in the majority of such cases he wins acquittal for his clients. That lawyer is accepted as an honourable member of the bar, a clever man, and an able advocate. But in the eyes of God's law, he is a liar who will not be able to hide behind the cliché he uses to shield himself from press criticism: "My client deserves the best defence I can give him." Lies and perversions of the truth are never a legitimate defence. They are deliberate breaches of the ninth commandment for which God will demand an account.

If this is applicable to the state, it is even more applicable to the church. In the church of Christ the standard of judgment must be truth. Even when the state establishes a different standard, the church must not accept it. The law of God sets its own standards of morality, standards that are radically different from those set up by the state. For example, in the matter of divorce, God's law maintains a strict standard, while the state has moved to ever more liberal standards. In some cases, those who adopt the state's standards stand condemned as adulterers according to the word of God. The church must minister to adulterers, but it must never permit any standard but God's law to define acceptable judgment within the body of Christ.

This is the major thrust of the ninth commandment. It condemns corruption in judicial proceedings. Truth—not opinion, vengeance, envy, or any other personal motive—must be the basis of judgment. *Mercy* may operate, but it can operate only on the basis of *truth*. Where truth is denied, it is not mercy that triumphs, it is total injustice. Once truth is made clear, no man should expect that position, money, influence, or friends will protect him from its just sentence.

But this ninth commandment goes beyond safeguarding the nation's courts of justice. It also governs every relationship of personal life.

Lying

The ninth commandment condemns lying: "Thou shalt not bear false witness." The word of God is strong in its denunciation of lying and liars. God will destroy liars (Psalm 5:6; Revelation 21:8). He commands us to speak the truth with our neighbours (Zechariah 8:16–17; Ephesians 4:25; Colossians 3:9). But what *is* lying? The Hebrew word *sheqer,* "false," used in Exodus 20:16, has the idea of a *lying, deceptive,* or *fraudulent* witness. In the restatement of the Ten Commandments in Deuteronomy 5, the Holy

Spirit substitutes the word *shaw'* (verse 20), meaning "vain," "empty," or "baseless." These terms show us precisely what God means by lying.

- Deliberately representing as true what we know or believe to be untrue, is lying.
- Wilful deception is lying. "Conceiving and uttering from the heart words of falsehood" (Isaiah 59:13) may appear to men to be clever policy, but God's judgment is altogether different: "He that worketh deceit shall not dwell within my house: he that telleth lies shall not tarry in my sight" (Psalm 101:7).

Wilful deception raises questions that moralists have long debated. Is deception ever morally acceptable? For example, must a terminally ill patient always be given *full* details of his condition, even if such knowledge may weaken his will to fight his illness? Does a partial answer to his questions—true as far as it goes, but incomplete—come under the censure of the ninth commandment? Again, is it deceptive and therefore lying to *tell* the truth in the way that does not *convey* the truth? A speaker may do this by employing a vocabulary, a euphemism, or a figure of speech of whose significance the hearer is ignorant. If the speaker is accurate in his expression, is he responsible for his hearer's ignorance of his language? The Lord Jesus Christ is "the truth" (John 14:6) and "the faithful and true witness" (Revelation 3:14). But He deliberately spoke the truth at times *with the intention that His hearers should not understand it:* "He said unto them [the disciples], Unto you it is given to know the mystery of the kingdom of God: but unto them that are without, all these things are done in parables: *that seeing they may see, and not perceive; and hearing they may hear, and not understand; lest at any time they should be converted, and their sins should be forgiven them*" (Mark 4:11–12). However, if we are ever to state the truth in a manner that does not actually convey it to our hearers, we must keep these truths in mind: First, we must have a very good reason for stating the truth in a way that our hearers do not understand. We will consider some possible reasons below, but in everyday life, it is the almost invariable rule that we should state the truth in such a way that there can be no doubt that our hearers actually grasp it.

Second, what we say must be accurate. It is better to refuse to answer than to practise wilful deception. Third, to impart partial information is not necessarily lying, but that information must be truthful. When the Lord commanded Samuel to go and anoint David to be king over Israel, the prophet feared that Saul would hear of his mission and kill him. The Lord's solution to the problem was to supply partial information to Saul and hide the rest from him: "Samuel said, How can I go? if Saul hear it, he will kill me. And the Lord said, Take an heifer with thee, and say, I am come to sacrifice to the Lord" (1 Samuel 16:2). This was precisely, exactly, but not *exhaustively* true.

The white lie is usually an utter misstatement of the truth, often an evasion to save our own or others' feelings. White lies are really black lies, fabrications that have no basis in truth and that corrupt our dealings with our fellow men. The so-called polite lie is another device employed to save face or feelings—for example, when we do not much enjoy the meal provided by a hostess and cloak our true feelings with words that she will interpret positively. Again, politeness demands that we commence a letter, "*Dear So and So,*" even when the person we address is far from dear to us. Are such "polite lies" actual lies? Truth does not demand boorishness or insensitivity, nor does it necessitate the overthrow of polite conventions. In the case of congratulating a hostess for a meal we did not enjoy, the statement that pronounces it *delicious* when we found it distasteful is a plain lie. But it is not a lie to find something good to say about it, for after all, our personal taste in food is not the final standard for deciding its goodness or healthfulness! In the case of addressing people we do not like as *dear,* we should strive to make the expression true, in that we should love even our enemies. Is there a precious soul that should not be dear to a Christian?

Malicious lies are always wicked and wrong. Doeg's implicating Ahimilech in David's flight from Saul, and his claim to have witnessed Ahimilech enquiring of the Lord for David, was a wilfully vicious misrepresentation, stated for the purpose of personal advancement (1 Samuel 22:7–19). Lies for personal advantage are usually of this order, including most *political lies.*

Humour often depends on a false or deceptive statement, or a "tall story," which some have labelled a jocular lie. It is doubtful that a joke, clearly intended to be understood as a joke, should be called a lie of any kind.

Various forms of literary work involve the use of fiction, which some Christians imagine to be intrinsically immoral because it is "untrue." A fiction is not necessarily a lie. When a novelist writes a story that he admits never occurred, does he lie? Not necessarily. After all, our Lord used parables—fictional stories—to teach some of His greatest lessons. So fiction may actually teach great truth. However, when it presumes to set contemporary or historical characters in a non-factual light, it becomes a lie. From this point of view, some writers and Hollywood directors are plain liars. The most glaring examples concern the treatment accorded to the Lord Jesus Christ in productions such as *Jesus Christ Superstar* and *The Last Temptation of Christ*.

We must now consider the ethical difficulties raised by such departures from the truth as the responses of the Egyptian midwives to Pharaoh (Exodus 1:17–20), of Rahab as she hid Joshua's spies from the king of Jericho (Joshua 2:4–6), and of the woman who hid David's allies from Absalom's supporters (2 Samuel 17:19–20). Augustine, Calvin, and many other Christian ethicists have inveighed heavily against these women and all who in similar circumstances would follow their example. Some go even further and condemn those who escape such dilemmas by subterfuge—for example, Hushai, David's friend who used deliberately ambiguous language to escape detection and secure David's victory over Absalom (2 Samuel 16:16–18).

To denounce such stratagems goes beyond Scripture, for God's word does not criticize but pronounces blessings on people like Rahab. It actually praises her faith in hiding the spies (Hebrews 11:31). It is easy for moralists who have never had to face a situation in which not only their own lives, but those of innocent people, depended on their response to the questions of a foe bent on destruction. Where subterfuge can procure the safety of the innocent, it is not culpable but commendable. Athanasius was not sinning when he misled pursuers bent on arresting him for his stand for truth. When they overtook him, they did not recognize him, but asked, "Where is Athanasius?" He replied, "He is not far away; with a little effort you can find him!" They made off, and so did he! The Mennonite Hans Busscher, travelling in a cart with others, was detained by pursuers charged to arrest him. As he saw them approach, he *stood up*, and when they inquired, "Is Hans Busscher *sitting* among you?" he replied, "No," with perfect honesty!

Is such deception reprehensible, as so many moralists assure us? We cannot adopt the position that deception is always sinful. The Lord Himself commanded Joshua to employ military tactics to deceive his enemies (Joshua 8:1–19). What then is the rule to direct us when it is allowable and when it is evil to deceive? The wording of the ninth commandment supplies the answer: "Thou shalt not bear false witness *against thy neighbour*" (Exodus 20:16). Who is my neighbour? The parable of the Good Samaritan teaches that my neighbour is anyone to whom I may do good (Luke 10:29–37). Upon such, it is wicked to practise deception. But to save my neighbour by misleading those who would do him harm is not a sin but a service. Consider two real-life cases from twentieth-century history. During the Second World War, Christians in Holland hid Jews from their Nazi persecutors. When German soldiers came to Christians' homes, they were met with bland but misleading statements, or with all sorts of obstructionist ruses to allow the Jews for whom the soldiers were searching, time to hide more securely. Similarly, in the Warsaw ghetto, Jews trapped by the Nazi army had to resort to every means possible to deceive the sadists who were determined to exterminate them and who did brutally kill many thousands of them. Did those Christians and Jews break the ninth commandment? Were the Nazi occupiers and murderers their neighbours *at that time?* Did the Germans have any right to hear the truth when they asked the whereabouts of any Jews? Would those who gave the desired information not have been collaborators and accessories to murder?

Such questions are apt to become very personal in the violent society in which we live. If we were faced with an intruder whose intention was to rape and murder our wives and daughters, would we be wrong in deceiving him into thinking there were no women in the house? Would we not rather have the moral duty to do all we possibly could to mislead him? We must not lie to our neighbour. We must not, as Abraham and Isaac did, expose others to sin by lying out of fear for our own safety. But there are times when it may be our duty to deceive evil men who have no right to the information they ask of us and whose only use of it will be to do us or others great harm. Such times are similar to wartime, when it is our duty to deceive the enemy. Cases of deception such as we have just been considering, therefore, are not examples of lying at all. To call them "necessary lies" or "pious lies," as many moralists do, is to misrepresent them and to apply to them a standard that the Scriptures do not appear to apply.

Some Christian commentators disagree and maintain that even this deviation from strict truthfulness is in itself an evil—but that when it is the lesser of two evils, it is necessary. Others, such as Augustine, Calvin, Timothy Dwight, and A. W. Pink, abominate any excuse for the so-called necessary lie.

The difference covers only those hard cases that, thankfully, occur only very infrequently. We must not make the hard cases an excuse for lowering our personal standard of strict truthfulness in dealing with our neighbours. We must not lie for money, advantage, comfort, to save face, or for any other self-serving reason. The ninth commandment condemns lying.

Slander

It also condemns slander, for that is another form of lying. The Bible says, "He that uttereth a slander, is a fool"(Proverbs 10:18). Writing to Titus, Paul warned that Christian women should not become false accusers (Titus 2:3). The Greek word he used was *diabolos,* which gives us the English word "devil." The devil is a slanderer, the accuser of the brethren (Revelation 12:10), and false accusation—slander—is a diabolical work. It emanates from Satan, for "no lie is of the truth" (1 John 2:21).

Backbiting

The ninth commandment also condemns backbiting. Psalm 15:1–3 warns us that backbiting destroys fellowship with God. It is a particularly destructive sin. The Hebrew word *ragal* in this passage means to go about as a spy. Proverbs 25:23 uses the Hebrew word *sether,* "secret," to describe the backbiting tongue. That word emphasizes the fact that backbiters operate under cover and love to trade in secrets. In the New Testament the word for backbiting is *katalalia,* "evil speaking." In Romans 1:30, backbiting, or evil speaking, is linked with hating God, boasting, and inventing evil things. What a low, vicious habit backbiting is! Yet it is a widespread sin among God's people. Snoopers, those who love to obtain and spread secret information or who delight secretly to spread defaming stories, fall under the censure of the ninth commandment. This comes as quite a shock to most backbiters, for they typically pride themselves in "being blunt, loving the truth, and telling the truth whether others like it or not." God's description of their sin is altogether different. It is not love of truth that drives a backbiter, but love of self. Backbiters are abominable to God and injurious to the health, happiness, and holiness of the church of Christ, for gossip has no place there. The Bible is very clear about this: "Speak not evil one of another, brethren. He that speaketh evil of his brother, and judgeth his brother, speaketh evil of the law, and judgeth the law: but if thou judge the law, thou art not a doer of the law, but a judge" (James 4:11).

Talebearing

The ninth commandment also condemns talebearing: "Thou shalt not go up and down as a talebearer among thy people" (Leviticus 19:16). We should always beware of a scandalmonger, one who goes about whispering some tidbit of information or gossip. He *goes up and down* like a merchant, and his trade is scandal (the Hebrew *rakîl,* "up and down," comes from *rakal,* "merchant"). He may flatter us with his information today, but he is just as likely to slay our reputation tomorrow. We should be particularly on our guard of the scandalmonger who covers his sin in tones of religious sincerity. Often he will approach us with the pretence of sharing a need for prayer: "I thought you would like to know this about so-and-so, so that you could pray for him." This *whispering,* as the Bible terms it (Romans 1:29), is a great evil. We can almost hear the hiss of the serpent in the sibilants in the Greek word *psithuristes* in this text. If Christians would eschew talebearing, determining neither to be a talebearer nor to give one a hearing, they would do an immense service to God's church: "Where no wood is, there the fire goeth out: so where there is no talebearer, the strife ceaseth" (Proverbs 26:20).

These and other misuses of the tongue—for example, flattery, vain boasting, denigrating others, twisting words—deal with human relations, though the Lord declares them to be breaches of His law and therefore sins against God. But there are other classes of false witnessing that make a direct attack upon the Lord Himself.

Lying in the Lord's Name

The command "Thou shalt not bear false witness" covers not only lying against our neighbour but against our God. Lying in the Lord's name, one of the worst forms of which is false prophecy, is a particularly evil breach of the ninth commandment. In the Old Testament, the Lord exposed it for the vicious lie it is: "The prophets prophesy lies in my name: I sent them not, neither have I commanded them, neither spake unto them: they prophesy unto you a false vision and divination, and a thing of nought, and the deceit of their heart" (Jeremiah 14:14); "They prophesy falsely unto you in my name: I have not sent them, saith the Lord" (Jeremiah 29:9); "Thus saith the Lord God; Woe unto the foolish prophets, that follow their own spirit, and have seen nothing!" (Ezekiel 13:3).

In the New Testament, the Lord Jesus Christ warned against false prophets and prophesied their increase before His second coming: "Beware of false prophets, which come to you in sheep's clothing, but inwardly they are ravening wolves" (Matthew 7:15); "Many false prophets shall rise, and shall deceive many" (Matthew 24:11). Paul (Acts 20: 29–30; 1 Timothy 4:1) and Peter (2 Peter 2:1) continued the warning. John (Revelation 16:13) speaks of *the* false prophet, who by the exercise of supernatural powers will deceive millions.

Deuteronomy 13 describes two ways to identify false prophets. First, there is *the test of fulfilment:* If their prophecies do not come to pass as they said, they are false. Second, there is *the test of orthodoxy:* Any prophet who seeks to lead us away from God as He has revealed Himself in His word, is a false prophet, even if his prophecies come to pass and are attended by miraculous signs. "To the law and to the testimony: if they speak not according to this word, it is because there is no light in them" (Isaiah 8:20). That is the ultimate God-given standard by which every professed prophet must be judged. If Christians today would heed the plain safeguards established by Scripture, they would not be easily led astray, as so many are, by the claims of the false prophets of the so-called end-time restorationist movements, with their claims to the possession of apostolic gifts and supernatural powers. The Bible gives us perfectly straightforward ways of identifying false prophets. In Galatians 1:8–9, for example, we learn that any preacher who fails to preach Paul's gospel—which in context means the gospel of justification on the ground of the imputation of Christ's righteousness, received by faith alone—is accursed. By that standard, what are we to conclude about the plethora of self-styled prophets today who claim all kinds of miraculous powers but who, almost without exception, never preach anything remotely like the Pauline doctrine of justification? We must conclude that they are divinely accursed and are therefore false prophets who lie in God's name.

Lying to God

Unfulfilled vows are lies uttered directly to God. Frequently made under the pressure of extreme need, these vows are often forgotten or neglected. "Be not rash with thy mouth, and let not thine heart be hasty to utter any thing before God: for God is in heaven, and thou upon earth: therefore let thy words be few. . . . When thou vowest a vow unto God, defer not to pay it; for he hath no pleasure in fools: pay that which thou hast vowed. Better is it that thou shouldest not vow, than that thou shouldest vow and not pay" (Ecclesiastes 5:2, 4–5). The Psalmist stated what should be the holy determination of every believer: "I will pay my vows unto the Lord now in the presence of all his people" (Psalm 116:14). This commitment is especially appropriate for those who, having heard the gospel call, have vowed to obey it, and yet have failed to close with Christ. In the parable of the two sons, the Lord Jesus warns against lying to God, especially by promising to heed His call, yet failing to do so: "A certain man had two sons; and he came to the first, and said, Son, go work to day in my vineyard. He answered and said, I will not: but afterward he repented, and went. And he came to the second, and said likewise. And he answered and said, I go, sir: and went not. Whether of them twain did the will of his father? They say unto him, The first. Jesus saith unto them, Verily I say unto you, That the publicans and the harlots go into the kingdom of God before you" (Matthew 21:28–31).

D. L. Moody told of a young man in his meetings who sadly exemplified the sin of lying to God. The young man felt that he could not serve Christ where he worked, and therefore continually put off acknowledging Christ as his personal Saviour. Moody pleaded with him, but he would not come to Christ. Late one night the preacher received a call to go to the young man's home where, according to his physicians, he was dying. Again Mr. Moody pleaded with him to be saved. The young man still would not come, but he said, "If God will raise me from this sick bed, I will receive Christ and will serve Him." God in His mercy did restore the young man to health, but he still did not come to Christ though the preacher exhorted him to fulfil his vow. Some months later Mr. Moody received another call. Late in the night he went to that same home, to the same bedroom, and bent over the same bed. This time the death angel was certainly approaching and would not turn back. Again the evangelist sought to minister the gospel, but to no avail. Then the young man's lips moved and Moody bent low to catch what he said, hoping to hear a cry for mercy. What he actually heard was a miserable lamentation, for as he went out into eternity, the only thing the young man could say was, "The harvest is past, the summer is ended, and I am not saved." Lying to God can have dire consequences. He demands that we keep our solemn word of promise to Him, for He certainly keeps His to us.

The Reality of Truth

The ninth commandment teaches us that truth is objectively real. It is not an abstraction. It is not relative. Truth is absolute. Yet the absoluteness of truth is not found in man, or in mere facts, or in any philosophical interpretation of facts, but in God. The Bible makes this abundantly clear. Four times it speaks of the "God of truth," five times of the "true God," and three times of "the truth of God." As the eternal Word made flesh, the Lord Jesus Christ claimed, "I am the truth" (John 14:6).

Thus, *the more we know of God, the more we know of truth.* God is not the last link in a chain of reasoning about what Cornelius Van Til called "the brute facts" of creation. He is the truth underlying all the facts, the ground upon which they exist and have any meaning at all. He *is* the ultimate truth, and if we are to know anything truly, we must know it in Him in whom "we live, and move, and have our being" (Acts 17:28).

The only way to know God is in the Lord Jesus Christ. Only in Christ is the living and true God revealed to us (John 1:18). Apart from the Son, the Father is not known (Matthew 11:27). Christ defined His entire mission in terms of making His Father known to His elect: "Thou hast given him power over all flesh, that he should give eternal life to as many as thou hast given him. And this is life eternal, that they might know thee the only true God, and Jesus Christ, whom thou hast sent. . . . I have manifested thy name unto the men which thou gavest me out of the world: thine they were, and thou gavest them me; and they have kept thy word. Now they have known that all things whatsoever thou hast given me are of thee. For I have given unto them the words which thou gavest me; and they have received them, and have known surely that I came out from thee, and they have believed that thou didst send me" (John 17:2–3, 6–8).

The only way to know the Lord Jesus Christ is by the written word of God, "the word of the truth of the gospel" (Colossians 1:5). Jesus prayed to His Father, "Sanctify them through thy truth: thy word is truth" (John 17:17). God's word is objectively, eternally, and immutably true. Today it is popular among even conservative theologians to speak of the Bible as "historically conditioned." Usually what they mean is that the Bible *as written* is limited to the historical setting of its time of writing—that is, its expressions are governed by that historical milieu, and therefore we must get underneath the verbal expressions to the enduring theological message, which alone is of continuing authority. But the Bible is not historically *conditioned.* It is historically *mediated,* in that God progressively revealed Himself through actual historical circumstances. Its language necessarily reflects the time of its writing—and is a major proof of its authenticity—but that language continues to be the divinely chosen garb of the gospel revelation. Any interpretation of the biblical message that must disparage, contradict, or set aside the actual words of Scripture is a counterfeit.

Truth is real and is grounded in God, who is revealed in Christ alone, who is revealed in Scripture alone. It is of vital importance for us to grasp this, for we are by nature prone to falsehood and deceit. *The devil is the father of lies and of sinners:* "Ye are of your father the devil, and the lusts of your father ye will do. He . . . abode not in the truth, because there is no truth in him. When he speaketh a lie, he speaketh of his own: for he is a liar, and the father of it" (John 8:44). If God had left us to *find* the truth, He would have abandoned us to eternal darkness. Sinners can never find truth by investigation or by meditation—and especially not in the meditation skills taught by Eastern mystical religions that are so alluring today to many Westerners disillusioned by the crass materialism of modern society. Sinners receive truth by divine revelation, from the Spirit of God opening their hearts to the written word of God. The gospel of Christ is the sole hope of darkened souls. It alone has the word of truth to deliver us from the lie of the devil. Christ is the true light (John 1:9; 8:12), whose witness is true (John 8:14; Revelation 3:14), and whose gospel is truth without error (Colossians 1:5). The Lord Jesus emphasized the power of this truth: "Ye shall know the truth, and the truth shall make you free" (John 8:32). As Peter says of the gospel, "This is the true grace of God" (1 Peter 5:12). All who receive it enter into the experience of which Paul spoke to the Ephesians: "Ye were sometimes darkness, but now are ye light in the Lord" (Ephesians 5:8).

Walking in the Light of Truth

The ninth commandment demands that we walk in the light of truth. Those who know the truth must not leave its light to live again in the darkness of sin or deception. Having reminded the Ephesian Christians that they were now "light in the Lord," Paul immediately commanded them to "walk as children of light" (Ephesians 5:8). This is the duty of all who know the truth. "This then is the message which we have heard of him, and declare unto you, that God is light, and in him is no darkness at all. If we say that we have fellowship with him, and walk in darkness, we lie, and do not the truth: but if we walk in the light, as he is in the light, we have fellowship one with another, and the blood of Jesus Christ his Son cleanseth us from all sin" (1 John 1:5–7). Walking in the light means *walking according to the gospel,* as Paul makes clear in Galatians 2:14 and 20, where he exposes Peter's inconsistent walk as contrary to the gospel and where he shows us that the only way to live the Christian life is by faith in Christ crucified.

Every Christian should covet Hezekiah's testimony: "I have walked before thee in truth and with a perfect heart, and have done that which is good in thy sight" (Isaiah 38:3). The apostle John speaks for the Lord Jesus when He says, "I have no greater joy than to hear that my children walk in truth" (3 John 4). That is how He expects us to fulfil the ninth commandment.

CHAPTER TWENTY-THREE

CONTENT, NOT COVETOUS
THE TENTH COMMANDMENT

"Thou shalt not covet thy neighbour's house, thou shalt not covet thy neighbour's wife, nor his manservant, nor his maidservant, nor his ox, nor his ass, nor any thing that is thy neighbour's."
Exodus 20:17

The beginning and end of the Ten Commandments are strikingly similar. They begin by probing the covert attitude of the heart before proceeding to overt acts of wickedness. After enumerating many acts of sin, they come full circle to make a final search of the heart and its inmost inclinations. They commence by prohibiting *idolatry,* and end by condemning covetousness, "which is idolatry" (Colossians 3:5).

The word *covet* means "to desire" or "to set one's heart upon." It may indicate an innocent or even a righteous desire, as for example, when the Lord Jesus Christ said, "With desire I have desired to eat this passover with you before I suffer" (Luke 22:15). When Paul exhorted the Corinthians to desire the best spiritual gifts, he employed the term *covet* (1 Corinthians 12:31). He used the same language when he spoke of a man's *desiring* the office of a bishop: "This is a true saying, If a man desire [Greek, *oregomai,* 'lust,' or 'covet,' cf. 6:10] the office of a bishop, he desireth [*epithumeo,* 'lusts for'] a good work" (1 Timothy 3:1). Obviously the tenth commandment does not forbid strong desire. The Bible is not a book of stoic or Buddhist philosophy that glories in the removal of desire. In its proper place and rightly directed, strong desire is a very good thing. However, when that desire is directed to what belongs to our neighbour, it is sinful. Thus, this commandment forbids concupiscence, or cupidity, a craving after what God has prohibited. The *Shorter Catechism* comments on what the tenth commandment forbids and requires:

> *The tenth commandment forbiddeth all discontentment with our own estate, envying or grieving at the good of our neighbour, and all inordinate motions and affections to anything that is his.*
>
> *The tenth commandment requireth full contentment with our own condition, with a right and charitable frame of spirit toward our neighbour, and all that is his.*
>
> (Questions 81, 80)

John Calvin, with his usual penetration into the meaning of Scripture, said, "Since the Lord would have the whole soul pervaded with love, any feeling of an adverse nature must be banished from our minds. The sum, therefore, will be, that no thought be permitted to insinuate itself into our minds, and enflame them with a noxious concupiscence tending to our neighbour's loss."

Thus, *the tenth commandment condemns covetousness and commands contentment in loving service to God and our neighbour.* In considering this proposition we will observe that the commandment, "Thou shalt not covet," impresses three important truths upon us.

The Depths of Our Sinfulness

This commandment exposes the depths of our sinfulness. We have to wonder why the Lord included it among the Ten Commandments. After all, if we understand it to mean, "Thou shalt not look with desire upon thy neighbour's wife," isn't that covered in the seventh commandment? According to the Lord Jesus it is, for He said, "Whosoever looketh on a woman to lust after her hath committed adultery with her already in his heart" (Matthew 5:28). If we understand the tenth commandment to say, "Thou shalt not set thy heart upon thy neighbour's possessions," isn't that covered by the eighth commandment? Surely if the *intent* to commit adultery is adultery, then the *intent* to commit theft is theft. So, why does the Lord apparently repeat what He has legislated in prior commandments? Why does He choose this as the consummation of "The Ten Words" (Deuteronomy 4:13; 10:4, Hebrew) in which He summarized all His law?

There are very good reasons for His doing so. First, we need to have the lesson repeated that spiritual obedience does not consist merely in outward observances, but in heart holiness. Second, this commandment is more than mere repetition; it carries the teaching of those earlier commandments a stage further. Desire may or may not lead to action. The seventh and eighth commandments condemn desires that plan, produce, and lie behind the actual commission of sin. The tenth commandment teaches that even when evil desire does not produce action, or even a fantasy of action, the very desire is sin. In other words, as *The Marrow of Modern Divinity* says, it not only *commands the binding* of lust, it *forbids the being* of lust. "Thou shalt not inwardly think on, nor long after, that which belongs to another, though it be without consent of will, or purpose of heart to seek after it" (*Marrow,* p. 312). That is, though we do not actually choose it or make any real plan to seek after it, we should not dwell upon, or long for, anything forbidden to us by God's law.

The tenth commandment, therefore, sets the standard by which the Lord judges the true state of our obedience to His law. He is unimpressed by our observance of mere outward forms, but examines the state of our minds and wills. This is a devastating discovery for any man to make. It kills our innate pride and self-righteousness and makes us see how vile and wicked we really are in the sight of a holy God. This was Paul's experience. As a good Pharisee he had thought himself righteous. "Touching the righteousness which is in the law," that is, judging himself by the strict observance of all the standards of behaviour that the Pharisees understood the law to demand, he was "blameless" (Philippians 3:6). But then something happened to shatter the illusion: "The law came." By that he means that God began to apply to his conscience the spiritual fulness of His law. Paul came to understand its real meaning. He testified, "I had not known sin, but by the law: for I had not known lust, except the law had said, Thou shalt not covet" (Romans 7:7). Dr. Martyn Lloyd-Jones understood Paul to be saying two things by these words: First, "I would not have known that lust was sin, in and of itself, if the law had not taught me so"; second, "I would never have understood . . . the meaning of lust, and the part it plays in a man's life, were it not that the law had said, *Thou shalt not covet.*" Dr. Lloyd-Jones significantly added, "In other words, the law not only brought Paul to see that to lust was to sin, it had brought him to see the terrible power of lust in his own life." The tenth commandment stripped away Paul's Pharisaic self-righteousness, and made him look beyond the surface of his actions to examine his secret thoughts, feelings, and desires.

The Bible teaches, "The thought of foolishness is sin" (Proverbs 24:9). We may translate *thought* as "lewd or wicked thought." In a society that bombards us with images calculated to stir impure thought and desire, it is easy to excuse or accept such things as normal. Immoral thought may titillate. The hidden desire for what is another's, or for what may be ours by evil means, may seem like harmless dreaming, but God calls it *sin.* He terms it idolatry and links it with heinous wickedness: "Know ye not that the unrighteous shall not inherit the kingdom of God? Be not deceived: neither fornicators, nor idolaters, nor adulterers, nor effeminate, nor abusers of themselves with mankind [homosexuals], nor thieves, *nor covetous,* nor drunkards, nor revilers, nor extortioners, shall inherit the kingdom of God" (1 Corinthians 6:9–10). This states God's view of the wickedness of covetousness in the clearest possible terms. It is a great sin.

Where is the person who does not stand indicted as a foul and guilty sinner when judged by God's standard? The tenth commandment reveals the dismal depths of our sinful state. Even when we try to clean up our behavior, we are unclean. Charles Wesley felt this when he penned the couplet in his famous hymn "Jesus, Lover of My Soul": "Vile and full of sin, I am, Thou art full of grace and truth." The law drags out every motion of the soul from the dark places of hidden lust and holds it up to the light of the holiness of God. To use the expression of Genesis 6:5, "God [sees] . . . that every imagination of the thoughts of his heart [is] only evil continually" (Genesis 6:5). *Every imagination* of the thoughts of the heart of man *is evil continually.* Such is the depth of our depravity and sinfulness. That depravity corrupts our very being. It pollutes everything we say and do. It scars every relationship we have on earth. It desecrates even our holiest attempts to worship God. It bars the road to heaven. And it fits us, body and soul, for hell. Douma quotes a seventeenth-century Dutch theologian who states the case with heart-searching clarity: "If we measure by the outside, the Pharisee looks like a saint; if we survey from the inside, the best of saints is worthy of hell" (*The Law,* p. 350).

The Extent of Our Duty

In exposing our depravity, the tenth commandment does not lessen our responsibility but rather emphasizes the extent of our duty. When it says, "Thou shalt not covet anything that is thy neighbour's," it lays down some far-reaching rules of conduct.

First, it *commands us to bring every thought and every affection under the control of the word of God*. We must not indulge even the *thought* of sin. When that thought comes into the mind (this is the crucial stage where we lose many a battle), do not nurse that thought into a desire. That desire may or may not lead to wicked action, but it is still corrupting. Worldly psychologists see little or no danger in such secret desires. Some of them even applaud the "liberating" results of an interest in pornography. But the word of God says, "Thou shalt not covet."

Second, the tenth commandment *calls on us to learn Christian contentment in the enjoyment of all that God has given His people in Christ*. He has "blessed us with all spiritual blessings in heavenly places in Christ" (Ephesians 1:3). He has "given unto us all things that pertain unto life and godliness" (2 Peter 1:3). He has promised to meet our daily needs. Jesus said, "Seek ye first the kingdom of God, and his righteousness; and all these things shall be added unto you" (Matthew 6:33). Paul therefore could state with confidence, "My God shall supply all your need according to his riches in glory by Christ Jesus" (Philippians 4:19). Christians should therefore "rejoice in the Lord alway" (Philippians 4:4), for in Christ we have all that we need for life and happiness, both in this world and in the world to come. "Godliness with contentment is great gain (1 Timothy 6:6); therefore, "Let your conversation be without covetousness; and be content with such things as ye have: for he hath said, I will never leave thee, nor forsake thee" (Hebrews 13:5).

Third, "Thou shalt not covet" *instructs us to love and serve the Lord from the heart.* It emphasizes the importance of heart obedience. It calls us not only to avoid evil and to do good, but to do so from the heart. *Saving faith* is marked by heart obedience: "God be thanked, that ye were the servants of sin, but ye have obeyed from the heart that form of doctrine which was delivered you" (Romans 6:17). *Serving faith* has the same mark: "As the servants of Christ, [do] the will of God from the heart" (Ephesians 6:6); "Whatsoever ye do, do it heartily, as to the Lord, and not unto men" (Colossians 3:23).

Fourth, the tenth commandment *requires us not to envy others in their possessions.* Envy is the absolute denial of Christian love, for "charity envieth not" (1 Corinthians 13:4). It is a work of the flesh (Galatians 5:21), and a particularly rotten one: "Envy [is] the rottenness of the bones" (Proverbs 14:30). It produces an evil brood of confusion and corruption: "Where envying and strife is, there is confusion and every evil work" (James 3:16). In the light of all this, our duty is evident: "Let us not be desirous of vain glory, provoking one another, envying one another" (Galatians 5:26).

Fifth, the tenth commandment *commands us to be careful, especially in our attitude to money.* There is no crime in being rich if our riches are lawfully acquired—though they may bring trials, for there are few people to whom God can entrust great wealth. But there is a crime in being consumed with a passion to become rich. "They that will be rich fall into temptation and a snare, and into many foolish and hurtful lusts, which drown men in destruction and perdition. For the love of money is the root of all evil: which while some coveted after, they have erred from the faith, and pierced themselves through with many sorrows" (1 Timothy 6:9–10). So, *thou shalt not covet* teaches us not to become greedy. "He that is greedy of gain troubleth his own house" (Proverbs 15:27). And it lays upon us the absolute duty to refuse to entertain the thought of gaining anything in any way that is hurtful to others or to our fellowship with God. Gain motivated by covetousness attacks both God and man. Achan's coveting and stealing what he saw in the conquered city of Jericho (Joshua 7), and Ahab's lusting after and laying hold of Naboth's vineyard (1 Kings 21) are two outstanding examples of men making great material gain to their own spiritual detriment and to the hurt of their fellow men. This is what makes gambling so wrong. As we saw in studying the third commandment, gambling is a blasphemous presumption upon the providence of God. Here in the tenth commandment, we see its roots in idolatrous covetousness and in utter disregard for other people. No man can hope to win in gambling without hurt to his neighbour. The law of God, therefore, condemns gambling. Woe to the man who tramples on God's law for this evil gain! Woe to the state that makes gambling a part of its official policy! Politicians may claim that state lotteries provide funds for education and a host of other good causes, but the truth is that they prey upon the poorest, neediest, and most vulnerable members of society. Any gain that hurts others and is spiritually detrimental to the one making the gain is a breach of the tenth commandment.

Sixth, the tenth commandment *implies that we should avoid responding to any form of manipulation aimed at making us desire things that we cannot afford*. The advertising industry exercises its immense power and virtually unlimited resources to ensnare the weak and unwary. It employs great artistic skill and an understanding of psychological techniques to induce millions of people, including Christians, to satisfy cravings they cannot afford, for things they do not need, with money they do not have. Their debt becomes a millstone about their necks, a detriment to them, and an insult to God for it plainly states their rejection of His level of provision for them. It is a wilful breach of God's law. The tenth commandment is not the instrument of a killjoy, but the shield of a loving Father. In the matter of borrowing, buying, desiring, and getting, we ought to obey God rather than men by avoiding the manipulations of slick advertisers who prey upon the innate lust and covetousness of the human heart.

Seventh, the commandment "Thou shalt not covet" emphasizes the superior importance of spiritual consideration over material, for it *teaches us not to allow the love of the things of this life to blind us to the greater need of being rich toward God.* Jesus said, "Take heed, and beware of covetousness: for a man's life consisteth not in the abundance of the things which he possesseth" (Luke 12:15). The Lord employed this warning as the text for His parable of the rich fool who gloried in his possessions and planned a long life of enjoying them, without thought for God or for eternity. Just as he talked to himself about having many years to enjoy his riches, God said, "Thou fool, this night thy soul shall be required of thee: then whose shall those things be, which thou hast provided?" (Luke 12:20). These are solemn words and they press some searching questions upon us. Amid all our efforts for material acquisitions, have we forgotten to lay hold of the "true riches" (Luke 16:11) that are in Christ? If God called us into eternity today, what wealth would we have to take with us? A good way to evaluate the *things* of earth is to use them in the constant realization that *this night* God could summon us to leave them all. We greatly abuse material possessions if we concentrate on them to such an extent that we neglect making sure that we are rich toward God—that is, that we have personally received by faith the benefits of Christ's coming into the world to save sinners (2 Corinthians 8:9) and that we are living for His kingdom and laying up treasure in heaven.

The Perfection of Our Saviour

The tenth commandment brings us full circle. It is addressed to the heart. In effect, it is a call to observe the two great fundamental commandments of the law—to love the Lord with all our hearts and to love our neighbour as ourselves. Dr. Ian Paisley well remarked in his commentary on Romans, "As love is the fulfilment of the whole law, so lust is the violation of the whole law." Here then is our double condemnation. The law exposes our depravity and is inexorable in emphasizing our duty. Can it do anything but condemn us? It can, because it points us to one who has perfectly fulfilled its highest standard as our Saviour and covenant representative. Every beam of divine glory from Sinai that exposes our sin and depravity reveals just how utterly different the Lord Jesus Christ is from all other men. In other words, the tenth commandment compels us to consider the perfection of the Saviour.

At the commencement of this study we noted the *inwardness* of this commandment. It legislates not only action but attitude; not only conduct but character. In Christ it finds its perfect fulfilment. He not only "did no sin" (1 Peter 2:22) and "knew no sin" (2 Corinthians 5:21), but "in him is no sin" (1 John 3:5). He said, "The prince of this world cometh, and hath nothing in me" (John 14:30). That is a glorious statement of the impeccable sinlessness of our Saviour. When the devil comes to any other man, he finds lust in his nature, something on which he can take hold and which he can use to tempt him into sinful action. But when he approached our Lord Jesus Christ he found that there was no innate depravity, no inbred lust, nothing on which he could fasten. Our temptations proceed from the outside *and* the inside. Christ's temptations were just as real as ours, but they proceeded from the outside alone, for the prince of this world had *nothing in Him.* "For we have not an high priest which cannot be touched with the feeling of our infirmities; but was in all points tempted like as we are, yet without sin" (Hebrews 4:15). *Yet without sin* in the Greek text is simply "apart from sin" or "sinlessly." Christ can stand in the fullest glare of the light of the law of God, endure its strictest probings into his innermost soul, and still hear His Holy Father say, "This is my beloved Son, in whom I am well pleased." No unworthy or impure thought, no selfish motive, ever found a place in the soul of Christ. His holiness of soul was absolutely perfect. His obedience to God's law was not only external, but internal. He could say with absolute honesty, "I delight to do thy will, O my God." He perfectly satisfied every precept of the law. He embodied every perfection the law ever envisaged. That is what gives such beauty to His example and such value to His sacrifice. And that is what makes the truth of His imputed righteousness so glorious. Because of Him, the law declares utterly depraved sinners guiltless by faith in Him. "For he [God] hath made him [Christ] to be sin for us, who knew no sin; that we might be made the righteousness of God in him" (2 Corinthians 5:21). It is on that basis that we can make Paul's triumphant statement in Romans 8:1 our own: "There is therefore now no condemnation to them which are in Christ Jesus" (Romans 8:1).

The righteousness of Christ is the procuring cause of our justification; that is, it merits justification for us. And the Christ who justifies us also gives us power to obey the law from the heart. Acts 15:9 speaks of hearts "purified by faith." The object of that faith is Christ, so that ultimately the tenth commandment—indeed, the entire law—calls us to Christ. It shuts us up to grace for salvation in all its parts. When God says, "Thou shalt not covet," He exposes our depravity, expresses our duty, and points us to our only Deliverer. He calls us to confess our innate depravity, to trust in Christ's perfect righteousness for our acceptance with Him, and then to set our affections on things above and not on things on the earth (Colossians 3:2). Thus shall we love God and our neighbour and so fulfil the whole law.

POSTSCRIPT
THE LAW, THE CROSS, AND THE CHRISTIAN

At Mount Sinai we have looked upon the chariots of God's majesty—His law and commandments written on tables of stone. At Mount Calvary we have seen that law fulfilled and satisfied by the Lord Jesus Christ in His obedience unto death. Perhaps the simplest way to explain the relationship of the law to the cross and the Christian is to visit another mount where, at God's command, His law was written on stones. In Joshua 8:30–35 we read of a very significant event that took place immediately after the battles of Jericho and Ai: "Then Joshua built an altar unto the Lord God of Israel in mount Ebal, as Moses the servant of the Lord commanded the children of Israel, as it is written in the book of the law of Moses, an altar of whole stones, over which no man hath lift up any iron: and they offered thereon burnt offerings unto the Lord, and sacrificed peace offerings. And he wrote there upon the stones a copy of the law of Moses, which he wrote in the presence of the children of Israel. And all Israel, and their elders, and officers, and their judges, stood on this side the ark and on that side before the priests the Levites, which bare the ark of the covenant of the Lord, as well the stranger, as he that was born among them; half of them over against mount Gerizim, and half of them over against mount Ebal; as Moses the servant of the Lord had commanded before, that they should bless the people of Israel. And afterward he read all the words of the law, the blessings and cursings, according to all that is written in the book of the law. There was not a word of all that Moses commanded, which Joshua read not before all the congregation of Israel, with the women, and the little ones, and the strangers that were conversant among them."

The significance of this passage for Christians is not difficult to grasp. Ebal and Gerizim stood within Canaan, not far from Shechem. According to the Lord's command to Moses (Deuteronomy 27:12–13), half of the tribes of Israel were to stand on Mount Gerizim and cry "Amen" at the reading of each blessing that the law pronounced on obedience to God, and half were to stand on Mount Ebal and cry "Amen" at the reading of each curse of the law on disobedience to God. On Mount Ebal, the mount of the curse, Joshua raised his altar upon which no tool of man was employed. On that altar he wrote the Ten Commandments and offered sacrifices of atonement. Then he read the law with its blessings and its cursings in the ears of all the people.

This story is more than history. It is prophecy veiled under typology. The New Testament records the fulfilment of the types depicted in Deuteronomy in the death of the Lord Jesus Christ. Our greater Joshua—the Hebrew form of the Greek *Jesus*—raised a greater altar on another mount, Calvary, where the law was powerfully operative and where God fully expressed His curse on sin.

The Cross, God's Answer to the Curse

The breach of God's law brought a curse (Galatians 3:10). No attempted obedience by sinners could ever remove that curse, but the gospel is that Christ raised His cross on the ground of the curse of the broken law to procure God's blessing for His people. By bearing its curse, He removed that curse and redeemed His people from it: "Christ hath redeemed us from the curse of the law, being made a curse for us: for it is written, Cursed is every one that hangeth on a tree" (Galatians 3:13). Henceforth, the curse of the *broken* law is replaced by the blessings of the *fulfilled* law for all who are covered by Christ's atonement.

The Law, the Cross, and Justification

The law written on Joshua's altar provides a dramatic illustration of a glorious theological truth: The cross of Christ meets every demand of God's law, and thereby procures the justification of His believing people. The cross *magnifies* the righteousness of the law. It does not offer salvation by avoiding, evading, abrogating, or otherwise destroying the law

(Matthew 5:17). The cross also *satisfies* the law, for the death of Christ was a penal satisfaction for sin (1 Corinthians 15:3; 2 Corinthians 5:21). The great message of Hebrews 9 is that the offerings of the Old Testament sufficed to purify the worshippers from ceremonial defilement and give them entrance into the earthly tabernacle, but they could not remove moral guilt and corruption. Only the death of Christ, the fulfilment of the Old Testament's typical sacrifices, could do that. Hebrews 9:19–20 mentions a significant detail: Moses "sprinkled both the book, and all the people" with the blood of sacrifice, saying, "This is the blood of the covenant." What a rich type of the death of Christ! What Moses did pointed forward to the day when Christ would shed His own precious blood and thereby confirm the covenant of grace for all His people by entirely satisfying the book of the covenant of the law. Having magnified and satisfied the law, the cross of Christ *justifies believers according to the righteousness of the law* (Romans 5:17–19; 8:1).

The Law, the Cross, and Sanctification

The scene in Joshua 8 reveals that God's people—redeemed by Christ's blood from the curse of the broken law and justified according to the law's absolute standard of righteousness—should never forget that both the law and the cross sustain an important relation to Christians. Both the typical teaching of Joshua 8 and the plain statements of the New Testament (see chapters 2 and 6) show that *God's redeemed people have a duty to obey His law*. But in seeking to do so, they should always remember that *they must use the law in the light of the cross*. This is the only lawful way for Christians to use the law (see chapter 5). Christians do not stand on Sinai, or between Sinai and Calvary, but they stand on Calvary and on Christ's finished work. It is from this vantage point that they view Sinai. They do not deny or despise God's law, but delight in it after the inward man (Romans 7:22). They see that in fulfilling the law as a covenant in their behalf, the Lord Jesus Christ justified them fully "that the righteousness of the law might be fulfilled in us, who walk not after the flesh, but after the Spirit" (Romans 8:4).

Here is the true majesty of the law: It is never more fully expressed, satisfied, fulfilled, and vindicated, than in Christ's obedience unto death.

Because of our depraved nature, the law could never justify or sanctify us, but Christ has accomplished both by His perfect obedience to it. "What the law could not do, in that it was weak through the flesh, God [accomplished by] sending his own Son in the likeness of sinful flesh, and for sin, [and so] condemned sin in the flesh: that the righteousness of the law might be fulfilled in us, who walk not after the flesh, but after the Spirit" (Romans 8:3–4).